TWICE-DIVIDED NATION

TWICE-DIVIDED NATION

National Memory, Transatlantic News, and American Literature in the Civil War Era

SAMUEL GRABER

University of Virginia Press
CHARLOTTESVILLE AND LONDON

University of Virginia Press
© 2019 by the Rector and Visitors of the University of Virginia
All rights reserved
Printed in the United States of America on acid-free paper

First published 2019

1 3 5 7 9 8 6 4 2

Library of Congress Cataloging-in-Publication Data

Names: Graber, Samuel J., author.
Title: Twice-divided nation : national memory, transatlantic news, and American literature in the Civil War era / Samuel Graber.
Description: Charlottesville : University of Virginia Press, 2019. | Includes bibliographical references and index.
Identifiers: LCCN 2018044532 | ISBN 9780813942384 (cloth : alk. paper) | ISBN 9780813942407 (pbk. : alk. paper) | ISBN 9780813942391 (ebook)
Subjects: LCHS: United States—History—Civil War, 1861–1865—Press coverage. | United States—History—Civil War, 1861–1865—Press coverage—Great Britain | United States—History—Civil War, 1861–1865—Literature and the war. | Collective memory—United States.
Classification: LCC E609 .G725 2019 | DDC 973.7/1—dc23
LC record available at https://lccn.loc.gov/2018044532

Cover art: Reynolds's political map of the United States, designed to exhibit the comparative area of the free and slave states, William C. Reynolds and J. C. Jones, ca. 1856; Horace Greeley, Currier & Ives lithograph, ca. 1872; Walt Whitman, ink drawing by Valerian Gribayèdoff, ca. 1870. (Library of Congress, Prints and Photographs Division)

For my parents,
and for my person

He says to the past, Rise and walk before me that I may realize you.
—Walt Whitman

CONTENTS

Preface		xi
Acknowledgments		xvii
Introduction		1
Part I. Revival and Revolution: The Modes of Modern Memory		25
1	Memory for the Masses: Sacred History and the National Press	31
2	Enslaved to the Past: Emerson and the Spirit of Antislavery News	53
3	The News and Walt Whitman: Poetry of the Divine Present	74
Part II. War Stories and Memory Circuits: Hypernationalism and the Transatlantic Time Lag		99
4	Palaces of Memory: Global Information and the Specter of Catholicity	105
5	Wars and Rumors of Wars: Kansas and the Presentist Crusade	130
6	"Transatlantic Latter-Day Poetry": Nationalist Anxiety and the Memory Circuits of *Leaves of Grass*	161
Conclusion		195
Notes		219
Index		261

PREFACE

There is no such thing as memory: the brain recalls just what the muscles grope for: no more, no less.
—William Faulkner, *Absalom, Absalom!*

Nationalism is news again. To our great surprise, the idea seems to be urgent and everywhere on our crowded planet, from Moscow to Glasgow, from the street corner to the house next door, from our Facebook likes to our Twitter feeds. In the United States and Britain, common themes resound: we must make our country great again, must take our country back, never mind from whom. Our enflamed passions for the nation may well destroy the nation-states we claim to venerate. Political parties and agreements are being broken and remade, economies shaken, by nationalist desire. Brexiting the EU in the name of the British nation has threatened to break a United Kingdom that has existed for centuries. Trumpism has threatened to leave the twenty-first-century United States less united than it has been in generations. This violently divisive nationalism filling our news seems entirely without precedent. Yet it surprises us in part because of how we have been trained to think and feel about our shared American past, especially about our great mid-nineteenth-century American upheavals. We assumed all this had been settled long ago.

One lesson of the recent Civil War sesquicentennial was that the war did not really need an anniversary to be remembered. It was present with us all along, and more uncomfortably active than we realized. Though the war arose from a mid-nineteenth-century global unsettling, most of us had been taught to recall its battles and speeches as part of a firm and indivisible American heritage. Clearly, we forgot a great deal when we remembered a civil war in this way. Especially we forgot that a refusal to acknowledge the binding authority of the national heritage we commemorate had given millions of erstwhile Americans a reason to fight the battles we now remember. The intensity of white southern repudiations of a former nation-state, and violent defenses of a new one, necessitated speeches celebrating a national rebirth in a time of pervasive death. Thus the forgetting began before the war was over, at places like Gettysburg, where the dead themselves were made to speak for the abiding reality of what their fighting so obviously called into question. Speeches like Lincoln's were pronounced, sometimes literally, over the graves of those who fell; half of the battle's dead (those Rebels who were decimated in what later came to be known as Pickett's charge, for instance) would have scoffed at the president's notion that his version of the American nation could outlive such a war or even their rebellious determination to fight under a different flag. Lincoln was one of our greatest imaginers of national unity because he had to be, and he was assassinated by a Confederate partisan from a Union state.[1]

In a period when the party that Lincoln championed seems to be exploding with nationalist bluster and paranoia, it may also be a good time to revisit the disunities of that earlier era and the question of how and why we the people continue to remember the nation so fervently and so inaccurately. For in truth, nationalism's resilience has little to do with Lincoln's honored dead—or the accuracy of the Gettysburg Address's assumption that the American nation's life would continue not only in spite of but also because of war's carnage—the mystical as well as the practical power of the fallen. Nationalism's power has to do not with the dead but with the real subject of Lincoln's speech, "us the living": we who in living remember not so much the dead as ourselves, we who collectively forget even as we remember—today much more so than when Lincoln spoke. Though we may pause to mark the anniversaries of a "great civil war," we do so from a safe distance, a distance that has allowed us to take for granted the same nationality those events so deeply troubled, and even when recalling a war that made a mockery of many nationalistic assumptions, we continue to adopt them. When we are being conscientiously rigorous about the war's implications for nationalism, we will sometimes allude to a significant alteration in national essence by describing the conflict as a second American revolution or observing the United States' grammatical shift from a plurality of states to a single unified noun.[2] But these are minor adjustments within a dominant historical view that sees American history in the way that Lincoln did, as a more or less continuous saga involving one entity. It was this national personality, born in a revolutionary founding, that had sustained a midlife crisis followed by a conversion experience four score and seven years later, without ever suffering an actual death. This is the living American nation that triumphs over its own historical mortality, insisting (perpetually it seems) on its capacity to be made great again.[3]

But where, among the northern and southern populations, would we look for signs of that nation's life and indications of its cohesion in, say, the spring of 1863—just before the clash of armies marked the ground around Gettysburg as a future memorial site? If we assume that the nation was ever more than the shaky claim of sovereignty made by a particular federal system, then viewing the Civil War as merely a trial of the antebellum nation rather than its death sentence seems ahistorical and irrational.

Yet we must also conclude that seeing the nation in the way Lincoln suggested is not entirely absurd. If we take the political power of collective memory seriously, we can see how a common belief in America's survival through its bloodiest ordeal is precisely what makes that nation's "survival" a political reality, despite its dubiousness as an historical assessment. To the extent that nations always depend on present beliefs about the shared national past rather than on historical facts, speaking in the way that Lincoln did at Gettysburg eventually becomes a self-fulfilling prophecy.

From the perspective of a memory scholar, the public refusal to count the founding fathers' America as the Civil War's first casualty seems neither surprising nor blind. Rather, such creative ahistoricism forms the foundation for the cultural work that nationalists need collective memory to do. Recent as well as distant history shows us that nationalist beliefs are often unbothered by stubborn facts and national memory will never accord with any strictly historical description of the past.[4] Thus our forgetfulness about the Civil War era not only obscures a history of divisions in that time but also simultaneously ignores how all articulations of national memory, in the antebellum as well as the postbellum United States, have had stubbornly to ignore supposedly stubborn facts.

Although the focus of this book predates most of the fighting, the book offers its own account of memory's relationship to the Civil War. Looming large in these pages is a belief about what the war indicated, namely that America during the Civil War era did not, by many measures, exist as a nation. Although the United States in 1861 had spent the better part of a century as an internationally recognized state, American nationality in the mid-nineteenth century represented as much an open question as an established fact. It was a question the war itself dramatically punctuated, and in a sense this book attempts to answer a version of it: How are we to understand

American national memory in a period when the nation itself could best be represented as a question mark?

Yet from another perspective this is the best and perhaps the only time to see national memory clearly for what it is. Politically stable nations, almost by definition, tend to obscure their own historical contingency.[5] When nation-states begin to fail, perhaps we can better recognize that the sort of consistency nations project, through us and upon us, has more in common with metaphor than institutions. In stable times, the nation stands as a great tree, with a visible trunk of a nation-state rooted in invisible substances, rising up into great branches of national culture and topped by all the emblems and symbols of a nationality fluttering like so many leaves in the sun. In eras of national uncertainty, perhaps we can better see how the nation also rests like a flat oceanic stillness cast over depths of dissent and diversity, how it presents an illusion of stable ground amid the great flood of modern cultural life. As many scholars have noted, nations appeal to the imagination, to feeling, and sometimes to fantasy; in this they resemble poetry.[6] And there is a spiritual poetry to nations that seeks to establish their empirically questionable reality as a truth more dependable than fact.

In short, our tendency to see the Civil War as a fiery test of a uniform nationality arises as a feverish symptom of a deeper syndrome that also helped spawn the war itself. We are reluctant to admit what the conflict proved and still proves about us: that we are not inherently one people, that we have always depended on national memory and its attendant forgetfulness in order to convince ourselves that America has existed and continues to exist; that when doubts about that nation's standing arise, we will often respond with deeper registers of nationalist fervor, even when doing so threatens the nation-state itself. This may have been more obvious during or just after the Civil War, but it was also equally true during the antebellum period this book explores most closely. And it is also true today. To the extent that America has always been a divided nation, it has always depended on national memory, and the forgetting that comes with it, to obviate if not overcome the distance between its parts—as well as its cultural proximity to the history made in other parts of the world.

Nevertheless, such memory worked in different ways in different times. This book's examination of the late antebellum years highlights how particular historical developments, especially the arrival of a modern news apparatus on the transatlantic scene, helped activate two characteristic and distinctive forms of modern memory, one of which was tied especially tightly to modern news. Because these modes of memory were so integral to American nationalism, and because they merged and meshed with previous ways of conceptualizing the shared past, complicated memory work in the period can sometimes resemble political clichés and jingoistic boilerplate. But what might otherwise seem to be politics as usual was only just being invented at midcentury, and this book argues that American politics were changing during the Civil War era partly because the foundations of memory were shifting.[7] It shows how new ways of sharing a common past in the mid-nineteenth century, especially through the phenomena associated with transatlantic news, provided grist for all manner of nationalist formations and frictions that helped make the war and the nation that emerged from it imaginable.

ACKNOWLEDGMENTS

Thanking all those who contributed to this book would far exceed my promised word count, which would irritate some of those I intend to thank—namely, the incisive editors and readers of the University of Virginia Press, and Eric Brandt in particular. Eric's patience and care in seeing this project through to publication were remarkable. In my immediate sphere, I am indebted to Dean Jennifer Prough for securing a course release at a crucial point in the project and to my colleagues at Valparaiso University and Christ College. Their hallway conversations and devotion to scholarship have guided me in countless ways. This particular project, however, owes a special debt to Gretchen Buggeln, mentor extraordinaire and all-around mensch. Gretchen read an early version of this project, and her constant encouragement has kept me hopeful and (mostly) sane even when teaching took me away from my research for long stretches. I also need to thank two stellar undergraduates, Halina Hopkins and Ethan Grant, as well as Ed Uehling and Mel Piehl, who as my former chair and dean permitted me to harness Halina's and Ethan's talents as researchers. I must also mention the University of Iowa, the Virginia Historical Society, the Mellon Foundation, and the Lilly Fellows Program for supporting the research behind my dissertation and this manuscript. Finally, I wish to thank the *Walt Whitman Quarterly Review* for publishing an article that contained portions of chapter 6.

This book began as an interdisciplinary dissertation, and it would never have existed without the faculty, staff, and willing collaborators of Iowa's Department of American Studies—an oasis of interdisciplinary thinking within the larger academy. Patrick Naick, my dear friend and fellow American studies grad student, was a constant conversation partner and the first respondent for most of the ideas in this book. Nick Yablon and Mark Peterson read the dissertation and offered support and many suggestions along the way. Ed Folsom's legendary Whitman seminar, and Ed's humility and generosity as a scholar and teacher, taught me to respect not only the poet's work but also the responses of his innumerable readers; I now realize that the germ of almost every insight I've had into Whitman's writing took root at Ed's seminar table in my first year of graduate school. Even before that, John Raeburn encouraged me to come to Iowa, and he later served as my dissertation director. Now that I'm a professor, I can only wonder at the care John put into his mentoring. I will never forget his meticulous handwriting on the drafts he spent so much time reading, responding to, and editing. His unsparing and tireless pencil showed me the good in my own writing, and the weaknesses that remain in this book only prove I've been apart from his advice for too long.

Kathleen Diffley taught me to revel in periodical research. She was the first to imagine these chapters as an independent book and has continued to shepherd my work beyond graduate school. It was Kathleen who introduced me to an incredible group of Civil War scholars by organizing and maintaining the Midwest Modern Language Association's Civil War caucus and by inviting me to participate in its inaugural panel with Jane Schultz, a great scholar with whom I was later lucky to share space at several conference tables. Significant portions of this book emerged directly from papers I delivered at the MMLA and benefited from the work of other caucus members, who generated not merely comments and criticisms but also great conversations. I am deeply grateful to all of them for their generosity and good fellowship, for restoring my faith in the academy each year, and (indirectly) for my family. My wife Anna and I had our first date during the St. Louis caucus of 2009, and though we've had to juggle kids at some subsequent meetings, we've been going strong ever since. Knee-deep in countless revisions and conflicting impulses, I often felt as if this book was its own sort of civil war, and I suppose these acknowledgments are the armistice. To Anna, who has put up with my sleeplessness and orneriness for too long, I can say that there's no one with whom I would rather share the coming peace.

TWICE-DIVIDED NATION

Introduction

I will never perpratrate [sic] anything foreign in England again.
—A. W. N. Pugin, 1840

The power of the newspaper is familiar in America and in accordance with our political system.
—Ralph Waldo Emerson, 1856

In the summer of 1851, Horace Greeley, founder and editor of the *New-York Tribune*, was called to the Palace of Westminster in London.[1] The British Parliament, housed in the palace, had invited Greeley to testify as an expert witness before the Select Committee on Newspaper Stamps. By 1850, the committee members could easily have read a special European edition of the *Tribune* that regularly shipped out of New York via oceangoing steamer, but they were curious about more than the paper's content.[2] Their hearings were delving into the political and social effects of newspaper pricing, and this was a subject about which Greeley knew a great deal.[3] A mogul at the age of forty, a critic and editorialist who spoke to hundreds of thousands of readers each week, Greeley had based his career on the market for cheap but high-quality American newspapers and had built a media empire from scratch in less than a decade. Yet he was also a man who had been made—professionally, politically, even spiritually—by the news he printed. He might not look it, uncomfortable as he was in anything more formal than his three-dollar topcoat, but Greeley had come to Parliament as a power to be reckoned with and as a herald of the modern era that had empowered him.[4]

Despite the *Tribune*'s transatlantic footprint, Greeley was out of place in Parliament. In fact, as a news publisher operating within a culture addicted to the latest information, the American newsman presented the veritable antithesis of his physical surroundings. A fire had destroyed much of the Palace of Westminster in 1834, and since 1840 workmen had been busy with the "renovations"—a term that rang more than a little false given the willful lack of novelty in the structures they were erecting.[5] For reasons that went to the heart of nineteenth-century British national culture, the Westminster reconstruction planners were refashioning the political center of one of the world's most advanced societies in the medieval style of the Gothic Revival.[6]

Greeley's appearance at Westminster presents one dramatic instance of the conflict explored in this book, a clash not only between a midcentury American revolution in news and a British mania for medieval revivalism but also between two contrasting approaches to national memory that were shaping the transatlantic world of the mid-nineteenth century. These modes of memory, which this book terms "presentist" and "traditionalist," each developed in tension with the other, and their competing claims contributed to the construction of national identity on both sides of the Atlantic.[7]

The traditionalist version converted relics and false relics of the distant past, such as the Westminster renovations, into signs of common national heritage for sprawling populations with relatively little to bind them. The presentist version, by contrast, offered national memory in the form of news, an ongoing virtual experience of shared information that purportedly bound diverse individuals within a powerful knot of historical experience—even though no individual actually experienced this history directly. The standards traditionalists advocated were not really ancient; similarly, the exalted present the *Tribune* celebrated was really a representation of the recent past. Both were forms of memory that organized mass populations by addressing modernity's core anxiety: the perceived threat a networked world posed to traditional societies grounded in common religion, kinship, and local environments.

Despite their oppositional stances, the approaches exhibited important similarities that marked them as distinctly modern mnemonic endeavors. Each accounted for and depended on the new technology, economic systems, and political arrangements that defined the modern experience. Each offered the comfort of a common national past in response to the globalizing forces of modernity. Finally, and perhaps most importantly, each combined secular and religious appeals to offer mass audiences shared access to sacred national histories. Traditionalists trafficked primarily in a sacred national heritage that identified diverse constituencies vertically. This is to say that they summoned a national past distant enough to be held in common and infused it with spiritual content. Thus the traditionalist collaborators who built the New Palace of Westminster gathered a modern mass public around the re-created relics of an imagined national legacy of medieval religious forms.[8]

Within cultures influenced by Christianity, both modes of memory established contemporary national publics within a long history of divine action, but in mutually opposing ways. Presentism, in contrast to the verticality of traditionalist heritage, promoted immanent histories as the foundation of nations. As midcentury traditionalists toiled to connect masses of modern nationalists to designated anchor points in a sacred past, their presentist counterparts sacralized common access to the recent past as a means of fulfilling the prophetic promise of an immanent sacred history; thus they maintained a sense of stability and duration for their revolutionary endeavors.[9]

Greeley's appearance before the parliamentary committee demonstrated both the symbolic and instrumental power driving traditionalist and presentist projects. The image of the towering Gothic renovations and the owlish American commoner atop a burgeoning media empire each symbolized a very different sort of relation to national history. Yet Greeley's testimony, which would highlight the modern Anglophone news's uneven rate of acceptance, also demonstrated that more than symbolic power was at work in establishing traditionalist and presentist control over their respective national cultures. Presentist memorialists depended on harnessing the same mechanisms that allowed Greeley to cultivate a mass audience in the age of steam: mass printing, telegraphic communication, photography, and faster and more reliable transportation. In the United States such technology operated within a relatively unregulated market to make news both available and appealing to an increasingly democratic audience. In Britain, the special newspaper taxes levied by Parliament to prevent this development indirectly funded the Westminster renovations and necessitated the work of a special committee on newspaper taxation.

In this sense, the Gothic palace of British politics and Greeley's mass-marketed American newspaper were each in their way cathedrals built for modern times. Icons as well as instruments of vast social power at midcentury, they projected their own position at the heart of public life as a sure sign of the underlying reality they supposedly represented—the reality of their respective nations' abiding existence in the memory of millions. Yet the tension between them also contributed to novel nationalist arrangements and ultimately to the spiritual and social conflicts that made imaginable not only new nations but also a civil war fought in their name.

Greeley had founded the *Tribune* a decade before he had his say before the parliamentary committee; a decade later he would be relaying the first reports over the wire from the firing on Fort Sumter. This book is mostly about Americans, northerners in particular, in the intervening years. Yet one of its central arguments is that terms such as "American" can be deployed only anachronistically in the antebellum era unless we maintain an openness to a wide range of transatlantic attachments and divisions. This is what I mean by the "transatlantic world."[10] It is less a place than a world in search of place, which is one reason why writers can map it in any number of ways.[11] This was true of writers at the time, and also true of those who write about it today, as brilliant books by Robert Weisbuch, Elisa Tamarkin, Christopher Hanlon, and Sam W. Haynes have amply proven, even as they have disagreed in their points of emphasis.[12]

Below I will briefly rehearse the key concepts and terms that have guided my own mapping project and in particular the spiritually potent forms of national memory that drew from and shaped transatlantic news and American literature. The essential wateriness of the transatlantic world, its protean fluidity, affects not just understandings of nations and nationalisms but all the terms we might associate with them.[13] This is one reason why I have maintained an interdisciplinary outlook, one which assumes that the generic forms and disciplinary approaches of literature, religion, politics, and journalism are historically contingent and interrelated regions of larger cultural fields. This book analyzes Walt Whitman's poetic literature at length, yet Whitman also wrote extensively for the papers, in prose as well as poetry, both before and after he published his masterwork in 1855. Furthermore, Whitman quite clearly was interested in muddying the divisions between literary and journalistic forms, and he wrote as he did partly to oppose definitions of literature he associated with the Old World. This was not merely because he valued literary originality; the formal innovations that *Leaves of Grass* would make famous arose partly from Whitman's developing interest in modern news as a spiritual mode of memory and from his political quest to justify the poem he and Emerson both called America.[14] To take such art seriously is to deny, at least provisionally, its status as art. American definitions and redefinitions of literature were also intertwined with the transatlantic aspects of the news, both with how news was imagined symbolically and how newspapers functioned socially as a kind of circulating artifact of a common past. Both literature and news, moreover, resonated with a sense of sacred histories derived primarily from Christianity. These interwoven cultural elements came together to shape an antebellum period when cultural categories as well as nations were breaking down and being reforged, and that we can only now recognize as the Civil War era.

That shaping potential arose from the inherent power of national memory, which was spiritual in both an expansive and a narrow sense. It was spiritual because it helped to address the deepest feelings of alienation and isolation experienced by modern individuals. And it was also spiritual because it presumed that history, however chaotic or threatening it might appear, was governed by some higher principle—a spirit moving over the dark waters of the transatlantic world.

Memory Loss: A Modern Predicament

As it is most typically defined, national memory borrows from and contributes to other historical discourses, but it can be most clearly distinguished by its modern political purpose. Some scholars have suggested that the perceived loss of authentic tradition lies behind every distinctively modern memory project. According to this view, premodern peoples were bound together by a collective past that remained a constant presence in their everyday lives. Modern societies, on the other hand, became increasingly separated from the intimately shared sense of the past that primitive traditions provided. Faced with this irretrievable loss, moderns would feel compelled to actively memorialize and commemorate, constructing islands of memory in a sea of alienated histories. In the well-known formulation of Pierre Nora, these are *les lieux de mémoire,* sites that appear to project a vision of a shared past for a dissociated modern public. Under the auspices of a large nation-state, these "realms of memory" provide the powerful social bonds of a proposed national community to innumerable individuals who will never meet face to face.[15]

As John Gillis observes, such "national memory is shared by people who have never seen or heard of one another, yet who regard themselves as having a common history."[16] Because there are so few actual commonalities in personal experience or remembrance among an entire population of national size, national memory must base itself on the largely mythical but durable belief that a mass of largely unrelated individuals can in some sense hold particular memories in common—through a vision of the shared past they locate at places like the Palace of Westminster, for instance, or in the pages of a great national newspaper like the *Tribune.*[17]

Why would disparate persons acquiesce in "remembering" a past that they never actually experienced? In fact, such acts of collective memory are not restricted to nations. Communities of all sorts and sizes will claim to share histories to which they are only unevenly connected. Even family members can never apprehend or recall the same family event in precisely the same way, and individuals remember their own histories differently at different times in their lives. Memory's rather obvious heterogeneity means that any notion of shared history, even among the smallest social group, must rest to some degree on a kind of communal fallacy: fallacious in the sense that events can never have appeared to individuals precisely as they remember them together, communal in the sense that an individual believes in such fallacies partly in order to conform and belong to a particular community "in his nature as a *zoon politikon*."[18] Yet the social animal's predictable turn to the social terrain of memory's communal fallacies explains neither the precise relationship between individual and group memory in the modern context nor the modern turn to national memory specifically.

This book makes at least three basic and interlocking assumptions about the extremely complicated relationship between modern individuals and collective memory.[19] The first is that the connection between individual memory and collective memory is not wholly metaphorical: we do not, obviously, share a hive mind, but society plays a real role in determining individual mnemonic functions and practices; conversely, our capacity to remember as individuals clearly shapes the forms of our collective remembrance.[20] The commonplace notion that collective memory does not exist, at least neurologically speaking, expresses an accurate assessment from one perspective and a dangerous misrepresentation from another; in fact, collective memory is reciprocally linked to individual memory in ways that have real effects. Modernity's diminishment of local traditions coupled with an enhanced ability to record and transmit historical events certainly has altered the way modern individuals recall their pasts, just as their individual mnemonic experiences as moderns influence the forms of collective remembrance that develop around them.

A second premise is that individual memory and collective memory both serve as means of relating past and present identities but carry inherent and recognizable limits that reflect uncertainty and anxiety upon the identities they forge.[21] One scholar has described the limitations of individual memory as "sins," which might seem a fitting description for capacities that signal our fallibility while remaining fundamental to our sense of ourselves.[22] As a practice that both constructs and constrains our identities, our remembering creates both psychological security and deep anxiety that ultimately relates to our consciousness of ourselves as mortal. The development of collective memory in the modern era thus bears a relation to how modern individuals and societies address these mortal limits, and death in particular.[23]

A final related assumption is that in order to understand what motivates the modern turn to national memory, we must take into account the spiritual appeal of national continuity and exclusive national commonality. Theorists of nationalism have exhaustively analyzed modernity's role in its development, and many have suggested that the nation is a creature of the modern world. Others have insisted that nations have existed in identifiable forms since long before the modern era. Thus a cloud of uncertainty hovers over the precise relationship between modern forms of national identity and prior expressions of political affiliation.[24]

This academic debate about the literal provenance of nations should not obscure the vital interplay between the modern nation and its ancient precedents that clearly occurs at the level of popular memory. There can be little doubt that modernity had a major impact on how nationalist feelings, ideas, and practices were organized at the mass level. Yet it is also clear that modern nationalism depended on the sense of continuity and commonality that the idea of venerable nations and the practices of nationalist commemorations provided.[25]

It was partly this sense of abiding continuity in the face of modern disruption that gave nineteenth-century nationalism its strong spiritual overtones. National memory (like nations themselves) certainly took some form prior to the modern era; nevertheless, in addition to modern cultural capacities such as expanding print and global capitalism, the peculiar spiritual and social upheavals of modernity gave the forms and fallacies of modern national memory their particular shape. Nineteenth-century individuals were spiritual as well as social animals, and also animals whose spiritual and social natures were challenged in new ways by a modern situation. In particular, they faced the threat of individual alienation from the common pasts they shared within an increasingly open and fluid global culture. What Richard Terdiman has aptly labeled the modern "memory crisis"—the perceived loss of a deep connection to the past—was also experienced as a kind of spiritual crisis.[26]

Participation in modern memory, and modern national memory in particular, thus became part and parcel of a modern individual's larger existential battle against oblivion.[27] Yet this raises a disturbing historical irony, for if national memory arises partly as an escape from mortal dread, it has often amounted to a death trap. In straining the generally dubious notion of shared historical experience far beyond the local scene of face-to-face interactions and kinship relations, national memory achieves enormous political potency, producing a "remarkable confidence in community in anonymity which is the hallmark of modern nations."[28] This "problematic reality in people's minds of an unreal past" is never more poignantly expressed than during violent nationalist conflicts of the sort that defined the mid-nineteenth century in America and Britain, when thousands and sometimes millions of citizens were said to die in the name of national memories that no one actually shared.[29]

The Modes of Memory and the Anglo-American Midcentury

We can explain this conundrum better by recognizing national memory as a spiritual field that influenced nineteenth-century beliefs about everything from shared land to blood lineage, as well as organized religion. Narrowly defined, religion—as cult, scripture, and dogma, for instance—forms only one component of national memory. Nevertheless, a deep background of spiritual concern infuses all the various elements of national memory with the quality of sacred history. Understood in this way, presentist and traditionalist remembrance addressed a widespread suspicion that the modern individuals of the Anglo-American world were rootless souls, floating amid uncertain and fleeting social connections.

This spiritual foundation often appeared clearest among traditionalists of the sort who rebuilt Westminster and who tended to be fairly open about their religious objectives. But restricting our understanding of national memory to traditionalist commemorations alone overlooks a presentist imaginary that, while differing significantly in its forms, nevertheless shared traditionalism's basic purpose: organizing mass societies through the propagation of histories that could be shared by millions as a spiritual balm. As the theorist of religion and memory Jan Assmann points out, the shared past is not merely the hegemonic and coercive invention of states but also holds considerable attraction for groups of disparate individuals as a "bonding memory" that appeals to "man's desire to belong." If, as Assmann asserts, memory's power comes "not from tradition but from feeling" and if the common past is only needed in a social and psychological sense "because it imparts togetherness in the present," then it would seem any such past, regardless of its actual duration or chronological position, can serve memory's central purpose.[30] The historian's exercise of exposing the recent provenance of "invented traditions" often fails to enervate their power "to establish a chain of felt or willed continuity" for precisely this reason. As

Anthony Smith suggests, "The quality of living memory in a population [is] more critical for the meaning and success of a nationalist enterprise than any amount of well-documented but un-resonating evidence" of their belated fabrication.[31]

The spiritual need to forge national memory became especially intense among the people of the United States and Britain during the middle decades of the nineteenth century, partly because the audiences for nationalist messages were rapidly expanding along with new media and transportation technologies, and partly because violent conflicts were threatening to redraw lines of national affiliation throughout the Anglo-American world. As midcentury technologies provided more rapid physical and virtual access to distant locales, they increasingly disrupted the mnemonic authority of local culture while helping maintain and publicize the broader international connections of standing nation-states and their citizenry. Especially in the Anglo-American context, where so much common culture crossed international borders, the intense political ferment of these years tended to leave previous nationalist identifications on shaky ground.[32] Even as they wondered at the technological "annihilation of space and time," nineteenth-century audiences were forced to reconsider their own place in the world.[33]

Modern Anglophones in particular confronted national identities under threat of dissolution, and this provided an opening for traditionalist memorialists who advocated a return to the safety of a distant national past. Yet the essential contradiction involved in looking back to face a modern problem intensified as the traditionalist movement literally "gathered steam" by utilizing many of the same modernizing forces that were straining the seams of nineteenth-century community life. Nineteenth-century traditionalism should not be confused with a return to a traditional society, any more than a Gothic Revival project should be taken for its medieval original; after all, both movement and monument were intended for mass audiences impossible to imagine in a premodern world. As many scholars have pointed out, nationalist traditions were necessarily constructed using the same modern advancements against which they often railed, and traditionalist nationalism's strength in the mid-nineteenth century relied partly on modern innovations that spread, funded, and framed its message.[34] As traditionalist memory developed its freshly minted versions of a shared national past for contemporary audiences, its ancient standards often mingled uncomfortably with the modern technologies and economies that reaching the masses required. This left traditionalists strangely "equivocal" about the modern times in which they operated, but they could nevertheless legitimate their movement as a reaction against an alternative mode of memory on the Anglo-American scene, a mode that more openly championed the new engines of mass communication.[35]

Thus while traditionalists tended to regard their relationship to modern tools and institutions as incidental or embarrassing, memorialists operating in the presentist mode made these modern technologies and techniques the instrumental and symbolic basis for belonging. In particular they proposed that modern news—powered by telegraph networks, steam-driven cylinder presses, and railroads—could become its own sort of common history to nineteenth-century British and especially American masses. Nineteenth-century information networks expanded unevenly and could undercut as well as enhance the authority of nation-states.[36] Nevertheless, papers that made these networks manifest provided a foundation for common history to which modern nationalist audiences might belong, both by making the most recent past widely available and by publicizing how news was being shared.

Just as Gothic recoveries of medieval precedents must be viewed with skepticism, presentists' bold acceptance of a boundless modernity should not be taken at face value; indeed presentist memory typically carried its own nostalgic insistence that the traditional (though not traditionalist) model of community could somehow be retained—even if only through a national audience addressed as a unified body by news that enveloped localized experiences as part of an emerging national history.[37] Americans of Greeley's persuasion often cast an aura of provincial community around their presentist endeavors and concealed the obvious contradiction within their metropolitan enterprises by attacking traditionalism as an elite attachment that was unrepresentative of the ordinary folk who made up the true national public. Thus the *Tribune* marketed itself as a national paper that circulated in local "clubs," and Greeley, while consciously and openly addressing a mass readership, would eventually become known as "Uncle Horace" to innumerable American everymen and women.

The paradoxes and equivocations apparent on both sides of this memory war suggest that traditionalist and presentist movements, in placing the national category at the heart of their dueling visions of common history, were both responding to more basic social challenges of global information and migration. Each mode of memory sought to recover, in the name of the nation, the conviction of shared blood, land, and god that a disruptive modernity had left shaken throughout the Anglo-American world at midcentury.

Casting themselves as antipodes, both presentists and traditionalists were marketing memory and its corollary, a durable sense of communal belonging, to the masses. Each responded to a basic social need to belong to a shared past and provided a profoundly meaningful sense of human communion, one that addressed the mortal limits and losses that individual memory created in a modern person. Thus the modes of modern memory sanctified forms of communal belonging to deliver a palliative if not an outright cure for a memory crisis that was also a spiritual crisis.

The Memory War and the Paradox of Christian History

Not surprisingly, then, the modern modes of national memory would rely heavily on religion, though not necessarily in a form that all theories of religious nationalism would recognize. Rather, both drew on a rich religious context that linked the nation and its memory, both implicitly and explicitly, to a complex but widespread understanding of sacred history that derived from Christianity. Christian culture did not merely influence national memory in the nineteenth century but also managed to support both sides of the memory war, imparting spiritual energy and divine authorization to the conflict between presentist and traditionalist modes.

This was because Christianity, in its basic formulation as a messianic religion that maintained continuity with a sacred past even as it diverged from it, had developed a paradoxical sense of divine authority and action in history. On the one hand, it sanctified the traditionalist attachment to a distant past. Membership in the church implied participation in a sacred tradition that descended from ancient times; to call oneself a Christian meant participating in a communion that began in the first century, whose biblical roots extended nearly to the creation of the world. On the other hand, that history contained an essential presentist thrust; from doctrines of the Incarnation and the Trinity to the canonization of the books of the New Testament alongside the Old to the widespread understanding of the gospel as good news and especially the belief in the abiding involvement of the Holy Spirit and divine Providence within an ongoing sacred history, the faith defined itself in partial opposition to traditionalist claims. By some lights, then, Christianity's most authoritative version of sacred history lay in the recent rather than the ancient past and in a gospel that was good because it was news.

One could experience Christian history and therefore identity through either a presentist or a traditionalist access point, each of which defined the collective experience of the contemporary church through a different kind of relation to the Christian past. Moreover, it was not merely the case that authentically Christian versions of sacred history came in two distinct forms but also that tension between the two was inevitable. The traditionalist vision defined itself as a limit on the organizing authority of current events, just as the presentist alternative contained within it a traditionalist foil. Both could claim to be legitimate interpretations of Christianity, and either could be activated through appeals to the central pillars of the faith, for the traditionalist/presentist paradox inhabited the basic structure of Christian scripture, sacramental ritual, and Trinitarian godhead. In theory, Christianity effectively contained the tension it carried within itself. In practice, the most zealous adherents of either perspective were bound to regard the other as fundamentally misguided at best, heretical at worst: each could easily become in the other's eyes "blasphemers against the Holy Ghost."[38]

It seems inevitable that notions of national identity developing in a largely Christian cultural context would borrow from Christianity's paradoxical sense of sacred history, especially given Christian associations with the biblical nation of Israel. Yet many descriptions of the rise of nationalism tend to obscure religion's contributions to deep nationalistic unities and distinctions in the mid-nineteenth century, partly because theorists often associate the presentist potential with modernity and a turn to secular temporality.[39] Particularly problematic is the premise central to Benedict Anderson's work, that modern nationalism arose from a fundamental difference in the way medieval and modern peoples understood history, the former which Anderson terms "messianic" and the latter which he describes as "homogenous." Anderson borrowed both these terms from Walter Benjamin and the basic scheme from Eric Auerbach.[40] Anderson's theory rests to a large degree on a historical transition from a medieval Christian form of simultaneity to a modern secular one. Drawing on Benjamin and Auerbach, he argues that medieval Christian temporality was organized around a sense of simultaneity that collapsed past, present, and future in reference to the eternal authority of Providence. Anderson asserts that this "simultaneity-along-time" amounted to a form of temporality "wholly alien to our own," for it was replaced in the modern era by "cross-time" simultaneity "marked not by prefiguring and fulfillment, but by temporal coincidence, and measured by clock and calendar."[41]

As Anthony Smith observes, the influence of Anderson and other members of the "modernist" school of nationalism studies led to a situation in which "nations and nationalism are treated as wholly recent and novel phenomena, and a secular, anthropocentric, and anticlerical modernity is always counterposed to tradition and traditional society with its emphasis on custom and religion."[42] Yet as Annika Hvithamar suggests, "modernists [who] explain nationalism from the outside and concentrate on measurable empirical facts" often fail to convince those who "describe nationalism from within, on the basis of the conceptions of their adherents," in part because those adherents experience religion as profoundly compatible with their nationality.[43]

Furthermore, notions of secularism hinge on the modern development of a secular "horizontal" temporality through the auspices of newspapers and other forms of mass printing; thus modernist models tend to ignore the possibility that modern national communities could organize themselves around a spiritual connection between the past shared through news and more ancient iterations of sacred history they derived from their religious tradition. Yet the resources for horizontal engagements with Christian notions of sacred history are, quite literally, endless. The Christ of the New Testament (prefigured though he may be in the Old) is also a news event, and temporal coincidence was fundamental to the understandings of the gospel that permeate the New Testament epistles; Paul's letters reek of "cross-time simultaneity," as he imagines with great relish the simultaneous actions of the Holy Spirit in the religious communities he had founded throughout Asia Minor, in Jerusalem, and in his own time and place. Many modern Christians would continue to see the recent contemporaneous past as a region of sacred history infused with prophetic spirit, and they would have every reason to regard such simultaneity as consistent with the ancient church to which scripture bore witness.[44]

Though sound in many ways, the "modernist" thesis of a fundamental rupture, through which Anderson and others have identified nationalism with a Reformation turn to vernacular culture and print capitalism, conflates and thus elides a paradox at the heart of Christian doctrine with a clear-cut division in European history.[45] Thus theology becomes chronology, and it becomes more difficult to grasp the many ways in which modern and supposedly secular imagined communities depended upon the imagined continuity of Christian history for their development. Yet, as Mircea Eliade contends, Christianity's *"redemption* of Time" made all of history sacred, including the shared contemporary experience that lay at the heart of secular simultaneity.[46]

It was not merely that modern nation-states retained residual elements of premodern religiosity, although this was certainly true. It was that modernity allowed national publics to collectively experience and imagine their common religiously infused continuity in traditionalist and presentist modes. The sacred aura that the Gothic style attached to nationality is as difficult to imagine in a world without mass print as the reformist zeal of Greeley's national newspaper; yet this does not mean that the religious content of either form of memory was innocuous or inert. We do not need to assume that the Gothic Revival was successfully reimposing a medieval temporality, or that the *Tribune* was channeling the eschaton, in order to recognize that modern traditionalists and presentists experienced the forms of piety they advocated as authentic connections to the ancient faith. Thus Smith rightly criticizes Anderson's work because, though recognizing the originating linkage between Protestantism and secular nationalism, it subsequently and "resolutely turns its back on religion and the sacred, in favour of print and vernacular language."[47]

This, though, is a false choice, for print and vernacular language continued to facilitate nationalist involvements in sacred history throughout the modern era. This book's analysis of antebellum national realignments accords with Anderson and other modernists in arguing that nineteenth-century nationalism grew in response to the spread of an increasingly democratic print market, especially the market for cheap news. But it also proposes that this market created bonds that were religious and mnemonic as well as emotional and political and that the modern experience of simultaneity retained a fundamental quality of spiritual history that the modern news fostered. Christianity's continuing influence provided Anglo-American nationalists with presentist as well as traditionalist strains of history to draw from and bolstered their truth claims even when they turned in relatively heterodox or secular directions.

Thus both modern modes of memory upheld the spiritual continuity between the national present and past. Yet their dueling claims on sacred history, combined with the seemingly fundamental antagonism between their points of emphasis, supported sectarian distinctions among nominal coreligionists and Anglophones in the United States and Britain. Indeed, from one perspective presentists and traditionalists evinced a rift deeper than any that lay between the churches of greater Christendom, for they disagreed about where to locate ultimate authority in time as well as space. Yet however virulent their disagreement, neither presentists nor traditionalists had to abandon their connections to sacred history, because their respective models of national memory corresponded to a division contained within Christianity itself. Both could effectively tether claims of national authenticity to an exclusive spiritual unity with ancient Christianity, and American presentists no less than British traditionalists could merge a Christian ideal of the true church into the political quest for the true nation.[48]

Thus Charles Taylor, though he follows Anderson and Auerbach to a significant degree in his descriptions of secular time, notes an American tendency to experience the "immanent frame" that characterizes modern life as "open" rather than closed to some degree of transcendent authority. This admission, however, may not go far enough. Due partly to the transatlantic contrast nineteenth-century Americans drew between presentist and traditionalist varieties of sacred history, their Americanness could appear as a primary avenue for maintaining that transcendent connection, in zealous opposition to the deadening cant of an Old World traditionalism they associated with British contemporaries.[49]

The Mechanics of Transatlantic Memory

It would be easy to dismiss such transatlantic distinctions as mere nationalist clichés if they did not also depend on particular national institutions and understandings of church and state. For while Christianity was dominant for both transatlantic populations, it bore a different relationship to national culture on either side of the pond. Americans could combine the presentist strain of Christianity with their experience of democratically oriented popular news and the nationalist myths of the Revolution and the New World. Similarly, Britons working against the presentist impulse during the same period could lift up a traditionalist form of sacred national history that roughly mirrored the institutionalized connections between relatively ancient national churches and the British state.

This deployment of a common Christian religion as a means of distinguishing between the nationalities of coreligionists may seem contradictory. Yet as Azar Gat points out, "Official or unofficial national churches of the universal faith were very much the norm wherever a multiplicity of national states existed. . . . Rather than conflicting with the national idea, as it is conventionally and erroneously assumed to have been, religion was one of its strongest pillars."[50] This was partly because "universal faiths" are inevitably complex enough to be interpreted in fundamentally different ways and thus to be integrated with relatively distinctive areas of national culture.

Anglo-American distinctions in the production, circulation, and consumption of transatlantic news magnified this truism by gravitating toward the dueling points of emphasis inherent within Christian history. These distinctions will be examined in depth below, but two that were grounded in the mechanical limitations of news sharing deserve mention here. First was the increasing Americanization of cheap English-language news on the transatlantic scene in the early nineteenth century through the mid-1850s. American dominance in cheap journalism in this period benefited from a combination of restrictive British taxation and the profitability that cheap news had demonstrated in the United States. Thus more than prejudice led British papers to assume dismissively that "in the United States every one reads the newspapers, and many read nothing else."[51]

The second mechanical distinction involved the long quest to lay a transatlantic cable and the stubborn transatlantic time lag. Although it was an improvement over previous centuries, a full transatlantic news circuit took the better part of a month until the laying of a successful Atlantic cable after the conclusion of the Civil War. The regularized but anachronistic circulation of transatlantic news had several effects that influenced the development of the presentist strain of American memory. Beyond the obvious fact that British news was never new by the time Americans read it, its arrival often reinforced the transatlantic divisions in shared history by producing and publicizing mutually exclusive cycles of news sharing, or "memory circuits." In part because the British press, and in particular the *Times* of London, became increasingly popular and politically powerful in the decade before the Civil War, transatlantic news conveyed evidence of uncommon histories constructed around alternative national communities. As long as the transatlantic time lag endured, these uncommon histories could readily stoke popular beliefs in a common American history built around news sharing.

Indeed, inasmuch as this structural division in US Anglophone news was a function of the actual space between the United States and Britain, it seemed to ground American national memory in geographical factuality. Keen as they were for news from abroad, American audiences were acutely aware of the daunting Atlantic span and its alienating effects. American papers published the specific duration of the time lag alongside the names of oceangoing ships that carried old news from Europe; this was reprinted beside much more timely domestic news to which American readers could more effectively respond and to which they were far more closely and literally connected. Thus the news's transatlantic division transformed the material realities of raw Atlantic distance and domestic proximity into an ever-present image of nationally distinctive shared history. Yet due partly to the transatlantic cable's potential to end the transatlantic time lag and thus bridge the gap in news sharing, a strong undercurrent of communal anxiety arose from late antebellum transatlantic news. The coming cable suggested that national histories organized around the Atlantic span were tenuous and subject to revision and that therefore the ground beneath the national imagination might also prove unstable.[52]

These worries meant that transatlantic news became a natural launching point for what I refer to as hypernationalist reactions. Such nationalist constructions and restorations threatened the institutional power of nation-states by attempting to connect to a true nation deeper than any information flow and thus secure from global impingements on unstable national news cycles. Furthermore, these new nationalist alternatives tended to frame themselves in relation to the dueling modes of national memory. Because those modes corresponded to competing understandings of Christian history, they ultimately encouraged hypernationalism as a kind of modern crusade to recover an imagined holy land. Such struggles combined a desire for deeper nationalist commitment and an appetite for violent conflict and political disruption; though sometimes framed as moral crusades against infidel powers, they also responded to more mundane geopolitical uncertainties arising from transatlantic factors, including the global expansion of news and the perceived deficit of ethnolinguistic distinctiveness among Anglo-Americans.[53]

The search for a stable national memory, whether undertaken by presentist or traditionalist Anglophones, displayed a zeal for perpetual reform; thus both sides of the memory war tended to destabilize the political status quo by expressing more expansive political concerns than the narrow spheres of government policy and party systems could contain. While they might disagree about whether revivalist architecture or the modern telegraph system should serve as primary engines of national history and social change, both presentists and traditionalists deployed them to challenge as much as support the political structures of standing nation-states.[54] Because the concerns of presentism and traditionalism transcended any particular political group, party, or ideology, their influence often created independent centers of gravity within established state institutions that in turn generated waves of schisms.

This inherent fractiousness often led British revivalists to reject party lines in the name of deeper orthodoxies; even when they stood as conservatives for Parliament, as they had in the Young England movement, they often did so as insurgents.[55] Operating as a dedicated presentist, Greeley was even more notorious for refusing to be bound by strict party doctrines. When he testified at Parliament he was helping preside over a Whig Party that was already heading toward the dissolution he would help finalize. Over three decades as a major political figure, Greeley was never fully at home in any party, becoming embroiled in nearly every major intraparty revolt and some of the minor ones, first as a restless Whig, then as an unreliable ally of the first Republican president, then as a "Liberal Republican" running against an incumbent President Grant. But while Greeley's policy positions and party alignments might shift, his commitment to the socially binding power of news and the authority of America's most recent history over its distant past remained firm; thus he would tellingly describe the so-called "nativists" not as the natural-born Americans they insisted they were but rather as motivated by "old-world feelings and prejudices," a form of traditionalism that was antithetical to true Americanism.[56] To a great extent Greeley's presentism was his politics.

The first part of this book explores this form of presentism by examining the first stage of the presentist/traditionalist division as a kind of holy war that was influenced by Christian history and belief but not restricted to it. Focusing on the 1840s and 1850s, the first three chapters explain how northerners operating in a transatlantic context might discern a single spirit behind presentist correspondences at the heart of their common culture, including the distinctive US news business, its colonial and revolutionary origins, and the presentist potential of Christian history. Greeley, Emerson, and Whitman ultimately passed beyond the organizational bounds of the faith traditions that had originated in the struggle to reform and then replace medieval Catholicism. Yet following through on a Protestant impulse had helped bring them there, and to the extent their traditionalist foes were sometimes pejoratively associated with Roman Catholicism (whether or not they had actually converted), it is tempting to cast American presentism as not only fundamentally Protestant but also anti-Catholic.[57]

The more important form of anti-catholic reaction in this book, however, comes with a lowercase *c,* and the resistance to catholic universality is a driving concern of part II. The transatlantic time lag would continue to divide the sharing of Anglophone news until after the Civil War; nevertheless, by the 1850s Anglophone news sharing seemed likely to rapidly transcend national as well as sectarian lines. This prospective catholicity of news troubled efforts to wed national identity to domestic news sharing, contributing to powerful hypernationalist reactions that included a crusade to capture the imagined holy land of a unified national geography. The three chapters of part II address how the transatlantic memory war helped initiate this more violent stage of American civil conflict as the 1850s ultimately gave way to what the British would call "the American War."

Chapter 1 identifies the diverging modes of memory endorsed by two contemporary cultural figures who effectively channeled them, Horace Greeley and A. W. N. Pugin. It analyzes Greeley's 1851 testimony about the divergent American news business and locates it within a larger cultural conflict over sacred national histories. Thus it links the *Tribune*'s development to a spiritually infused American presentism, a mode of memory that defined itself against the British alternative that endorsed Gothic Revivalism even as it constrained the free circulation of news.

Chapter 2 then tracks this spiritual strain into the more recognizably literary realm of Ralph Waldo Emerson and the historical experience of antislavery news. It shows how Emerson redirected a national spirit of presentism that he located at the heart of Christianity into a broad cultural critique of traditionalism as a moral and political heresy. Emerson's approach implicitly elevated the news to the level of sacred history. Thus his reformist efforts eventually converged with an antislavery struggle that had its own reasons for championing the recent past as a revolutionary front, source of divine action, communal bond, and index of the nation's moral health. Just as the *Tribune* helped shift the antislavery movement into the mainstream of American public life, Emerson helped frame abolitionist news as a distinctly American spiritual struggle. By bringing these forces of presentism into the same frame, the chapter shows how an increasingly nationalized antislavery movement, a distinctively American news model, and an argument for an independent national culture were drawn together and sacralized as a campaign to free America from traditionalist oppression.

Chapter 3 assesses Walt Whitman's early poetic contribution to this presentist campaign. Through a close analysis of a group of religious-themed poems published in Greeley's *Tribune* in 1850, it demonstrates that Whitman both understood and participated in the sacred national history taking shape in the popular press. Furthermore, by framing the national struggle in transatlantic terms, Whitman situated traditionalist proslavery forces as an alien power as well as a heretical one.

Chapter 4 examines how the Anglophone news's asymmetrical memory circuits shaped Great Exhibition news coverage during Greeley's 1851 tour. It focuses on the press controversy over belated contributions to the American exhibit, a battle over Anglo-American news that illustrated how transatlantic reciprocity shaped presentist memory in the 1850s. This transatlantic press battle shows how catholicity of news and the transatlantic time lag produced heightened nationalist anxieties and hypernationalist reactions that undercut the exhibition ethos and its celebration of the international news network. Even writers with internationalist inclinations and affiliations resisted the global network's full extension and rooted their embattled presentist memories in nationalist geographies. The chapter argues that the transatlantic time lag, which affected the transfer of news in much the same way it restricted the transportation of American exhibits, facilitated these efforts by producing geographically distinct and mutually alienating memory circuits that transatlantic news activated and made visible. In the hands of Greeley and his British peers these circuits became vital tools for sustaining nationalist inclinations at home by establishing shared history around a clear sense of place.

Chapter 5 follows this current of nationalist anxiety and hypernationalist reaction into Bleeding Kansas and the broader territorial misadventures and international crises that characterized transatlantic news in the mid-1850s. Against a backdrop of news from the Crimean War and several major Anglo-American controversies, Greeley and other presentist prophets promoted the so-called civil war in Kansas, generating nationalist uncertainty and hypernationalist zeal throughout the northern news media. The *Tribune* in particular promoted reading and responding to Kansas news as a hypernationalist engagement that threatened the political institutions of the nation-state. Ultimately, the broader Kansas conflict narrative encouraged a mass audience to regard their response to increasingly mainstream antislavery news as an experience of sacred national history and a crusade to regain the nation's moral and geographical integrity. By 1856 that history was literally grounded almost exclusively in the North but would soon come to include the image of a conquered South as the ultimate objective of the presentist crusade.

Chapter 6 focuses on Whitman's response to this situation by examining the first two editions of *Leaves of Grass* as a presentist memory circuit that defined itself against transatlantic traditionalism. It tracks Whitman's complex entanglements with American news and transatlantic influences by examining an overlooked poetic treatment of antislavery news in the 1855 edition and by analyzing early British and American reviews that Whitman collected and ultimately republished in the 1856 edition. Through all these efforts, Whitman transferred the worrisome prospect of renewed intersectional violence onto the well-established framework of a transatlantic memory war, and through the circulating artifact of his own book he offered himself as the sacred ground on which the presentist crusade would stand or fall.

The conclusion turns to the Civil War to show how war news, diplomacy, and literature all combined within the transatlantic field in presentist opposition to implicitly traditionalist British judgments. It argues that questions of national recognition that structured relations between Britain and the American sections drew inspiration from the transatlantic memory war of previous decades. Similarly, questions of national recognition in wartime shaped American national culture in ways that went well beyond military or diplomatic objectives. While British production and consumption of war news unsettled northern visions of the conflict, the transatlantic time lag placed limits on transatlantic communication that ultimately confirmed northern control of the war's presentist memory and provided Whitman with a fresh argument for an independent national literature.

Together these chapters aim to trace the broader cultural implications of transatlantic news while tracking the rise of two modern modes of memory. Drawing on the influences of a culture grounded in Christian temporality, mid-nineteenth-century presentist memorialists hoped to enact a more stable communal future through the increasing availability of news—a past so recent that it was very nearly the present and so pervasive that it could encompass nearly any locale. Their traditionalist counterparts, by contrast, were building their common national history around a past ancient enough to belong jointly to nearly all citizens or subjects. Presentists sacralized the idea of the past's common dissemination to bind the national public; traditionalists worshipped the image of its common provenance. Both gathered bodies of stone and paper, crowds and congregants, to complement their abstract beliefs. Inventing and imagining, they also rendered memory tangible. Masking the nations as they made them, they provided the unquestionable realities that modern individuals desperately desired. Thus the dueling modes of memory worked to construct their nationalist pasts out of the protean stuff of the mid-nineteenth-century transatlantic world.

Yet, in the United States at least, a twice-divided nation where conflicts proliferated along the border with the transatlantic East as well as the boundary between North and South, this was a story of destruction as well as construction, in which memory designed to foster national unity helped produce the ironic outcome of national dissolution on a grand scale. Though both presentists and traditionalists hoped to build a coherent national community upon the foundation of a shared past, they shaped an era when nations would be broken as well as forged, as what was once imagined soon had to be reimagined out of the ashes of lost histories. Presentist and traditionalist revivalists in various guises would play leading roles in these developments, and the tension between them would inspire some of the United States' most distinctive writing and the career of its most influential poet.[58] Yet to the extent that they trafficked in the metaphors of nationalism, all presentist writers were poets; thus my story begins not with Emerson nor with Whitman but rather with an equally prolific presentist writer upon whom both depended. It was Horace Greeley, after all, who made the nation's news and therefore the history in which the former minister found his church and around which the poet would spin his songs.

Sitting at his parliamentary hearing in 1851 Greeley could hardly guess that he would precipitate a revolution in his own country a decade later; that his paper would bring to such violent self-consciousness the "young North" to which Whitman and Emerson also appealed; that his own national influence would soon help a western lawyer and political dark horse upset far better-known rivals to become president of the United States; that as a chief herald of the modern era, the *Tribune* would preside over the rise and then the fall of nations. For the war, too, it would turn out, was a way to remember—was not merely a story for newspapers to cover but also one of the modern news's chief results. When those who formed million-man armies set out to make history, it would be unlike any history yet seen, and their national causes would take shape through a new kind of media in which they already saw themselves represented. This modern war would help produce its own common history of the most recent past, and most Americans would encounter it not in the field or in personal stories or historical tomes but rather in newspapers that had become their daily bread and their national communion meal.

Yet despite the rise of the news and the erosion of local traditions under the onslaught of modernity, traditionalism would also never disappear. Offspring of the modern world, its anachronistic reaction would continue to coexist beside a presentism that sought a solid basis for community in a sea of pulp. Equally absurd when subjected to reasoned analysis, these dueling modes of modern mass memory would nevertheless wield a great power based on a need deeper than reason: the need to belong, to share a history in common, to hew together over time, to escape a common mortal fate. National monuments, mass-produced newspapers, and civil wars were the colorful biproducts of this intense and essentially human desire, lodged deep in a social animal whose identity rested on the dual footings of a recollected past and a present will. Tapping into wellsprings of consciousness and communal desire, the modern era's traditionalist and presentist reactions could never be exhausted, as long as there were human audiences to respond to their call.

Those same desires buttressed the Palace of Westminster as Greeley sat testifying about the public's passion for telegraphic dispatches and morning news. Soon after he departed, the common communal impulse behind both traditionalist and presentist modes of memory would manifest itself in the gigantic clock tower rising high over the Stamp Committee's meeting room in the new Houses of Parliament. Traveling to London from far and wide, visitors from both shores of the Atlantic and both memory camps would discern more than merely the hour behind the face of the five-ton clock, nested among its novel Gothic arches. Later called Big Ben after its main bell, the timepiece that became London's most globally recognizable landmark would present an uneasy epoch with a symbol of unceasing change, housed in an image of unyielding permanence. Visible from great distances, audible from miles, the clock with its Roman numerals would reassure Britons drawn to an imperial metropolis. Though their communal traditions might be rapidly vanishing, though their hold on their personal past might be increasingly fleeting, each moment passed secure within the framework of a common national history. Whatever changes the modern world or their daily papers might bring, the nation promised its modern people that it would never lose control of time.[59]

PART I

REVIVAL AND REVOLUTION
The Modes of Modern Memory

Give me the writing of a nation's newspaper, and who pleases shall make speeches in its House of Commons.

—*Illustrated London News*, 1851

The history of architecture is the history of the world.... The belief and manners of all people are embodied in the edifices they raised.

—A. W. N. Pugin, *An Apology for the Revival of Christian Architecture in England*, 1843

When Horace Greeley testified before Parliament in 1851, he was standing on what was arguably some of the most sacred ground in Britain. It was not just that the new Houses of Parliament were being made up to look like a giant Gothic church. Although the renovations going on around him were new, English kings and churchmen had been erecting shrines near that bank of the Thames to the west of London for a thousand years or more. Legend held that a church built at the site of Westminster Abbey by the sixth-century Saxon king Sebert had been miraculously consecrated by St. Peter himself. A somewhat more historically credible partnership between church leaders and the ninth-century English king Edgar had erected a monastery at the site, and Edward the Confessor had elevated it to new prominence by raising a Norman-style building there and also a royal palace nearby; this last significant Anglo-Saxon king had consecrated his abbey only a year before the Norman conquest would open its doors to both William the Conqueror, who was crowned in the abbey on Christmas Day 1066, and the Gothic style that followed them across the channel.[1] In future years further cooperation between political and religious leaders yielded a rich harvest of monumental structures in what would become the Westminster borough of greater London: Westminster Abbey, the Palace of Westminster, the Palace of Whitehall (which had burned to the ground at the close of the seventeenth century), Buckingham Palace, and numerous other smaller sites that housed Britain's secular government and symbolized its connection to church tradition.[2]

Clearly the physical environs around Westminster arose from the weaving together monarchical, parliamentarian, and ecclesiological elements into a potent form of sacred history. Yet the nature of the bond between the history of a nation and a faith can be difficult to identify. This is partly because the connections between religion and politics, in modern as well as ancient times, cut both ways, yielding "an affinity not only between forms of polity and forms of religious organization but also between political forms and how religious phenomena are imagined."[3] Indeed, the threads of religion and politics are not only tightly woven but often organically fused, for their mutually defined myths, memories, rituals, and traditions tend to overlap and influence one another. Thus the site of Westminster suggests a process of mutual appropriation that has been taking place on the banks of the Thames for a millennium. The faith to be found there can be identified with neither church nor state as isolated entities. Rather, the sense of sacred history such sites produce relies on the overlapping narratives and reciprocal involvements of a political state and Christian church, each with peculiar constitutions that evolved in relation to each other.[4] In such a context, popular forms of sacred history are likely to emerge through overlapping practices and narratives that actively conflate political and religious elements. Through such combinations they help explain the origins and prospects of national life and address modern spiritual concerns over the loss of tradition, rapid social change, and alienation from the past. Thus, even in modern nation-states where the institutions of church and state are nominally separate, it may be difficult to see where national politics end and religion begins.[5]

If the line between secular and sacred is never set in stone, the stones set up in Westminster built a bridge between the two, symbolically standing for the fundamental spiritual unity that upheld a British nation forged of warring tribes and waves of foreign invaders. The Gothic renovations of the mid-nineteenth century amounted to a belated attempt to rebuild that bridge of sacred national history. Yet in considering Greeley's testimony on the American news business, the text of which was duly recorded in the parliamentary records, we may be inclined to forget the place in which the testimony occurred entirely and the interlacing of religion and politics that it so clearly indicated. In doing so, we would be missing something important not only about the history of that interaction but also about historical experience in general—namely that it is always embodied, always active through material elements that carry their own symbolic weights and resonances and create their own practical effects. Where Parliament met mattered, and so did the building design its members had recently chosen as an explicit reinforcement of their belief in a sacred and durable national history. As Andrea Frederickson argues, the parliamentary committee members who determined to remain in Westminster "believed that by working with and reinforcing the area's ancient character, the [parliamentary] complex would provide a necessary connection with the past that would at once trigger the spectator's ancestral ties with Old England, and underline the continuity of the British Parliament."[6] Britain's ruling classes had intended the New Palace of Westminster to be a symbolic image and a social instrument, a material means to belong to a nation through a connection to a distant past. The way the MPs thought about news and the policies regulating it bore a relation to the physical place Parliament called home.

When Greeley arrived there in 1851 to testify about the unique character of the midcentury American news business, he was also describing a national symbol at least as monumental in its own way as Westminster. Liah Greenfeld has argued that nationalism, as "a particular perspective or style of thought" at the heart modern society's symbolic order, always involves elevating "the people" to an "elite" position as "the bearer of sovereignty, the basis of political solidarity, and the supreme object of loyalty."[7] Horace Greeley's *Tribune* was one of the chief vehicles of that symbolic elevation. In speaking in Parliament about the news business, he was also participating in an ongoing transatlantic debate about how the modern masses should be organized as nations and advancing his presentist cause on an important battlefield in the larger memory war.

Part I recounts how that memory war took shape during a period that roughly corresponded to Greeley's career. Focusing on several key cultural figures, including Greeley, Emerson, and Whitman, it demonstrates that the rapidly evolving news business in the United States was providing more than cheap access to the latest information. Rather, it was creating a conduit for a mass audience to share a sacred national history in a new way, one that set them apart from the Old World and in particular their British counterparts. In an American context that was bereft of monarchs and state churches, modern newspapers were seeking to unify the fractious tribes and the alienated individuals who constituted their readerships and thus to provide a viable alternative to the stones of Westminster. As they expanded their reach, they were not merely delivering bloodless information about the world to populations of national size; as icons and instruments of spiritually potent history they were creating the world and the nations within it. Like those who laid Westminster's stones, the purveyors of presentist memory were building bridges to a sacred past.

No single figure had more to do with this development than Horace Greeley, whose *Tribune* was sometimes referred to as a modern bible not because of its explicit moral and religious content but rather because it effectively sacralized involvement in national political life in the form of cheap, timely, high-quality news.[8] And no single figure represented the modern antithesis and foil to this nascent American form of sacred history than A. W. N. Pugin, the nineteenth-century British architect who had made his career a protest against modernity's destruction of traditional culture, and who had fashioned many of the Gothic details surrounding Greeley in 1851.

Children of the modern era, Greeley and Pugin were virtual contemporaries; born a year apart just before the most recent war between Britain and the United States, both were popular agitators and innovators who had shaken up their respective cultural fields. Both men also understood that they were giving mass audiences a place to belong within their respective national histories. Yet the modes of modern memory they crafted, Pugin's traditionalism on the one hand and Greeley's presentism on the other, could not have been more different. Part I begins with an analysis of Greeley's testimony about differences in the British and American news business in its material context amid the century's "most decisive intervention into the argument for Gothic revivalism."[9] By uncovering the spiritual and nationalist roots of a seemingly secular and mundane distinction in newspaper taxation, it helps explain the political power of a presentist/traditionalist split to build and also destroy political unities within the transatlantic world of the Civil War era.

1

Memory for the Masses

Sacred History and the National Press

The erection of the Parliament Houses in the national style is by far the greatest advance that has yet been gained in the right direction.
—A. W. N. Pugin, *An Apology for the Revival of Christian Architecture in England*, 1843

The telegraphic dispatch is the great point.
—Horace Greeley, parliamentary testimony, 1851

As Greeley sat in the Palace of Westminster, he was only a few generations removed from his family's British roots, and he still spoke and published in a fair approximation of the queen's English. What divided him culturally from his British peers was neither language nor ethnicity nor long separation. Yet by the mid-nineteenth century, a new gulf had opened between Britain and its former colonies. The country from which Greeley hailed had invested heavily in a different sense of time, a focus on the recent past that Greeley's paper marketed to the masses every day and through which he had made his name. Thus, as a modern news publisher from the United States, Greeley stood as a double contrast to the reverence embodied in the Gothic Revival, for his nationality as well as his business depended on establishing the cultural significance of the most immediate history. As a progressive reformer from the New World, his allegiance lay with a new republic, which he saw as struggling to emerge from a dense thicket of mostly British cultural traditions. As much as any other quality or disposition, this presentist focus was what made Greeley identifiable as an American. In testifying to the power of the American news he also bore testament to the myth of a nation grounded in the new and growing strong under an eternally dawning sun. Standing under the shadow of Westminster's Gothic monuments to a distant past, he appeared as the bold advocate of pulp rather than stone.[1]

Yet stone had its modern champions as well. Beginning in 1836, Augustus Welby Northmore Pugin's popular and influential publications had been arguing that a nation's buildings were inextricable from its social and cultural life and that the physical ugliness of the "buildings of the present day" mirrored Britain's more fundamental "decay of taste."[2] To Pugin, "there was only one style," the Gothic, and the diversity that marked the British architectural landscape bore sorry witness to the spiritual devastation of the modern era.[3] Pugin was a popular polemicist before he was a builder, and he struck a chord with like-minded Victorians who saw something amiss in modern British culture and so wove their artistic and social criticisms around a potent defense of a bygone age. His influence had helped win Charles Barry the commission for the new Houses of Parliament, and he was either directly or indirectly responsible for many of Westminster's towering anachronisms.[4]

Pugin and his fellow revivalists were neither simple antiquarians nor mere supporters of the status quo. Rather, they were radically conservative thinkers who sought to recover an authentic national culture that had been buried under the detritus of modern times. Unity, both aesthetic and political, was one of their movement's chief objectives. Pugin disdained the mishmash of British architectural styles not merely as aesthetic monstrosities but more fundamentally as violations of national coherence, dismal symbols of pervasive cultural "inconsistency" within a British nation in search of its soul.[5]

The consistency he sought was spiritual and national as much as it was artistic, and Pugin thought he had found it in a Christian architectural tradition that predated the schisms and innovations of the Reformation and the Renaissance—those communal disorders that had accompanied the revolution in printing and new learning and launched Western Europe headlong into the modern world centuries before Pugin's birth. In offering rare praise for the Parliament Houses' "national style" of Gothic excellence, Pugin also criticized the rest of the London cityscape for failing to "advance . . . in the right direction." Ironically, advancing on Pugin's terms meant a strategic retreat to the stylistic standards of a shared British past that lay far beyond the reach of any living memory. Only a uniform Gothic style of the sort materializing at the Houses of Parliament could express the British nation as a unified entity, avoid an aesthetics based on modern innovation or alien infiltration, and, in Pugin's words, "remind [Englishmen] of our faith and our country."[6] As he put it in an 1841 treatise, "God in his wisdom has implanted a love of nation and country in every man, and we should always cultivate the feeling.... We should never forget our own land." Europe had been beset, Pugin thought, by "a sort of bastard Greek, a nondescript modern style." The heedless rush to modernity was "replacing the original national buildings with unmeaning lines of plaster fronts, without form, without colour, without interest." Worse, "all places are becoming alike," leaving "national feelings and national architecture . . . at so low an ebb, that it becomes an absolute duty in every Englishman to attempt their revival."[7]

Pugin's nationalistic reminders leant strength to a resurgent mid-nineteenth-century British traditionalism that sought to make a recovered past a bulwark against perceived modern encroachments on the nation's integrity. In addition to a revived Westminster, coinciding signs of this groundswell had appeared in major ecclesiastical and political revivals such as the Oxford Movement and Young England.[8] As the historian Michael Alexander observes, this "larger Medieval Revival, that broad movement in general culture which was the parent of the architectural revival," has been largely ignored even by scholars interested in its discrete religious, literary, or artistic manifestations.[9] Yet an even more basic idea than medievalism connected the widespread Victorian interest in ancient roots, and it was hardly obscure. The spirit of traditionalist revivalism sought social unity in a past distant enough to be widely shared, even by the diverse and divided people of contemporary Great Britain. The leaders of the Oxford Movement circulated their *Tracts for the Times,* for example, to counter not only the state's increased meddling in church matters but also the social fractures that for them characterized the modern British nation; thus their notion of tradition was "not only a preservative idea but a quest for reform" that was closely tied to communitarian visions of "the ancient and undivided church."[10] This basic impulse to recover unity in antiquity was what such revivalists meant by tradition, and in pursuing it they adopted a pattern that innumerable commemorations would follow throughout the modern era.

Against this traditionalist backdrop Greeley would present his testimonial to an alternative way of organizing a mass public, one that built a sense of unity around shared access to the recent past. As founding editor Greeley had made the *Tribune* one of the United States' most important papers in only ten years; in the process he had both demonstrated and symbolized the increasing political power and democratizing potential of the rapidly expanding news business.[11] Greeley had hired talented writers and managers, paid his printers well, and made his key employees shareholders. He had helped organize the Associated Press to maximize the news-gathering potential of the telegraph and oceangoing steam ships. Most important, he and his business partner, Thomas McElrath, had determined to sell his paper at a price almost any American could afford and had devised creative price mechanisms to maintain a growing popular audience.[12]

With a street price of only a cent and a half, the daily *Tribune* sold more cheaply by subscription, and its eight-page weekly edition digested the previous week's news for just two dollars a year; if even this price seemed steep, any member of a local "club" of twenty subscribers or more could receive a year of the weekly for just a dollar. In this way two cents brought distant readers a review of the week's most important events plus the latest news off the wire in New York as fast as the mails could carry it. Priced to sell and already boasting more than fifty thousand subscribers and one hundred thousand readers, the paper's daily, semiweekly, and west coast editions would soon make the *Tribune* the first truly national American news outlet.[13]

Greeley was not the only news expert to testify that spring, and the committee called a number of British witnesses who might have taught the American editor something about the business. The news-gathering network of the *Times* of London still outstripped its transatlantic peers, and many American papers tended to treat Britain's most powerful daily as the final word in European news—or even as a surrogate international bureau. The center of pictorial journalism was also still in England, where for nearly a decade the *Illustrated London News* had been using sketch artists, photographers, and engravers to bring images of news stories to press.[14] The technical knowledge Greeley brought to Parliament, then, involved not some new mechanism for news gathering but rather a means of both reaching and galvanizing a politicized popular audience. He became the spokesman for a profitable model that combined mass production, aggressive pricing, and the democratic commitment to a national readership into a potent social identity.

This was no minor business innovation. By producing the *Tribune* for the masses, Greeley was proving that high-quality journalism could be sold to a much broader and larger audience than any British paper possessed, and his example indicated an opportunity for similar growth to his British counterparts. Nevertheless, because the *Tribune*'s growth arose from a widespread and politicized readership, there was a real question about whether the British papers could enjoy similar success without violating the basic political assumptions governing Britain's more hierarchical society. Thus the committee's questions revealed an interest not merely in Greeley's business but also in the national culture to which his paper was so well harmonized, and they were especially concerned with the American lower classes' powerful relationship to a history that was common in two senses: common because it was widely shared as news, and common because it relied on the political engagement of ordinary readers drawn from the lower social strata.

Parliament had practical reasons to consider increasing British news readership by lowering the tax on newspapers, for the economic benefits of Greeley's model were undeniable. By successfully embracing the modern era and serving a rapidly expanding mass audience, American papers had demonstrated the profitable synergy among major advances in news production, the rise of more democratic politics, and a nationalistic relationship to the most recent past. Unfettered by excessive taxes and regulations, the value of Greeley's already successful paper had doubled in the two years prior to his testimony.[15] Meanwhile the British market for cheap news was still largely untapped, so that at the time of Greeley's testimony in Parliament, there were likely as many copies of the *Tribune* in American hands as there were issues circulating of all the London dailies combined. Yet the committee members' assumptions that an expanded British news audience also would be more politically engaged, radicalized, and in short Americanized were giving some of them pause.

More was at stake than filling the coffers of publishers or the government; what the members were considering was a major adjustment in British social engineering. While Greeley's cheap paper had from its first issue sought an audience of rural farmers and urban mechanics, the largest British newspapers had avoided such a democratic orientation by governmental design, eschewing the market for a "pauper press" that the Crown and Parliament had long associated with radical politics at home and political revolutions abroad. American newspapers such as the *Tribune* had capitalized on an emerging mass market that new cost-effective technology had opened; yet by catering to that market they indirectly supported the sort of democratic political culture that still made many British politicians uneasy, especially in the aftermath of an 1848 resurgence of "Chartism" and revolutionary activity on the continent. Conservative paranoia over the news's social power had a long history of association with America as well as France, dating from the revolutions in the late eighteenth century, and centered on the worry that political unrest would cross British borders through the efforts of radical journalists.[16]

That worry had taken root in the previous generation, when governmental efforts to control mass media had increased in response to significant political challenges. The perceived danger posed by radical news publisher

William Cobbett helped inspire increased duties on papers that carried daily or weekly news in 1815. These "taxes on knowledge" were especially notable in that they singled out news, rather than commentary, as politically dangerous content. The new duties eventually brought down Cobbett's *Political Register*, but Cobbett adjusted by bringing out his *Two-Penny Trash*, which got around the prohibition on news by providing blistering commentary on stories that were already widely known, and which soon achieved a circulation ten times that of the *Times* of London.[17] The Six Acts of 1819 more directly countered such radicalism by allowing the seizure of any paper deemed seditious and extending duties to all weekly and daily publications regardless of content.

In the 1830s, however, radical publishers again began to circumvent the law by publishing unstamped papers. When extensive prosecutions only increased unstamped circulation, the government finally lowered the duty on respectable papers to allow these now trusted supporters of the establishment to answer the radical challenge in an affordable format. Nevertheless, Britain still taxed its papers with stamp duties in 1851. This additional cost had since the early decades of the century kept any publication carrying news intentionally "dear": too costly to become popular among the working classes that had historically formed the core market for radical news.[18]

Now a Select Committee on Newspaper Stamps was considering abolishing these taxes completely, partly due to the success of American papers like the *Tribune*. The unstated question before the committee members was whether by expanding what had been an elite privilege of reading national news, cheap papers would also engage a popular audience in the daily doings of national politics and so cheapen Britain's national memory. Americans had little choice but to find their common history in the daily news, but was such a thing either suitable or safe for an Englishman—who should proudly claim Westminster Abbey and all its entombed monarchs and heroes as a national legacy? A more widely available press might unhinge British identity from aristocratic traditions and long-standing social hierarchies by giving the British masses a readier means of sharing the nation's most recent past. Although, as Linda Colley observes, "Men and women living in or near town with some access to print . . . seem always to have been among the busiest and most reliable of [British] patriots," many powerful Britons were still reluctant to trust the political privilege of national news to commoners who had less personal access to other aristocratic privileges.[19] Repealing taxes on knowledge entirely would offer a working-class public the sense of engagement in national history that reading a paper like the

Times of London already fostered in the more elevated classes; it would also mean extending patronage and therefore control of the national news's distribution beyond dependable elites.

These were uncharted and therefore politically dangerous waters, and American success stories like Greeley's were cold comfort for conservatives. Revisiting newspapers' governance tapped into the transatlantic worry that nudging the British press toward an American business model would in turn Americanize other British institutions, including the government, while simultaneously reducing precisely that nationalist reverence for Britain's premodern past that traditionalism's disciples were hoping to strengthen. Recognizing that the *Tribune* represented not just a news venture but also a way of organizing a national public that transcended traditionalist class structures, the members of Parliament who questioned Greeley gave voice to their own long-standing political hopes and apprehensions.[20]

The MPs wanted to know first about the economics and logistics of mass producing newspapers. Could Americans receive a reputable paper for less than two pennies per issue? How had a half-penny newspaper, the *New-York Sun*, managed to sell its operations for an astounding quarter million dollars? Was it true that American steam presses were now printing faster than those of the great London papers? Greeley confirmed all they had heard and in the process showed his audience what the future of the British newspaper might look like. The American editor judged the *Sun*'s $250,000 price "very cheap," considering the huge advertising revenue the penny paper commanded. He had personally witnessed New York City's newest cylinder presses printing eighteen thousand sheets in an hour, and they needed every second to stand up to the staggering task of providing daily news to nearly a million paying readers.[21] Beyond New York's news center, Greeley guessed that the American news network included twenty-five hundred distinct journals.[22]

For Greeley's listeners such staggering statistics raised the same deep social and political anxieties that had given the British news business its peculiar shape since the early nineteenth-century suppression of the radical press. How was this explosion of information kept under control, his questioners wanted to know. Did all these papers lead to the publication of outrageous libels and the pirating of news by unscrupulous editors? On the contrary, Greeley answered, there were very few court actions for libel in the United States, and he rather enjoyed seeing the *Tribune*'s articles reprinted in other papers. Besides, Americans liked to get their news as early as possible, before it could be copied, in order to read it at the breakfast table before work.²³ "Every mechanic takes a paper," Greeley testified, "or nearly every one."²⁴

Greeley's description of a well-informed mechanic breakfasting on the daily news was a pointed reference to the American working class, which the committee must have recognized all along as the elephant in the room. In America, one member deduced, "the purchasers of daily papers must consist of a different class from those in England." In the teeming cities of the New World, the working classes must read the latest edition of their own "daily newspaper, just as the people of the upper classes do in England."²⁵ While the transcript of the hearings does not reveal whether this prospect struck the committee members as laudable or horrifying, Greeley responded with typically democratic enthusiasm. By his count, three-quarters of New York families read their daily papers diligently, and even humble agricultural laborers could take the weekly editions of a great New York paper such as the *Tribune*. Moreover, Greeley was convinced the practice did them and the country a great deal of practical good.²⁶

Had the committee's task been merely to adjudicate questions of taxes and revenue, its members might have been accused of exceeding its mandate. The larger social issues the questioners raised were justified, however, by the increasingly obvious fact that wherever they grew unfettered, newspapers were fast becoming the center of modern community life. Moreover, aided by new technology, such papers would be more difficult to restrain than any these British politicians had yet seen. Greeley insisted that even so powerful an editor as he could not play the role of locomotive to the endless train of the news. Newspapers had a greater impact on public opinion in the United States than Britain, Greeley admitted, but operated through a different sort of influence. "I do not know that any class is despotically governed by [the press], but the influence is more universal [in America]," he averred. "Everyone reads it and talks about it with us, and more weight is laid upon intelligence than on editorials; the paper which brings the quickest news is the one looked to."²⁷

Yet this did not mean that such information was politically inert. Greeley's subscribers were using his paper to become part of a network of shared information that was spanning the globe and to take their place as individual citizens of a new kind of community based on the most current intelligence. American newspapers—with circulations rising into the hundreds of thousands and encompassing the literate masses—were no longer strictly speaking the tools of the partisan editors who ran them, but the power they now represented was still profoundly political, even revolutionary.

As a required element at every breakfast table, the news itself had become the American masses' daily bread, the raw material of an ever-present yet transient past. And in that form news would provide the basis for a new version of common history organized along presentist lines. No paper more perfectly captured the news's potential to serve this communal function than Greeley's *Tribune*, in part because he had spent his career as a media entrepreneur redrawing the lines between politics and news in ways that fostered his audience's sense of communal attachment to the recent past. While not as recognizable as the Gothic renovation of Westminster, a cheap newspaper like the *Tribune* was also providing a cathedral for the modern age.

Daily Bread: Greeley's Entrepreneurial Engagement with National Memory

British news had periodically sparked social unrest and had sometimes been suppressed, and traditionalists of Pugin's ilk sometimes demonized newspapers as diabolical impediments to all that was wholesome in their own Christian nation. The *Tribune*, however, was hardly irreligious. Greeley saw its role as providing a positive moral counterweight to the worst offenses of his industry, and by 1851 it had arguably become one of the primary conduits of a poly- and postdenominational religious movement.[28] At an even deeper level, he was providing a spiritual tether for Americans who were losing their sense of place amid modernity's upheavals, and in this basic purpose of addressing the loss of tradition Greeley stood closer to the Gothic renovators than he might appear.

Greeley had first come to New York City from the American backcountry, and he had found many thousands who had only just arrived in the budding metropolis. His early career there was marked by several innovative attempts at marketing different sorts of periodicals, from penny papers to weekly miscellanies, to a rapidly growing urban audience that included migrants from across the Atlantic as well as native-born Americans drawn to the nation's largest city.[29] These mostly failed innovations merely set the table for his eventual collaboration with the Whig leaders Thurlow Weed and William H. Seward, which gave Greeley the chance to reinvent the genre of the party paper with the displaced masses in mind.

The job put Greeley on the ground floor of a new national political culture ideally suited to a presentism centered on news. The modern drift away from the security of tradition would destabilize American politics, driving the political press and the parties it benefited in new directions. Greeley seemed to recognize the needs of his readership earlier than most, including his partners. When he began working on a state party paper with Weed and Seward in 1838, he had surprised them by naming the paper after Jefferson, the founder of the rival Democratic Party. If this represented a cheap bid to fool democratically inclined voters, it was also an effort to democratize the Whigs' tone if not their agenda. Moreover, it signaled what would become Greeley's lifelong quest to develop a new kind of antitraditionalist political paper.

Greeley would remain a seemingly loyal Whig and nominal conservative throughout the 1840s. Yet as a Whig editor he was contributing less to a political establishment than to a constant state of political flux, and out of a chaotic mix of elements in 1840 he would help organize a new Whig identity around election news. By then he had become well enough positioned within the New York Whigs to help drag the national party into the rough and tumble world of a more democratically directed politics and a "marvelously imaginative presidential campaign" that "raised sloganeering and political song making into a high art."[30] One of the major engines driving this shift was Greeley's campaign journal, the *Log Cabin*, and it was no ordinary paper. Benefiting from Greeley's authorship of everything from biographical sketches to jokes and songs, the *Log Cabin* achieved a weekly print run of eighty thousand issues and a success "entirely beyond precedent," according to one of Greeley's rivals.[31] Thanks partly to the journal, "every town in America seemed to have a log cabin, a Harrison club, and a chorus singing Whig songs," and its national scope helped elect President William Henry Harrison in the most raucous campaign the Whigs had ever run.[32] Greeley's publication of political news and editorials rose well above the level of information and opinion; it created a material focal point of democratically oriented presentist memory and opportunities for a mass public to affiliate not just with a presidential candidate but with each other around a common history.

Greeley had guessed that the American masses of future years could not simply be molded by elite opinions or past party affiliation. The Whig's reputation for elitism had contributed to election losses in the Jacksonian era, and shaking off the elitist stigma had stoked more recent Whig successes. That lesson would remain important as the resulting two-party system disintegrated under sectionalist pressures in the coming decades. After the political tumult of the 1840s and the first rumblings of the Free Soil movement, Greeley could see that those still willing to call themselves Whigs nonetheless "will prefer Freedom to Party."[33] Yet modern audiences who aspired to greater freedom also seemed to yearn for conformity in the feeling and practice of reading and responding to the news. The *Log Cabin* and the election of 1840 had proved that a paper's political power lay not merely in the acceptance of its positions but in how its audience experienced it viscerally as a collective engagement with history; a paper had a political life of its own that could not be constrained to its opinion pages. In 1840 that had meant the sort of print that could become manifest in all manner of material objects and social interactions: printed songs, sketches, jokes, and insults had become choruses, medals, laughter, and fistfights. Slogans had become soap. This was the modern politics that Greeley "helped invent" in 1840 as a moral crusade and means to embody political news as a common history as much as a successful campaign for government office.[34]

The *Tribune* would follow in due course. Determined to expand on the *Log Cabin*'s success, Greeley would provide not only a Whig alternative to the largely Democratic penny press of New York City but also a national paper of unprecedented scope by channeling the kind of communal spirit he had cultivated during the 1840 campaign. Launched in 1841, in only a few years it would stand nearly on par with the city's leading paper, the *New York Herald*, building a broad audience by filling his low-priced sheets with political commentary, cultural observations, and the latest news.[35] In these early years, European and especially British news was a primary draw, as it was for other major New York papers. By the time transatlantic news arrived, however, it was hardly new, and as it turned out, the more significant movement for the *Tribune* was not eastward across the water but westward across the continent.[36] The telegraph and steam engine were tying the country together even as it expanded geographically, converting local events into items of national interest within days, sometimes minutes. Yet the ties that bound were not only iron and copper, for the network's lifeblood was political. Indeed, Samuel Morse's telegraph had only proved its worth, which many had previously doubted, by serving as a medium for the latest political news, transmitting the outcome of the 1844 Whig convention in Baltimore to an eager crowd waiting in Washington, while a train raced to provide the same information.[37]

Greeley had welcomed these advances, even as his paper had literally embodied them. It was he who had championed homestead legislation and proclaimed "Go West, young man!" to the urban masses, and those men and women who followed the advice brought Greeley's paper with them. Thus the speed of steam, electricity, and Greeley's tireless pen combined to both establish the transplanted populations of new states and link them with each other and the places they had left behind.[38] Greeley's weekly edition of the "New York" *Tribune* became a constant in a sea of change and was as near to a national paper as America had yet produced. Following telegraph lines and railroads into the West, by 1850 its weekly edition advertised its sales to clubs in Ohio, Wisconsin, Michigan, Illinois, Iowa, California, and Oregon.[39]

As it expanded, the *Tribune* became the visible evidence of a modern information network and the symbol of the national community that relied upon it. In the process it formed its own sort of political society that overlapped with the Whig Party but did not always exactly align with it. Greeley's early work for the Whigs had demonstrated that the party could no longer depend on simple partisan fidelity and needed to cater to the popular desire for a more direct line into national politics. Just as he had successfully established the *Log Cabin* as an alternative to traditional conservative party politics, he now launched and positioned the *Tribune* as an effort to free the press from overt political influence, aiming for a "happy medium" between "servile partisanship" and "gagged, mincing neutrality."[40]

This stance helped make the *Tribune* a political revolution in its own right, one that bound together hundreds of thousands of readers and gave them a conduit for shared history and more intense political participation. Crucially, the *Tribune* offered its audience a means of making as well as reading news through collective political action. In its pages a mass public not only imagined themselves represented but also saw their political engagements reported as the cocreators of an embodied news cycle of call and response. Thus it fostered popular political involvement that arose in in the midst of degenerating party structures, weaving a powerful domestic memory circuit around a national spirit of reform.[41]

Sometimes ridiculed for converting his paper into a testing ground for the latest social experiments, Greeley's various pet projects—from homesteading to Fourierism to spiritualism—were outgrowths not just of his personal obsessions but also the thirst for new forms of community that defined his far-flung audience of displaced modern individuals.[42] As he would write to Thurlow Weed explaining his socialist leanings, the Whigs would only make themselves irrelevant if they came to be seen as "the enemies of improvement," and "the bulwark of an outgrown aristocracy in this country."[43] Thus he steered the editorial course most in keeping with the new social fact that the success of his paper implied: his mass public was ready to claim national news as their common history. Progressive social ideas were an important part of his agenda, but as a powerful organ of presentist memory, the *Tribune* was always Greeley's greatest social experiment. He had wagered the success of his paper on America's presentist spirit, and with each new reader he was proving the wisdom of that wager. The question Parliament was deciding in 1851 was whether such a bid would pay off—socially and politically, as well as economically—for John Bull.

Antitraditionalist Strains

When the historian of journalism Frank Luther Mott insisted that Greeley's chief power was as "a journalist," he was also crediting him with making American journalism an unprecedented social power.[44] For by the time of his testimony, Greeley was giving his audience a new way to belong within a wider national history by circumventing previously insurmountable political and geographical divisions. Americans east and west shared the news and therefore a sense of history and placed the editor at the heart of an information revolution that was also political. For some of Greeley's parliamentary listeners, his example represented an opportunity rather than a threat. On the surface there seemed to be no reason why the presentist form of national memory should necessarily remain particularly American, for Britain had its share of papers and journalistic entrepreneurs who would have appreciated ready access to an underserved domestic market. Many questions for Greeley seemed to arise from the assumption that the American way of doing news could be imported largely through the adoption of cheaper pricing.

Nevertheless, things were not so simple. Cheap news was actually part of a larger American picture and owed both its success and influence partly to transatlantic distinctions that ran deeper than tax policy. Some of these concerned literacy rates and reading habits. Some merely offered convenient ways for chauvinists to maintain a sense of exceptionalist nationalism. But the transatlantic distinction in modern news also arose from what seemed a peculiarly American propensity for collective identification with newly minted histories. This affiliation with presentist memory expressed itself in multiple areas of national life, from popular notions of a revolutionary heritage to religious cultures of revival. Yet all involved a reaction against a traditionalism associated with the Old World and Britain in particular.

For one thing, transatlantic distinctions based on the relative length of perceived national histories carried a kind of inertia. While no nation had a monopoly on either the distant or the recent past, most nineteenth-century

British nationalists had a far greater stake in a long-standing history; by contrast, American nationalists of Greeley's generation proved increasingly willing to regard the latest history as their distinctive legacy. Robert Weisbuch has argued that forward-looking American nationalists, spurning the traditionalist claims and ancient aristocratic titles they perceived to be at the heart of British national culture, instead made a virtue of their lack of ancient traditions by spinning their "thin history" into a national connection with the immediate past—and, by extension, with the future.[45]

Similarly, the distinctive mythos of a colonial and revolutionary past also contributed to Americans' presentist attachments to modern news. A hemispheric understanding of history had accompanied European exploration and colonization and still clearly shaped nineteenth-century transatlantic culture.[46] Almost by definition transatlantic exchanges, contrasts, and comparisons had to contend with this typical division of the world along a temporal as well as a spatial boundary, as "new" and "old" as well as "eastern" and "western." Prior to 1776 that division might have been partially mitigated by a provincial understanding of the New World as an arena in which the Old might stage its fantasies and enact its social experiments. Nevertheless, the idea of separate worlds (only one of which was new) laid the literal ground for a revolutionary nationalism. Once the final political breach opened between Britain and its colonies, in a time when mass printing was becoming endemic in North America, the American stake in the most recent past seemed planted in the firm ground of the New World.[47] Thus both the Revolution and a breakaway nation's distinctive affinity for news became more comprehensible as natural outcomes of geographical location.

Combined with a potent hemispheric identity, America's history of revolution helped guard a permeable transatlantic border that kept English speakers from considering themselves Englishmen and Englishwomen. Although a shared English language, the sense of British lineage, and continued transatlantic migration worked to perpetuate the British affiliations of many Americans, presentist appeals to revolutionary history could encourage the "young nation" to dispense with its largely European heritage and revel in its prospects. As a "nation of nations," made up of revolutionized former colonials and immigrants who had left their pasts behind for a New World, the United States could become the place to discard the dusty trappings of old Europe's tired habits, outmoded social divisions, and antiquated traditionalist tendencies—and thus the place to make a common history out of the news.[48]

Such an assumption, of course, was based on nationalist myths that would still be familiar to almost any American schoolchild. Yet its familiarity can mask one of its most salient features: it was not only a myth about a unique national history (of the sort every nation-state must claim and bequeath on its citizens); it also contained a more significant claim about a unique national experience of history that could be lived out through concrete contemporary practices.[49] Those who saw sharing the presentist orientation as a sign of their American identity also transferred their primary nationalist allegiance from the hazier myths of a distant past and onto readily tangible social realities packaged in newspapers that arrived by the week and by the day. In the static form of a Gothic edifice, a national heritage might inspire contemporary political unity based on common reverence for a distant past; the Revolution's true heirs, however, were those who believed unity was to be found in a perpetual refusal of tradition and a common engagement in the most recent past. The revolutionary imperative for a constant transatlantic reaction against the Old World implicitly elevated the news as the most relevant national history, and it was reinforced in the mid-nineteenth century by significant developments in American Protestantism.

Puritanism long held pride of place in identifying the religious roots of American identity in the nineteenth century and beyond; in explaining the development of American nationalism, however, assigning primacy to any particular religious tradition proves difficult to sustain for obvious reasons.[50] It may be nearer the mark to suggest that something like an antitraditionalist strain existed within multiple forms of Christian belief and practice and that this strain could be activated in a religiously diverse American environment to create a sense of religious and ultimately political unity. The nonsectarian communion that resulted could more easily overcome divisions vested in more traditionalist attachments of their various members because the Christian tradition itself authorized such a stance. Indeed, the paradox that shapes authority within the Christian tradition arises from a tension between old and new. While its most profound theological expression might lie in the Christian elevation of the second and third persons of the Trinity, it is most dramatically communicated through the gospel witness that the recent past had become the axis of all sacred history. Politically, this presentist potential within Christianity provided not merely a common concept or practice to American Christians but rather a common way to relocate the Christian tradition's unifying power in a diverse population's sharing of the immediate past.[51]

In Greeley's lifetime, the long string of multidenominational religious revivals sometimes called the Second Great Awakening offers perhaps the most obvious historical demonstration of how the presentist impulse within Christianity might be activated and what it could achieve politically. Though rooted in Christian belief, this form of revivalism distinguished itself from Pugin's traditionalist variety by locating the unifying element of Christianity in the most recent rather than the distant past. American revivalists' emphasis on immediate conversion recentered all sacred history onto a novel experience that was both deeply personal and highly public. The appearance of divine grace at a camp meeting, for instance, involved a private conversion. Yet coreligionists expected that conversion to generate a public display of divine intervention in the social setting of the wider revival and beyond.[52]

By providing such testimony, converts actively participated in the same sacred history upon which biblical truth was founded. Indeed, a converted soul demonstrated the power of both the scriptures and the divinity behind them by publicly manifesting its response to the divine word's proclamation in the present age. Only divine grace, active in one's own lifetime and revealed among one's contemporaries, allowed a Christian to claim biblical history as authentically true and powerful. By extension, the biblical tradition validated itself largely through its capacity to regenerate souls within the present community and thus incorporate itself in the nation's most immediate history.

Locating the crux of a salvation history in a new community's common past helps explain why revivalism achieved great energy on the southern and western frontiers, where it gave uprooted individuals a shared connection that transcended sectarian distinctions. Yet it was also a power east of the frontier. There, the divine stamp it placed on the recent past might similarly unify a variety of religious persuasions under a great antitraditionalist tent. As Nathan O. Hatch has argued, the American "challenge of adjusting existing denominations to the realities of disestablishment paled before" the more pervasive challenge to traditional authority that permeated the American scene in the early national period. "This stringent populist challenge to the religious establishment included violent anticlericalism, a flaunting of conventional religious deportment, a disdain for the wrangling of theologians, an assault on tradition, and an assertion that common people were more sensitive than elites to the ways of the divine."[53]

In stressing the importance of conversion experiences, revivalists also "incorporated popular religious elements [that] differed greatly from the teachings and practices of the parent denominations."[54] Although revivals often occurred under the auspices of sectarian groups, with Presbyterians, Methodists, and Baptists prominently represented, they also tended to resist creeds and ecclesiastical structures. When prior orthodoxies exerted themselves too forcefully over fresh converts, revivalist preachers and congregants sometimes responded by simply founding new branches and sects based on the authenticity of their immediate spiritual history.[55] The implicit rationale for such shifts lay in the transfer of a more abstract sacred history onto a concrete awakening of personal "lived religion"; the prescribed orthodoxies and hierarchies of an organized church could be tolerated and even celebrated as augmentations or explanations after the fact of the awakened soul, but they could not deny its authority as a fact to a true believer.[56]

This tendency to resist church authorities has earned revivalism a reputation for populism, but this term can easily be confused with the relatively superficial characteristics of democratic governance or the cultivation of a popular audience. Revivalist populism did not merely fling open the doors of religious authority to the masses who dared enter its tents; on a more fundamental level revivals anchored the sacred history on which such authority was based to their own collective experience of saving grace in the recent past. Thus among revivalists "knowledge of the specific time, day, and place in which this experience occurs is accorded preeminence, as though such knowledge [of conversion] was itself a central aspect of the salvation process."[57] This was and still is so because personal conversion, and more broadly revivalism, represents not merely a change of heart but also a sign of divine action in the most immediate history of a person and, more broadly, in a people.

Even American Protestants who were relatively indifferent or hostile to revivalism were potentially open to presentist influences, partly because demographic pressures and the raw fact of religious diversity tended to impose a measure of creativity on American religion. Mainline churches that upheld their Old World denominational affiliations also demonstrated the potential of New World variants. Thus even conservative church figures tended to locate American Christianity's unifying element in the protean potential of the immediate past. The Swiss German expatriate Phillip Schaff, who was closely associated with one of the foremost critics of American revivalism, John Williamson Nevin, could still report to his European coreligionists that American Christians were destined, as a "motley sampler of all church history," to bring about "something wholly new," for "the Spirit of God broods over them, to speak in time the almighty word: 'Let there be light!' and to call forth from the chaos a beautiful creation."[58]

This divine presence, ordaining the chaotic scene of America's recent past, also conveyed an authority on the ordinary believer. In step with increasingly democratic antebellum politics, it also traveled a parallel course to an increasingly popular American news business that spurned established social hierarchies. To regard these similarities as merely analogical connections between discrete arenas of American society would be a mistake, just as it would be a mistake to assume that Gothic Revival architecture could be explained without reference to British religion or romantic literature.[59] Each mode of memory, though various in form, shared a common spirit; like the identifiable currents of British traditionalism, presentist associations of the American press, political culture, and religion tended to bleed into one another. This constant presentist undercurrent is one reason Catharine Albanese can speak of an American metaphysical religion coalescing from the muddle of reformist impulses at midcentury, a religion that "would function, literally, in a borderland at the edge of liberal Protestantism—and with, sometimes, even bits and pieces of more conservative and evangelical Protestantism added."[60]

Again, the Second Great Awakening offers instructive though not exhaustive evidence of a presentist turn that took shape across a variety of religious commitments and a multitude of cultural fields. For the intensely personal religious experience at the root of revivalism demanded a public and ultimately a political response to verify the spiritual proof it contained; "turning private drama into collective explanation," American evangelicals who were personally touched by the awakening became energetic observers of "what happens when converts and continuing believers make their impact on public culture."[61] Not surprisingly, nineteenth-century revivalism quickly bore fruit in reformist social and political movements, which in turn filled newspapers with narratives of moral struggle and good works, testifying to Christian revivalism's divine provenance by demonstrating its positive effect on national life. Thus seemingly separate spheres of American politics, religion, and journalism converged in the mid-nineteenth century around common notions of an emergent and immediate sacred history, a presentist mode that both borrowed from and bolstered nationalist understandings of hemispheric temporality and the revolutionary heritage.

Like any exclusionary credo of American exceptionalism, this presentist doctrine of a distinctively American relationship to the recent past masked significant transatlantic connections and similarities: newspapers, like evangelical Protestantism, clearly played a significant role in British as well as American national culture. Yet the differences in how news operated on either side of the Atlantic were not merely imagined, as Greeley's testimony, and the existence of the parliamentary committee that heard it, clearly demonstrated. By bringing a US editor to speak for a distinctly American variety of news under Pugin's Gothic nationalist structure, Parliament underscored the tendency of Anglophone presentism and traditionalism to align with opposing hemispheres. The Anglo-American border was organizing time as well as space, and Greeley's testimony showed that the United States' exceptionalist association with presentism arose partly from a material basis: the asymmetrical production and consumption of modern Anglophone news. National policy, in other words, had helped solidify the dispute between traditionalists and presentists about the appropriate way to connect mass audiences to a shared history, "stipulating" the form as well as the content of collective memory.[62] For pennies, cheap newspapers were providing ordinary Americans with a share in a form of national history that remained an elite privilege in Britain.

Greeley's status as an American "new man" temporarily moored in the Old World clearly strengthened his warrant for critiquing an outdated British newspaper industry. But that same status helped to demonstrate why Britain's taxes on knowledge were necessary, for they helped obstruct not just the American model of news but also the accompanying cultural reliance on immanent history that helped make a person like Greeley such an important political figure. The disputes over the taxes and market innovations were about more than the changing news business; they flowed from the notion that each Anglophone nation required the support that only a distinctive approach to memory could provide.

As long as British news reading remained in the hands of the elevated few, the majority of Britons might continue to rely on relatively ancient traditions as their primary connections to a shared national past. Meanwhile, American nationalists could claim unique access to presentist memory as a means of distinguishing themselves from their British cousins in a way that resonated with their hemispheric, revolutionary, and religious imaginations. In part because modern news had not yet been adopted in Britain, US-style presentism gained a material basis for an exceptionalist trinity of revolutionary origins, evangelical Christianity, and New World novelty. Undergirding this potent combination, the distinctive American relation to news would have a profound impact on American culture and literature in the mid-nineteenth century, generating energy for iconoclastic agendas and grist for the transcendentalist mills of the American Renaissance.

"The Spirit Also Helpeth Our Infirmities"

Early in 1848, a German expatriate who would soon become Horace Greeley's London correspondent, reflected on the displacement of local and national traditions that the modern world had wrought. Compelled by the globalizing requirements of industrial capitalism, this devaluing of traditional social attachments formed one of the many aspects of the mass alienation that characterized the writer's midcentury world. Working with his collaborator, Frederick Engels, Karl Marx would survey the rapidly eroding ground of national history under the inexorable industries of the bourgeoisie:

> All fixed, fast-frozen relations, with their train of ancient and venerable prejudices and opinions, are swept away, all new-formed ones become antiquated before they can ossify. All that is solid melts into air, all that is holy is profaned.... The bourgeoisie has ... given a cosmopolitan character to production and consumption in every country.... To the great chagrin of Reactionists, it has drawn from under the feet of industry the national ground on which it stood.... In place of the old local and national seclusion and self-sufficiency, we have intercourse in every direction.

Global capitalism, in short, had produced a world without god or ground, a world without stable nations in which to tether, a world without roots.[63] *The Communist Manifesto* would premise its call for an international workers' movement partly on a violation of the national imagination, the disorienting disintegration of national borders and established social orders, and while many would doubt its prescription for escaping this modern predicament, fewer could argue with Marx's diagnosis of capitalist modernity's disruption of tradition and alienation of the modern individual.[64] As modernization brought unprecedented population flows and increasingly global communication, as well as more efficient international trade, it was removing modern individuals from their moorings in the more intimate forms of memory available in more traditional societies. It had sparked myriad revolutions and upheavals of the long nineteenth century that gave voice to the disaffected masses. But it was also creating a basis for various nationalist reactions.

A. W. N. Pugin, whose father had fled revolutionary France and who had been profoundly influenced by the social unrest of the early nineteenth century, had fashioned one powerful response.[65] Indeed, the Second Congress of the Communist League had convened just one mile north of the Palace of Westminster in 1847, and Marx had been tasked with writing the *Manifesto* very nearly under the shadow of Pugin's monument to nationalist traditionalism.[66] Looking around London and beyond it to Europe, Marx could assume that in the short term at least, a religiously infused traditionalist nationalism would continue to appeal to nineteenth-century individuals whose sense of social stability was dissolving under the pressures of mass migration and mass communication.

Yet if Pugin's career as a merchant of national memory had resulted from the constant change that surrounded him, Greeley's had as well. His early life had been shaped by migrations, and his move to the great eastern metropolis cut against the grain of a family defined by restless movements west and away from city life. His father's many failures as a farmer drove the family successively from southern New Hampshire to western Vermont and finally through western New York state and into the extreme northwestern corner of Pennsylvania, crossing the same burned-over district where revivalism had made perhaps its deepest impact. In previous generations the Scotch-Irish on his mother's side had been pushed from Scotland to Northern Ireland to Massachusetts and finally to New Hampshire, where Greeley was born.[67]

Throughout his groundbreaking career in journalism, Greeley would address the sense of community that many of his readers had lost. His work would give the temporal orphans of the transatlantic world a way to engage a common American history even as they migrated away from the intimate forms of memory associated with local societies. Just as Pugin and other Victorians self-consciously built renovated buildings, monuments, and public art to "remind" a national public "of our faith and our country," Greeley would produce a form of memory that brought together faith and country in the experience of national news.[68] The *Weekly Tribune* would eventually rise to be recognized as a second bible for a mass readership that had moved west much like Greeley's family, dispersing across North America in a mélange of denominational and ethnic groupings. Compelled to develop new forms of shared history in order to relate to each other as Americans, they would look to Greeley's paper as that history's source.[69]

While Westminster set up a national bulwark of stone to stand amid a torrent of historical change, the *Tribune*'s social power would arise from its capacity to keep pace with the rapid alterations of national institutions in the United States, corralling historical changes into the material form of its paper, and projecting an image of national consistency to which individual readers might associate. Yet the claims of both modern modes of national memory ultimately depended upon a spiritual appeal that linked them to a faith that was both timeless and grounded in history. Because neither the America served by the *Tribune* nor the Britain represented in the Houses of Parliament was empirically one people, national identity depended on memory's capacity to obviate long-standing fractures within the popular imagination, as well as to reorient more intimate prior experiences of community and commonality onto a modern mass public.[70] In this sense, memory had to be at once ancient and novel, and partly for this reason it was bound to intersect with a religious culture that understood sacred history as simultaneously old and new. The desperate midcentury need to combine contemporary identities with past attachments corresponded to a form of sacred history that grew from the core of Christianity, one defined by an ancient tradition's ongoing connection to recent events.

Yet that dependence on sacred history also had consequences that encouraged fracture and division, in particular between the forgers of traditionalism and the prophets of presentism. Their mutual reliance on sacred history, and each other's opposition, meant that the nineteenth-century memory war could also become a holy war. That war elevated the antislavery cause to national prominence as the forces of presentism sought to abolish human property as a legally and divinely ordained American tradition. The origins of this front in the memory war, and Ralph Waldo Emerson's ascendance as one of its chief theorists, form the subject of chapter 2.

2

Enslaved to the Past

Emerson and the Spirit of Antislavery News

Jesus is a Jew, sitting with his countrymen, celebrating their national feast.... I see natural feeling and beauty in the use of such language from Jesus, a friend to his friends; I can readily imagine that he was willing and desirous, when his disciples met, his memory should hallow their intercourse.
—Ralph Waldo Emerson, "The Lord's Supper," 1832

Heats and genial periods arrive in history, or, shall we say, plentitudes of Divine Presence, by which high tides are caused in the human spirit ... when the nation [is] full of genius and piety.
—Ralph Waldo Emerson, *English Traits*, 1856

In the months Marx was toiling over *The Communist Manifesto* in London around the turn of 1848, Ralph Waldo Emerson was touring and lecturing in Britain. Already a noted intellectual at home and abroad, Emerson was the center of the American transcendentalist movement and a prominent advocate of the development of national literature.[1] While in Britain he observed the same anxious and aggressive nationalism that Marx had described as the inevitable response to modernity's globalizing tumult. Yet the American thinker was also struck by the ways in which British nationality, and in particular British national memory, diverged from American alternatives. Returning home, he spent several years sporadically working up a full-length book based on the tour. Though he titled it *English Traits*, the text vacillates between the American's sense of genetic affinity with the British and a feeling of acute national distance, as if Emerson could not decide whether the English traits he was describing suggested a foreign culture or merely an alternative "seat" of the same "British race."[2]

Yet a deeper presentist concern shadowed the vexed national definitions and distinctions that marked his tour, for Emerson identified traditionalist memory as a profound threat to any authentic nation. This chapter shows how Emerson's battle with traditionalism arose from his heterodox but nonetheless serious religious commitment to a presentist vision of sacred national history. Furthermore, it demonstrates that Emerson's antebellum experience of a distinctive US news culture profoundly shaped a presentist understanding that he advanced as a spiritual truth as well as a nationalist creed. It is not surprising, then, that though he saw traditionalist memory amassing throughout the British Isles in 1848, it would appear most clearly within *English Traits* in two chapters on Britain's religion and its news business. Not coincidentally, these chapters would bracket his chapter titled "Literature" and his reflections on his British literary peers.

Emerson spent a good deal of time on tour exploring British churches, and his chapter on religion directly attacks the central premise behind Pugin's traditionalist reminders of faith and country. On the one hand, Britain's ancient Christian monuments impress Emerson as representations of faith and unity. "In seeing old castles and cathedrals, I sometimes say, as to-day in front of Dundee Church tower, which is eight hundred years old, 'This was built by another and a better race than any that now look on it,'" Emerson professed. "And plainly there has been great power of sentiment at work in this island, of which these buildings are the proofs." Emerson and Pugin would agree completely in this. Yet Emerson sees these ancient buildings, Westminster Abbey prominent among them, as "works to which the key is lost, with the sentiment which created them." The age of the great builders and reformers had ended. "The spirit that dwelt" in the Church of England, Emerson insisted, "has glided away to animate other activities." Worse, "they who come to the old shrines find apes and players rustling the old garments." Thus Emerson mocked the Gothic Revival as a gaudy charade that cheapened the nation that endorsed it, and the national church that "keeps the old structures in repair, spends a world of money in music and building; and in buying Pugin, and architectural literature," even while violently resisting "all change in politics, literature, or social arts."[3] Indifferent to the spirit of reform, the "part the church plays as a political engine" relies on imposing the vestiges of a national religion through force of habit. "From his infancy, every Englishman is accustomed to hear daily prayers for the queen, for the royal family and the Parliament, by name; and this lifelong consecration cannot be without influence on his opinions."[4]

Two chapters later, Emerson cites Britain's daily papers for failing to address the British masses raised on Britain's daily prayers. Thus the text suggests that religion and journalism were not merely discrete cultural arenas for Emerson but rather contributing factors in a pervasive British traditionalism. While on tour, Emerson had analyzed as well as read the British papers, and his notes from the time reveal a fascination with the *Times* of London, the influence of which was both titanic and strangely limited. Under the deceptively simple chapter title "The Times," Emerson would casually assert the social reality to which Greeley had also testified: that "the power of the newspaper is familiar in America and in accord with our political system."[5] The Sage of Concord would then wonder at Britain's simultaneous failure, despite the increasing news-gathering capacity of its press, to bring its political institutions into harmony with modern news.

The tension between the British appetite for news and the "feudal institutions" on which the British system rested had helped produce the phenomenon of the *Times*: it was a "power . . . more felt, more feared, [and] more obeyed" than any in England and a paper able to bring low those in high places in the name of truth; yet the paper still spoke not for "the majority, but [for] the commanding class" and thus partook in "all the limitations of the governing classes." To Emerson it seemed "a living index of the colossal British power" and a paragon of many English traits, yet it somehow failed to do right by the nation's soul, which was in dire need of conversion: "If only [the *Times*] dared to cleave to the right . . . and feed its batteries from the central heart of humanity," Emerson speculated wistfully, "it might not have so many men of rank among its contributors, but genius would be its cordial and invincible ally. . . . It would be the natural leader of British reform."[6]

Emerson's idea that a great national newspaper should speak for both national reform and "the majority," however, rested on ideas about nationality that many of his contemporaries would have regarded as deeply American. First, that a nation's identity lay primarily with its common folk rather than its "governing classes"; second, that the national press had a responsibility to express and respond to common experiences; third, that the truest expression of national genius lay not in standing institutions but in "social and political" reforms that could emerge only by exerting the natural power of the newspaper.[7] And finally, Emerson maintained the underlying premise that true national identity was vested in contemporary historical experience and therefore in news. This was at heart why the *Times*'s failures were so galling. The British state maintained its news as an elite privilege, even as the mainstream papers supported the state's traditionalist foundations.

At heart, Emerson's criticism of the *Times* shared the same spiritual grounds as his attacks on the Church of England in the era of Pugin. Like the established church, the establishment press had stifled the majority that constituted the true national public, and the *Times*'s incapacity to represent the whole British people was symptomatic of a larger failure to resurrect national memory from its traditionalist tomb. Emerson encapsulated this combined failure of the British press and church by recounting an evening he spent at the ancient cathedral in York "on the day of the enthronization of the new archbishop" in January 1848. A former minister himself, Emerson could cite the precise reading from Genesis he heard "in York minster"; but he also recalled feeling "strange" as he witnessed "the decorous English audience, just fresh from the Times newspaper and their wine . . . listening with all the devotion of national pride" in a great Gothic church. It was particularly strange because the date of the archbishop's installation was January 13, 1848. The Revolutions of 1848 had begun the day before in Italy. "That was binding old and new to some purpose," Emerson admits, but the purpose was hardly divine.[8] Even on a day that sparked a global rash of national revolutions, the *Times* and the church were both catering to the same tired traditionalist impulse that was, from Emerson's perspective, a perversion of nature and a sin against the spirit. British national memory, operating through the prescribed orbits of its news and its churches, was merely generating a new kind of pharisaic heresy. "The doctrine of the Old Testament is the religion of England," Emerson would conclude. "The first leaf of the New Testament they do not open. . . . They are neither transcendentalists nor Christians."[9]

As the thrust of his commentary suggests, Emerson's denigration of the British press and the English Church arose from a theory of national memory that Emerson derived from Christianity, one that deeply informed his presentist understanding of American culture and his resistance to British-style traditionalism at home and abroad. Yet it was more than a theory. Emerson saw Britain in 1848 as a symbol of a nation's potential to bury its spirit under the monuments to its venerable history, in part because his own career had been shaped by a presentist alternative operating through the lively form of American news.

In the decades before the Civil War American newspapers like the *Tribune*, whose form encouraged their consumption as a democratic and liberated manifestation of national history, merged with liberating content involving various movements for social reform. As the struggle against slavery became the central storyline in the American news cycle, the presentist strain within Christianity and the material context of the popular news were combining to form a powerful nationalist memory circuit. Ultimately an American struggle against Britain's "doctrine of the Old Testament" became associated not only with an imperative to escape traditionalism's trap but also with a highly publicized effort to combat American slavery. Because American news was becoming popular to a degree that the British could scarcely imagine, the pulpish pages of the nation's newspapers provided the distinctive substance that matched the spirit of America's national memory.

Yet if the nineteenth-century model of British nationalism amounted to a sham that mischaracterized the nature of sacred national history, it also remained influential within a shared Anglo-American sphere. This meant that, from a presentist perspective, the true American nation could only identify itself through a constant battle against traditionalism in the British style. Taking on religious as well as political import, the spark of presentist reform would ignite a holy war for the nation's past. Emerson was that war's primary theorist, and through his influence as a popular speaker, writer, and critic he fanned the flames throughout the 1840s and 1850s. Yet his first campaign in the memory war against traditionalist remembrance took the form of a sermon on Christian memory, preached on September 9, 1832.

The National Origins of Sacred Christian History

Emerson's image of national news as the source of the true nation's sacred history had shaped his early experience as a young minister in training and reached its fullest flowering in the transcendentalist movement that, like the *Tribune*, rose to prominence in the 1840s. Emerson had graduated from Harvard Divinity School in 1826, the same year that Greeley had begun his apprenticeship as a printer, and like Greeley he would move away from his ancestral denomination by the early 1830s. The influence of new historical approaches to biblical scholarship would contribute to a radical reassessment of what Emerson as a seminarian anxiously referred to as "the traditionary/legendary/greatness of Christianity."[10] The Unitarian Church that ordained him had by the early nineteenth century abandoned many Protestant orthodoxies, but it still maintained some doctrinal attachments to established dogma. These moorings would gradually erode under the influence of German higher criticism and homegrown insights that would fundamentally unsettle the young Emerson's understanding of Christian history. His decisive break with Christian traditionalism in 1832 would ultimately compel him to resign his pastorate. Yet his reasons for abandoning his post were hardly irreligious. In fact, in leaving Emerson would signal that he was bringing the heart of Christianity with him in the presentist form of sacred memory that he identified with his nation's spirit.

Something like this distinctively national sense of sacred history, facilitated by distinctively national news systems and all their compatible institutions, shaded his survey of the *Times* of London and the hollow traditionalist shell of the Church of England.[11] The spirit that had departed Anglicanism, and not yet fully invested British journalism, had left the British nation as well as its church absent its "genius"; it was a nationality replete with "apes and players" and "men of rank," but bereft of representative men. Yet both descriptions of these "English traits" were really oblique prescriptions for American alternatives based on a more authentic spiritual anchor point in the recent past.[12] Following the stark division scholars of nationalism sometimes draw between medieval Christianity and a demystified modernity, one might be tempted to cast Emerson's mature sense of history in 1848 as an incipient form of secular nationalism, one grounded in modern print rather than religion's hokum. The problem with this view, of course, is that Emerson did not think "the spirit" that had departed the ancient forms was dead.[13]

Indeed, he had left the ministry to look for it.[14] Though he did not publish it at the time, Emerson's farewell to Boston's Second Church set the presentist pattern he was to repeat in his more famous works in the following decade. The sermon makes several arguments against the traditionalist observance of the "Lord's Supper," which Emerson had informed his congregation he could no longer administer in good conscience. Yet though he refutes orthodox observance, he does so to advance an alternative mode of Christian memory, arguing that "remembrances of [Christ] should be pleasing, affecting, religious."[15]

The sermon's central argument against the ritual observance of communion hinges on two oppositions: between the religious "forms" of the past and "the spirit of Christ" and between Jesus's Jewish nation and Emerson's American one. In interpreting the meaning of Jesus's admonishment during Passover to "do this in remembrance of me," Emerson insists on the importance of the national history in which the words were spoken: "Jesus is a Jew, sitting with his countrymen, celebrating their national feast." It is only in this nationalist context among his contemporaries, that Jesus's directive to remember him in communion can align perfectly with nature: "I see natural feeling and beauty in the use of such language from Jesus, a friend to his friends," Emerson told his congregation. "I can readily imagine that he was willing and desirous, when his disciples met, his memory should hallow their intercourse." In the natural and national communion Jesus imagines for the earliest church of his followers, then, the sacred memory of the recent past is put to appropriate use to "hallow" the apostolic community.[16]

Emerson, however, cannot believe Jesus "looked beyond the living generation, beyond the abolition of the festival he was celebrating, and the scattering of the nation . . . to fasten it upon men in all times and all countries." Jesus's reference to body and blood was similarly appropriate for his nation and his era and therefore natural or "familiar in his mouth. He always taught by parables and symbols. It was the national way of teaching."[17] Clearly underlying all of Emerson's objections is his notion of a close connection between natural religious expression and a national society grounded in a particular time and place. Turning millennia of dogma on its head, Emerson insists that as an object of memory, Jesus can be holy only in his Jewishness, because authentic holiness must always be historically located and aligned with the contemporary realities of nature.

Because memory became holy through just such a temporal alignment, however, sacred memory cannot extend beyond generational and national borders except indirectly. Among Emerson's nineteenth-century American audience, "use of the elements, however suitable to the people and the modes of thought in the East, where it originated, is foreign and unsuited to affect us. . . . I apprehend that their use is rather tolerated than loved by any of us. We are not accustomed to express our thoughts or emotions by symbolical actions."[18]

This does not mean that Christianity can have no relevance to Emerson or his peers, but to do so it must take on the same presentist spirit that enlivened the first communion of the apostolic church, a spirit that revealed itself through its resistance to traditionalist forms. Understood rightly, the Apostle Paul (the figure who helped spread communion rituals beyond Palestine) becomes for Emerson a presentist saint and opponent of mere ritual observance. In Emerson's sermon, Paul assures the audience at Boston's Second Church that "the kingdom of God is not meat and drink, but righteousness, and peace, and joy in the Holy Ghost." Despite Emerson's rejection of the Trinity, the operative term in this verse is clearly the Holy Spirit. He explains, while "forms are as essential as bodies," to "exalt particular forms, to adhere to one form a moment after it is outgrown, is unreasonable, and it is alien to the spirit of Christ."[19]

Although the sermon may have been primarily a justification of Emerson's decision to leave the pulpit, it also propounds a religiously informed theory of national spirit that would animate Emerson's later career. That spirit had lived in the first national communion, which raised the recent memory of Christ's Last Supper over the Passover observance of his earliest Jewish followers, making them a community grounded in recent rather than merely ancient divine actions. But Emerson would suppose, decades later, that it had likewise lived in the English Church in various periods when "plentitudes of Divine Presence, by which high tides are caused in the human spirit," ensured that "the nation was full of genius and piety."[20]

Thus Emerson's denial of the sacred status of the English Church's traditionalism in the mid-nineteenth century does not deny the deeper validity of the sacred history traditionalists only claimed to uphold; neither does he deny the potential of a nation to partake in that history's spiritual power. Emerson instead asserted that the nationalized spirit he lauded in "The Lord's Supper" must reinvest the spiritualized nation he imagined in his great essays, the spirit that had once lived in the past but must also live in the present. National authenticity, for Emerson, must derive from the association between its political and cultural institutions and an immanent spirit of history that corresponds to the particulars of one's time and place; but that spirit was also divine, even for Emerson as a thoroughly unorthodox believer, precisely because it would not suffer to be constrained in tombs of cant and custom but would rise to live in every age.

For Emerson, Jesus's inspired determination to "spiritualize" the Passover was "full of solemn and prophetic interest, but never intended by Jesus to be the foundation of a perpetual institution."[21] In attacking the outgrown "form" of traditionalist Christian memory in 1832, Emerson was following a religious principle as deep as any to be found within Christianity and repeating a line of prophetic thought that predated the Christian era by a thousand years. He readily discerned it animating the history of the English Church during the Reformation and the Christian community of first-century Palestine. But he also looked for it in an American national culture he hoped was bold enough to deviate from the tottering British model and instead honor the presentist spirit that lay at the origins of all authentically Christian traditions.

Because Emerson drew a clear link between his own position and the ancient truths of church and scripture, the religiously informed presentism he conceptualized was not as indifferent to the sacred past as it might appear. Rather, it assumed that the spirit was discernable in history as a constantly regenerating source of truth within a national context. This is important for several reasons. First, some manner of continuity between past and present, preferably one that could claim sacred status, would seem vital to maintain within any nationalist ideology. Second, the link to the past suggests that for all his heterodoxy, Emerson was maintaining a bridge between American national identity and a viable image of Christian history. If we merely consider this event according to its outward form, as Emerson's final sermon, we may have difficulty taking the religious force of Emerson's nationalism seriously. His presentist model does not resist traditionalist forms, however, in the name of a secular vision of history. Rather it upholds a deeply religious principle that located divine "reality" in the present experience of divine action in history. In offering justification for leaving the church while insisting that "what I revere and obey in it is its reality," Emerson was also demonstrating how one could find the source of all true churches and all true nations in the spiritual vitality of the recent past.[22]

Though it is sometimes ignored today, the message was generally understood at least by the erudite among Emerson's contemporary audiences, who saw the transcendentalist "primarily as a religious thinker"; as Harold Bush observes, his highly popular "speeches were originally perceived as religious in nature."[23] Indeed, transcendentalism as a whole "began as a religious demonstration" and, as one of its late nineteenth-century interpreters suggested, was "more justly regarded as 'a gospel'" than a philosophy.[24] As a spiritual persuasion as well as a literary or philosophical school, Emersonian transcendentalism arose as a break not with religion, nor even with Christianity, but rather with a traditionalism that defined the church through deference to divine action in the distant past and a salvation history that centered on humanity's ancient fall. Moreover, this refusal maintained a "divine principle" at its core that, as Barbara Packer notes, Emerson never abandoned and thus could continue to celebrate as a soulful engagement with the historical experience of individuals in the present.[25]

The general term for this principle was "spirit," and in the years after leaving the pulpit, Emerson would find it in the news as well as nature. The explosive growth of American newspapers would reinforce the religious impulse in both Emerson's romantic band and many other Americans who remained organized within Christian churches. News, broadly conceived, had always been at least nominally central to the way Christians understood themselves. As members of a religion based on the authority of Jesus Christ—a figure who, as Emerson had noted, explicitly reoriented ancient Jewish ritual and scriptures around his own historical position—Christians were in countless ways encouraged to inhabit their own tradition in a uniquely antitraditionalist way.[26] This was perhaps especially true of Protestant Christians indebted to the Reformation objections to "Romanism," but it was not restricted to Protestantism.[27] Many of the central tenets of Christianity grounded themselves in an even more fundamental notion of a sacred history vested in the recent past: belief in the primacy of the New Testament, in the Christian gospel as good news communicated within a prior religious tradition, in Providence as heavenly involvement in in the most recent earthly past, and in the spirit as an experience of continuous divine connection to contemporary human culture.[28]

All of these pillars of the Christian tradition could be considered arguments against a rigid traditionalism, for all to some degree relocated the faith's organizing principle from an original revelation of divine truth to that truth's ongoing immanence.[29] Emerson associated his own beliefs closely with Quakerism; as he explained to a relative in the midst of his early success as an essayist in 1839, "I believe in the still small voice and that voice is Christ within us."[30] Americans who remained churched in an era marked by revival might also follow this presentist impulse into intensely religious interactions with current events. As Gail E. Husch suggests, "The language of apocalypse was, to pious antebellum Americans . . . the most natural and appropriate means—the only means they knew—to contend with the famines, plagues, and revolutions that confronted them in their newspapers." While Christians found end times in their contemporary experience of news, those on the outskirts of organized religion could also find signs of the divine operating within their everyday experience and the pages of their papers, locating their own notion of God within Emerson's ever-present nature and Greeley's timely newspapers.[31] Yet we should be careful not to assume that the newspaper was merely a delivery system for such troubling events, for it provided audiences with a material means of organizing and responding to, as well as conveying information about, events of the recent past.

From such a vantage point the news was America's sacred history. Those who held that perspective, and Emerson was certainly among them, could hardly applaud the Westminster renovators' traditionalist elevation of ancient forms and ancestral tombs. Nevertheless, Britain's flaunting of its medieval history did at least support American presentists' jingoistic insistence that their own favored mode of national memory represented a distinctive national "trait." Or as Emerson put it succinctly in his diary from the same European tour: "In England every man you meet is some man's son; in America, he may be some man's father."[32]

A Prophet in His Own Country

In actuality presentist and traditionalist memory grew on both sides of the pond, as did sons and fathers. In supposedly "young" America Emerson had to respond to traditionalists like the incomparable Daniel Webster, whose famous "Bunker Hill Monument Address" celebrated retrospective dedication and recommended the tombs of the fathers as the foundation for national unity. A monumental figure in his own right, Webster's famous oration had predicted that a common American reverence for the forefathers' tombs would mend the fractures already appearing in the national edifice during the early antebellum period. Though he came to prominence in a revolutionary land, Webster adopted a model of union grounded in traditionalist memory that functioned much like its British counterpart.

Just as Pugin would in Britain, Webster sought political unity in the safely deferential worship of an increasingly distant and therefore more easily shared past. Webster's 1825 celebration of the 1775 battle elided furious contests of the intervening years between federalists and antifederalists, Anglophiles and Francophiles, political parties, northerners and southerners, as well as divisions based on ethnicity, race, class, and gender. Nevertheless, his words were destined to embody the ritualized traditionalism he advocated; memorized by generations of schoolchildren, the oration's script became the point of return for future patriots who recited his "plea for the power of tradition" in mutual devotion to the fathers' tombs.[33]

This parroting of a sacred history, and the mode of traditionalist memory that lay behind it, clashed with Emerson's notions of divine truth, productive learning, and American nationalism. Small wonder then that in following his calling as a presentist prophet from the pulpit to a position as a public lecturer and prolific essayist, Emerson was forced to begin with some much-needed brush clearing. His introduction to 1836's seminal essay *Nature* encourages Americans to replace Webster's traditionalist mode of remembering the American founders with a presentist one. As Eduardo Cadava notes, "Webster [in the Bunker Hill address] appeals to the revolutionary rhetoric of America's beginning in order to encourage his audience to defer to the authority of the forefathers, whereas Emerson [in *Nature*] appeals to this rhetoric in order to persuade his listeners that they too may effect similar if not more spectacular revolutions."[34] Like the mass-produced newspaper he would celebrate in *English Traits*, the American Revolution became for Emerson a symbol of the preeminence of the recent past and a means to encourage Americans to avoid abject genuflection at the dusty tombs of the founding fathers.

This was political advice but it was based on a profoundly spiritual sense of time.[35] Emerson had ultimately emerged from his long wrestling match with Christian traditionalism marked by a powerful commitment to a sacred history of the present, one that eventually took shape in *Nature,* "The American Scholar," and "The Divinity School Address." Indeed, when the crisis over his calling came to a head in June of 1832, Emerson had described his clerical ministry using language that closely resembled the famous nationalist criticism that launched *Nature* and his literary career four years later: "The profession is antiquated. In an altered age we worship in the dead forms of our forefathers."[36] In *Nature,* this early criticism of orthodox Unitarianism's residual traditionalism would have expanded to include the traditionalist piety of a patriotic American citizen: "Our age is retrospective. It worships at the sepulchers of the fathers." In place of such traditionalism, *Nature* recommended seeking, as America's near-mythical revolutionaries had once sought, an "original relation to the universe" through a history written in the present tense.[37] Emphatically, *Nature* does not repudiate the revolutionary principles of the founding fathers, any more than the young Emerson had repudiated the spiritual principle that enlivened the revolutionary stance of Christ and his apostles. Webster's traditionalist version of that revolutionary impulse was not merely a misinterpretation: it was a heresy and a contradiction in terms, a fundamental misunderstanding of what made history sacred. It was a sin against the spirit, and thus a sin *Nature* could not forgive.[38]

Yet it was also a sin into which all of America seemed in danger of backsliding. *Nature* begins with a frank admission that later advocates of national literature would echo: the New World might not escape the traditionalist temptations of the Old World. Without first reforming their outlook, they would not be saved by their blood ties to their illustrious ancestors, or even their apparent proximity to New World wilderness or unvarnished nature. By choosing Webster's commemoration as the generative foil to introduce his great essay, Emerson showed he viewed the speech's traditionalist blasphemy as an existential threat to America's presentist spirit, and therefore American identity. The popular Webster had shown how quickly even a New World revolution could become another tired excuse for pledging eternal allegiance to an unchanging past. This abject slide from presentist revolutionary commitment into traditionalist genuflection required scarcely a generation to accomplish; Webster had managed to set it in motion with a cadre of revolutionary veterans sitting among his first audience at the monument site.

Despite the actual Revolution's break with British tradition, the deepest political purpose behind Webster's appeals to its memory were virtually identical to Pugin's traditionalist appeal to a national Gothic style: both sought to sanctify a unified nationality upon the altar of a safely distant past. Such a past might first obscure and then suppress the diversity and contesting perspectives within the nation-state. By linking the Revolutionary battle site to devoted retrospection, Webster had hoped to avoid the serious political schisms between states, just as the Palace of Westminster would surround all Britain's political factions within the same Gothic style.

Of all the contests Webster's traditionalist commemoration papered over, a slow-brewing conflict over American slavery would turn out to be the most irrepressible. It would come to a boil in the antebellum years partly because slavery's advocates had their own traditionalist vision of sacred history to deploy, but also because slavery's opponents would advance a viable presentist alternative, and the conflict between them would absorb the later careers of both Emerson and Webster.

The Ancient Church of Antislavery

When Emerson launched *Nature*'s broadside against Webster, whom he had idolized as a young man, he opened a new front in the memory war and launched an internecine antebellum contest over the meaning of history itself. *Nature* began by identifying the traditionalist heresy at home and reimagined the Old World as a domestic threat that needed to be purged before natural and national realities could be secured. Following its prophetic call to reform, *Nature* evangelized its readers with a presentist gospel; its rhetoric assumes that even in a retrospective age, individual readers were ripe for conversion. Yet Emerson, in recommending a turn to the present, was also locating national history in the antebellum news. Implicitly, the true spirit of the nation, which mirrored the true church of the apostles, would be found there. Moreover, that news would increasingly link the spirit of the nation to a new struggle for freedom.

In assessing the deepest truth to be found in the New Testament, Emerson had claimed in 1832 that "Freedom is the essence of this faith. . . . That form out of which the life and suitableness have departed should be as worthless in its eyes as the dead leaves that are falling around us."[39] This doctrine of divine freedom would ultimately merge with the struggle to free both the nation and enslaved African Americans from a slave system that increasingly became associated with traditionalist rhetoric. Though

Emerson worried about its results, the antislavery movement's presentist foundation would eventually provide him with a new spiritual home among a new sort of faith community and shatter Webster's allure as his traditionalism found common cause with slaveholders.

As the conflict over slavery increasingly became a battlefield in the broader memory war, the antislavery movement would rise in great measure through its capacity to channel the spiritual power of the recent past. Freedom from traditionalism's grip, as well as from the slave system, would march to the tune set by a liberated press under the banner of a sacred history of the present.

Among the chief agents in this development was William Lloyd Garrison, whose *Liberator* became an expression of his own prophetic ego and the diverse spiritual community that was coalescing around the antislavery impulse in the early antebellum years.[40] Garrison had abandoned the Baptist faith he had grown up with, but in many ways he transposed its sense of sacred history onto his work as an editor. "Above all else," David Paul Nord observes, "Garrison believed in God; and because he believed in God he believed in truth." Garrison's philosophy of journalism arose from a fervent faith in the efficacy of news to advance God's truth. Journalism was also a holy calling, and an editor who answered the call must also be a prophet.[41] Though he would attack the proslavery Christian churches, many of which had taken shape amid the storm of revivals, his newspaper was a conduit for the core impulses behind the Second Great Awakening, allowing him to "harness the conversionist energies of revivalism to the cause of institutional change."[42]

Guided by his own prophetic words and commitment to reform, Garrison would shape a history of the recent past in *The Liberator* as a sacred terrain around which a more authentic community could form. But he did not abandon his belief that America had a special role to play in aligning the present with the immanent reality of American history as it was coming to be. Thus he "treated Jefferson's 'heaven attested' Declaration as a revealed text on a par with the Bible" and though he remained "unrelentingly critical of American institutions" he did so "without ceasing to be fully American."[43] When it came time to launch his movement a few years after Webster's speech, Garrison would do so "within sight of Bunker Hill and in the birthplace of liberty."[44]

Garrison's antislavery version of a Bunker Hill ceremony pointedly placed the infant form of a new American revolution in Boston, the cradle of its old one. Yet in maturity the antislavery movement he helped lead relied not on the landmarks of New England's revolutionary past but rather on the power of newsprint to focus communal identity on the most recent past and shared contemporary experience. Furthermore, the era of violent struggle was far from over. As Ford Risley observes, abolitionists regarded their newspapers as "potent implements of modern political and moral warfare." "Castles fall before them," one publisher crowed, "cannons are silenced."[45] Emerson's *Nature* would follow the lead of Garrison's commemorative assault on Webster's sacred ground and would make the Revolution a fulcrum for reorienting American memory toward the most recent common past. Over the next quarter century, consideration of the present slavery question would increasingly challenge uncritical devotion to past glories. More and more Americans who had previously remained agnostic or silent would make the ongoing presence of slavery in the news the criteria for judging the nation's commitment to the founders' ideals.

How then did the abolitionists deploy the symbolic and instrumental power of the American press to forge a sacred presentism? Garrison and other abolitionists essentially superimposed the national news system over the national slave system in order to evoke an Emersonian style of presentist commitment. Garrison's genius lay in his determination to use news as a tool to "abolitionize" the broadest public sphere possible by showing how the evil of slavery transcended local and regional divisions, polluting the North as well as the South.[46]

The key to this front in the abolitionist battle plan lay in making a vast readership recognize slavery primarily as a current event. The strategic importance of the turn should not be underestimated, for it made the recent past the arbiter of national identity as well as slavery's morality. If slavery became a present concern, then American liberty could not be considered a settled issue and fodder for traditionalist apotheosis; freedom could not easily be commemorated when it had yet to be achieved. Thus when Garrison famously vowed "not to use moderation in a cause like the present" he also was making "the present" a cause and confronting the moral authority of slavery's traditionalist protectors by making news, a medium that matched his message.[47]

More than the effective manipulation of media, this amounted to a presentist shift in the axis of American national identity and the slave question in which it was deeply implicated. Treating American slavery as an eighteenth-century constitutional compromise had allowed gradualists to regard it as an antique fait accompli, doomed to a slow decline that made its swift annihilation unnecessary. Meanwhile slavery's defenders could uphold it as a potent combination of national heritage, long-standing legal right, dictate of a primordial natural history, and ancient scriptural ordinance. Virtually anywhere they encountered slavery's defenders or excusers, the problem for impatient abolitionists was really the past: the American worship of a freshly minted Constitutional tradition, abetted by either a perversion of science that cited an eon-spanning natural process as the author of both white supremacy and racial inequalities or by biblical acquiescence to slavery in the ancient world.[48]

The latter was especially challenging to slavery's opponents. As Mark Noll suggests, in addition to constitutional protections, proslavery advocates wielded biblical authority in ways that placed abolitionists on religiously dubious ground. Many found themselves compelled to abandon "the letter" of scriptural texts that countenanced ancient slavery in favor of the "spirit" that enlivened both the scripture as a whole and their own experience as religiously committed reformers. Garrison offered an extreme version of a more general abolitionist effort to turn the Bible's liberating spirit against its most offensive passages, or at least their literal application to modern American slavery. Exegetically speaking, this was a risky tactic. It seemed to fly in the face of the plain sense of the scriptural text, contradicting how the Bible had been read "in the history of a Protestant (and white) America," undercutting a central pillar of nationalist religion, and placing the believer on a slippery slope to all manner of infidelity.[49]

Yet exegesis was not the only way that Americans could grasp a gospel truth, and abolitionism eventually cultivated the news's power to share a sacred national history. The most effective and provocative antislavery publishers were not rank propagandists as their detractors charged, but neither were they mere purveyors of information. Rather they ingeniously harnessed and sacralized what Michael Schudson calls the news media's "capacity to publically include."[50] In the antislavery context, the news's inclusivity functioned as a form of presentist national memory to bind together an often unwilling public as participants in America's continuing history of slavery and iniquity. Whether masses of northern news readers wanted to or not, they were going to feel included in a nation compromised not by abstract legal principles or exegetical niceties but rather by the ongoing history of its own peculiarly horrifying institution.

This feeling would not be limited to subscribers. Committed abolitionist papers like Garrison's *Liberator* and Frederick Douglass's *North Star* never approached the circulation of the more moderately antislavery *Tribune*. Nevertheless, in the years before the mainstream northern press took up the cause, radical abolitionist editors were able to mitigate the limits of their short subscription lists by exchanging papers with their most vociferous opponents. These proslavery editors then reprinted the abolitionists' articles and editorials in order to refute them, and their adamant defenses of what many northerners considered abhorrent practices soon found their way into mainstream northern journals. In this way, abolitionists exploited an increasingly national news network in order to demonstrate the significant disagreements within the news-reading public. Although some northerners had no moral qualms about the dehumanizing treatment slaveholders meted out on African Americans, those who were at least moderately sympathetic had been sheltered by their capacity to remain largely ignorant of the slave's plight. Confronting northern readers who otherwise would be happy to forget about southern slavery, abolitionists provided unmistakable evidence of its continued obduracy. As they became tangled in the national news network, the institution's most vocal proponents provided its most damning testimony. Many northerners resisted acknowledging their own complicity in slave power, but the uncomfortable fact that slavery was growing stronger "on their watch" became undeniable when it arrived in the form of their daily paper.[51] If slavery's perceived entrenchment in an ancient past posed the problem, national news provided just the lever to pry it loose.

The broad social impact of the presentist memory of slavery registered in the fear such timely information generated among abolition's opponents, who condemned abolitionists as serious threats to "community" largely because they ran newspapers. This was the vexed culture of American news into which Emerson would step as a public figure once he renounced his ministry. The year after Emerson published *Nature*, proslavery mobs would martyr the antislavery newspaperman and minister Elijah P. Lovejoy, but before they did, they had already destroyed his printing presses three times. A proslavery gunman shot the controversial abolitionist dead only when Lovejoy had drawn a pistol in defense of his fourth and final press. This deadly combat over news, which occurred in the free state of Illinois, pointed to the potential for presentist national memory to involve a northern public in the ongoing American experience of southern slavery, to upset local social orders, and to overwhelm traditionalist interpretations of the Constitution and the founders—especially once more moderate and popular northern newspapers began to spread the word with presses that could print thousands of sheets an hour. The eventual shift of the antislavery frontlines from Garrison's *Liberator* to Greeley's *Tribune* signaled the early abolitionists' success in expanding the public for slavery news to the national arena.[52]

"National Style" and the Universal Faith

This was not, perhaps, the sort of success Garrison himself had envisioned. The irony of the strong bond between American presentism and antislavery at midcentury was that slavery in the Anglo-American world had only recently begun to seem a distinctly American problem. Although abolitionist print campaigns sought to develop and exploit a national news audience in the United States, and although Garrison's symbolic attempt to recapture Bunker Hill's commemorative power suggested a chauvinistic attempt to recover the nation's revolutionary break with Britain, the American antislavery struggle in its early period was hardly insular.[53] Garrison's conjuring of the spirit of 1776 implied an exceptionalism that Garrison himself avoided throughout the 1830s, as he focused instead on the antislavery movement's simultaneous appeal to the universal moral ground of Christian ethics and to an international human rights movement in which British cosmopolitans had led the way. The American Quaker and abolitionist pioneer Benjamin Lundy titled his antislavery newspaper the *Genius of Universal Emancipation*, a slogan he had taken from the Irish proponent of Catholic emancipation, John Philpot Curran.[54] The *Liberator* took its motto, "Our Country is the World, Our Countrymen Mankind," from the nationless radical Tom Paine, and Garrison openly acknowledged contemporary role models among more recent British antislavery pamphleteers and orators. Such international linkages cast abolitionism as one battle in a universal war for human rights and indicated how much publishers like Garrison were inspired by the international radical press's example. The push for American abolition, a struggle that was at once the nineteenth century's greatest battle over the meaning of the American Revolution and the single greatest test of the power of the exceptionally ubiquitous American news, also drew inspiration from the British experience of radical print and the Anglophone history of Christian reforms.

Nevertheless, those reforms were not quite the same, in part because the British antislavery movement achieved its success relatively early and in part because the visions of national memory and identity to which they appealed were structurally distinct. As Garrison discovered when he tried to leverage Britain's moral criticism of American slavery in the 1830s, such universalist appeals ran the risk of provoking an even more powerful Anglophobic backlash; even in antislavery strongholds like New England, critics of slavery seeking to hold up Britain's antislavery example found they sometimes needed to simultaneously attack the aristocratic decadence of an unjust British system.⁵⁵ Garrison and his somewhat less radical fellow travelers, however, found that the moral and material immediacy of news created an unquestionably national battlefield in the universal struggle for social redemption; while immediatists and gradualists alike based their commitments on their Christian convictions, the radicals' spiritual crusade gained power through the news's capacity to activate the liberating potential of presentist national memory.

Yet the press's proven potential as a liberating force was precisely what Parliament seemed intent on suppressing in the early nineteenth century, and the British government's determined exclusion of underrepresented news readers could make the news's power to publicly include seem like a distinctively American capacity. Although the British government prided itself on its relatively early repudiation of slavery, it had nonetheless restricted the popular news that had sometimes sought the elevation of the British working classes along with the emancipation of the empire's slaves. Though they might be proud of their nation's antislavery stance as a sign of their superior morality, most British leaders would find the notion of a perpetual revolution terrifying. That same fear also stoked the Gothic Revival that found religious authenticity and political unity in the distant national past.

Thus Anglo-American national cultures at midcentury revolved around a memory war, inspiring contrapuntal movements that were also nearly contemporaneous. The same year Emerson published *Nature*, A. W. N. Pugin published *Contrasts*, his popular manifesto that compared images of medieval society to diabolical contemporary alternatives. *Nature* and *Contrasts*, both of which were considered religious works in their time, each fashioned an argument for a revived national community infused by spirit, pitching their visions from opposite sides of the Atlantic and a vast gulf of time.⁵⁶ Each text arose from beliefs about sacred history and hopes associated with the Christian Church. Yet on the one side was a traditionalism that sought the nation's ancient unity by appealing to Britain's ancient place within Christendom. On the other stood a presentism with an equally dedicated faith that the spirit's power could make the true church and nation manifest in the rich spiritual terrain of the recent past. Each built its case through opposition to the other, yet each also in its way was arguing against the greater evil of modern rootlessness. Thus both grounded a nationalist recovery project in deeper beliefs about a divine spirit of history that they borrowed from the Christian roots of their faith and by which they sought to redeem modern experiences increasingly shaped by news.

This was the news that Greeley would ultimately create as well as champion. The same year Emerson was having his crisis of conscience over the Lord's Supper, Greeley had arrived in New York City, where his first print job was a pocket-sized New Testament.[57] Though a humble start for a future publishing titan, it was a fitting launching point for a writer who would soon bring a different sort of gospel to the American masses. While Emerson's tour of England would prompt an assertion that the English "do not open" even "the first Leaf of the New Testament," his tour of western states would lead him to declare "Greeley of the New York Tribune . . . the right spiritual father of all this region; he prints and disperses one hundred and ten thousand newspapers in one day,—multitudes of them in these very parts." Emerson had set aside his work on *English Traits* for his lecture tour in 1854 and had been both impressed and chagrined that Greeley had left his audience star struck. "People had flocked together, coming thirty and forty miles to hear him speak," Emerson exclaimed to his British friend Thomas Carlyle, "as was right, for he does all their thinking and theory for them, for two dollars a year."[58] Emerson's pique and condescension masked a history with Greeley that stretched into the previous decade, and their near miss in the western hinterlands suggested that by the mid-1850s the "Sage of Concord" and "Greeley of the New York *Tribune*" were no longer local figures but had become apostles in a church of American reform with the span of national news.

As Barbara Packer has argued, Emerson in 1832 left "one form of ministry behind . . . for the wider field of the lecture hall and published text." Yet in abandoning his pulpit, he entered an alternative spiritual region of moral and social reform, one in which the *Tribune*'s influence was destined to become ever more dominant, especially in the 1850s as the slavery crisis crested.[59] In the intervening years, the news surrounding the American antislavery movement gave the reform movement its mission and made it conscious to itself as the promulgator of a new kind of sacred history. As Packer has acutely perceived, Emerson's sense of religious and national authenticity lay in a potential conversion to a moral commitment lived out in the present moment. For Emerson the conversion moment came in 1851, the month before Greeley was testifying, with Boston's rendition of the seventeen-year-old fugitive Thomas Sims to slavery in Georgia. Emerson had been profoundly troubled by the Sims case, recognizing that it tarnished the names of the American statesmen who allowed it, as well as any celebration of America's present and future greatness. In his diary Emerson observed that "immense external prosperity is possible, with pure cowardice & hollowness in all the conspicuous official men." Despairing, he admitted that "I cannot read longer with any comfort the local good news."[60]

The national war on slavery, once he committed to it absolutely, finally "restored to Emerson . . . a sense that he could once again claim to belong to a community of believers."[61] In future years the memory war would converge with the antislavery struggle to recover American land from the scourge of slavery's imperial tyranny. Meanwhile Emerson would seek to liberate from traditionalism the same national spirit that had enlivened the ancient church and to hasten the emergence of a divine present as a national reality.

3

The News and Walt Whitman

Poetry of the Divine Present

The foremost watchman on the peak announces his news. It is the truest word ever spoken, and the phrase will be the fittest, most musical, and the unerring voice of the world for that time. All that we call sacred history attests that the birth of a poet is the principal event in chronology.

—Ralph Waldo Emerson, "The Poet," 1844

It asks no vague and visionary time,
No stale convention, no ideal clime,
But in the every-day of Life can see
The unblurred foot-prints of Divinity.

—William Wetmore Story, "Nature and Art," 1844

In March of 1842 a young reporter named Walter Whitman found himself standing in an audience with Horace Greeley, who had launched the *Tribune* the previous year. Both journalists were listening to a lecture by Ralph Waldo Emerson. At some point during Emerson's talk, Greeley became so enthusiastic that he began gesticulating somewhat wildly, or, as Whitman would rather uncharitably write for his paper, to "flounce like a fish out of water, or a tickled girl." The lecture that spurred Greeley to such ecstasy was titled "The Poet," and according to Emerson, America was in sore need of one.[1] In the version of the lecture that he published in his *Second Series* of essays in 1844, Emerson would call on the American poet to seek the secrets that "sleep in nature"; rather than serving the Old World meters and masters, the poet should become a "liberating god" in his own right, "that thought may be ejaculated as Logos or Word."[2]

Whitman's published report did not closely follow Emerson's speech, and years later he would try to minimize the debt he owed his literary forebear. Yet it is difficult to read much of Whitman's early work without hearing Emersonian echoes. Similarly, though Whitman mocked Greeley's colorful shows of enthusiasm at the lecture, he would later depend both upon Greeley's support and the political culture his paper represented. The *Tribune* editor admired Whitman's journalistic writing and, eventually, like Emerson, proved an ardent and early supporter of his poetic experiments. For his part, Whitman would absorb the presentist gospel that emanated from older writers like Emerson and Greeley and came to permeate the late antebellum period. Eventually he would stake a claim to the poet's prophetic mantle that Emerson's speech had described, and when he made his notorious decision to publish Emerson's private congratulatory response to the first edition of *Leaves of Grass*, he would send the letter to Greeley's *Tribune*.[3]

Between Greeley's chance encounter with Whitman and his positive response to the poet's masterwork, the *Tribune* would publish several Whitman poems that complemented its own increasingly bold antislavery stance. The year before Greeley's London visit the slavery question had exploded in the spring to consume the interest of the American public and virtually all its newspapers. Amid the controversies over the so-called Compromise of 1850, the *Tribune* would become a visible channel not only for the antislavery cause but for the sacred presentist memory Emerson had sought to foster in American poets. The *Tribune* poems Whitman literally placed in the midst of antislavery news exhibited his keen grasp of the spiritual force that had launched a crusade for American freedom. Drawing on the growing power of presentism evident in American religion, literature, and journalism, Whitman would cast the slavery question as a battle of the presentist spirit against a duplicitous and decidedly Old World traditionalist mode of memory.[4]

Though little noted at the time or since, it was an important development in nineteenth-century American literature. For while the editor, Walter Whitman, would leave it to Greeley to build a new kind of newspaper, the power of such news would inspire Whitman to create a new kind of poetry. Growing up in the age of Emerson, Whitman would ultimately base his later work less on any literary tradition than on the nineteenth century's version of the information age, especially the news's potential to bind readers together through their shared access to a sacred history of the recent past.[5] Coaxed by Free Soil politics and the increasingly resonant voice of the antislavery movement in the mainstream press, Whitman would insist on making the battle over slavery's expansion a struggle against the tyrannous traditionalism of the Old World and would begin to establish his place as an Emersonian poet by launching an attack on Emerson's once and future nemesis: traditionalism's American champion, Daniel Webster. As it had for Emerson, this early battle with a traitorous mode of memory would help set the terms for Whitman's later career.

Walter Whitman Reads the News

The relevance of this body of work to Whitman's poetic development can be easy to miss, in part because until recently poems published in newspapers have not garnered much critical attention, and Whitman printed only one of his 1850 *Tribune* poems in the 1855 edition of *Leaves of Grass*. That poem, titled "Resurgemus," first appeared in the daily *Tribune* on June 21, 1850. It recalls the European revolutions of two years before, which makes it somewhat difficult to place in the context of Whitman's work. Betsy Erkkilä has cited this poem as an indication of "the international frame, the workingman's movement—perhaps even the communist movement—and the global struggle for democracy out of which Whitman's Leaves emerged." These are qualities surprising to many readers who have been taught to regard Whitman primarily as a nationalist and an individualist. As Erkkilä notes, the heightened nationalism of Cold War–era Whitman criticism left many of his American readers ignorant of the poem's original connection to the European Revolutions of 1848.[6]

Yet a similar ignorance surrounds the uniquely American news apparatus of midcentury, one that had so thoroughly informed Whitman's *Tribune* audience about European political agitation that "Resurgemus" did not need to mention any country, ruler, or political figure in order to be understood. Virtually everyone who read the original poem knew those details, not because they were necessarily committed to radical politics but because the *Tribune* had exhaustively covered the story. While the poem clearly registers its author's attraction to the global struggle for democracy, its images of international radicalism actually highlight the national context within which the poem was literally situated. Like the other two poems Whitman placed in the *Tribune* that spring, "Resurgemus" (Latin for "will rise again") first rose as a sustained response to the Compromise of 1850, and in particular Daniel Webster's role in brokering it. Like those poems it also was thoroughly indebted to the *Tribune* for its presentist subject. Whitman intertwined all the poems with the sort of spiritually potent news Greeley was busy producing and clearly crafted them with *Tribune* readers in mind. Their original meaning, like the meaning of the title of "Resurgemus," depended nearly as much on their publisher as their author.

Like the rest of this early antislavery corpus, 1850's "Resurgemus" had its headwaters in a political awareness that began in the poet even before 1848. Martin Klammer has shown that, just when agitation for European liberty was reaching the point of crisis, Whitman determined to organize his political and poetic vision around slavery's challenge to American liberty. This decision seemed to have been based on a convergence of influences, many of them related to the impending collapse of America's two-party system, but also coincided with Whitman's reading of Emerson's essays.[7]

At the end of 1847 Whitman was reading and publishing on Emerson's work as the editor of the Brooklyn *Eagle*, a Democratic Party paper. But in January he lost his editorship over his sympathy for the Free Soil movement, the increasingly organized attempt to block slavery's expansion into the territories eventually acquired in the Mexican War. Although the movement would be defeated at virtually every level in subsequent elections, Free Soil managed to split the major parties and represented one of the first major victories in the abolitionist campaign to make slavery an ever-present news story and a national concern for both Whigs and Democrats. After his dismissal from the *Eagle*, Whitman went to New Orleans in early 1848 to become the exchange editor for the *New Orleans Crescent*, for which he cut and pasted news items from other papers published throughout the nation and the world. The major story that spring, other than slavery in the territories, was liberty in Europe.[8]

Upon returning to New York a few months later, Whitman reengaged with Free Soil, whose insurgencies within New York State politics were being carried in newspaper stories around the country. Before long Whitman became the editor of a Free Soil paper, the *Brooklyn Freeman*, but he was compelled to resign from that concern as well after New York Democrats compromised their Free Soil principles in favor of party unity in the fall of 1849.

The backlash against Free Soil had now cost Whitman two editorships, but his own convictions were unshaken. When national politicians began trumpeting the same two-note tune of compromise and unity, Whitman again found a way to respond through a newspaper, though now as an aspiring poet rather than an editor. Although some of the verses he published in New York papers seem to verge on the loose doggerel of a political hack writer, Whitman found ways to weave references to current political events into the deeper strains of American presentism. The poems are especially indebted to America's revolutionary opposition to transatlantic tradition and sense of participation in an ongoing sacred history. As such, they represent Whitman's first sustained attempt to develop the model of presentist national memory that would define his future work.

A common scorn for political compromises links all the poems, and they treat such conciliation as a refusal of America's revolutionary destiny in favor of European-styled traditionalism. The Compromise of 1850 included a series of such accommodations, all of which were designed to resolve the question that abolitionists and Free Soilers had put at the forefront of everyone's mind: Should slavery be expanded into the new territories? The legislation that finally passed in August and September after months of public debate and private deal making admitted California as a free state and New Mexico and Utah as territories without restriction on slavery; it also ended the slave trade in the national capital but significantly strengthened the Fugitive Slave Law. Whitman intervened poetically at several stages during the long controversy, publishing first in the *New York Evening Post* on March 2 and then placing three poems in Greeley's *Tribune* on March 22, June 14, and June 21. Each of the four poems addresses the slavery question in terms consistent with Whitman's Free Soil beliefs but does so obliquely, through the use of scathing metaphors, religious invocations, and unflattering transatlantic comparisons. As Klammer has suggested, the common origin in the expanding antislavery movement means the poems are best understood as a unified group, one that connected Whitman's journalistic career with the more formally adventurous but still openly antislavery voice evident in the 1855 edition of *Leaves of Grass*.[9] The three *Tribune* poems in particular demonstrate how Whitman's interactions with antislavery news underscored the same transatlantic distinctions and nationalist divisions between presentism and traditionalism that *Leaves of Grass* would take for granted. Each frames modern news as a basis for sacred national memory and a spiritual force to oppose the traditionalism of the Old World. Inspired by a moral and political crisis over slavery, the poems also spiritualize elements of nineteenth-century American news that Whitman would maintain at the heart of all his future poetic projects, including *Leaves*.

It therefore would be a mistake to dismiss these works as merely occasional poetry, for each is a "news poem" in at least four senses: their meaning depends on the newspaper for content, for framing, for audience, and most importantly, for spirit. While all borrow from contemporary news stories for their content, they also are framed beside those stories within a newspaper, and they intend, like the news items by which they are surrounded, to elicit an immediate response among a mass of politicized news readers (rather than typical readers of elevated verse). Although he did not yet have the editorial control he would exercise over *Leaves of Grass*, writing for the newspapers helped Whitman see how poetic arrangements on the printed page could create a material bridge to his readers' concrete experience of shared history. The poems repurposed journalistic subject matter, but they also demonstrated Whitman's keen appreciation for how, as timely artistic responses to recent events, they could encourage an audience to participate in a long-running news story as a medium of national memory.

Whitman's submissions to the *Tribune* are finally news poems because they explore the spirit of American news, and the poems themselves reflect on the American news's mnemonic power. The complex relationship between a mass audience and the form of common history that could be carried in a national newspaper comprises the group's central theme, making them an early foray into an arena of presentist memory that Whitman would rarely leave over the next two decades. The poetics made famous by *Leaves* would advance a similarly presentist mode by mixing direct address with the details of Whitman's contemporary experience to spur his audience through a highly engaged reading experience, one he hoped would be followed by new actions of their own. In this sense, the spirit of American news lay near the heart of his mature as well as his amateur experiments into poetry.[10] In each case, he sought to construct a presentist memory circuit around popular and politically oriented poetry.

While the news poems of 1850 unmistakably address the disturbance over slavery, on a more basic level they launch decidedly presentist attacks against an American traditionalism Whitman associated with monarchical European nations. In different ways, each of the 1850 poems unmistakably repudiates American compromisers for trying to define patriotism as a blind salute to a time-honored national union. Readers who have interpreted Whitman as essentially nationalistic may fail to recognize that throughout his early career he remained consistently hostile to nationalism's traditionalist strain. Such traditionalism forms the target for all 1850's poetic attacks, and at the center stood Daniel Webster, the same public figure who had drawn Emerson's presentist fire years before in the introduction to *Nature*. Webster's famous Bunker Hill speech had provided the leverage point for Emerson's great essay, and in March of 1850 Webster would offer a nationalist defense of American traditionalism that helped to inspire Whitman's presentist alternative.[11]

Bunker Hill Reprised: The Speech of March 7

Since the founding of the republic, northerners had found economic reasons to support slavery, and economic arguments for the Compromise of 1850 continued to circulate among the "Cotton Whigs" of Webster's Massachusetts. But the measure's supporters went further, arguing on the national stage that allowing slavery's expansion was patriotic; in the two major parties, the papers, and the Congress, compromisers insisted that deference to the national tradition and protecting the union of the founders required a compromise on slavery in the territories.

Leading up to that fateful summer, Daniel Webster's position on any compromise remained uncertain. But facing threats of secession from the South, Webster began his famous Speech of March 7 by prioritizing fidelity to national tradition over the North's Free Soil concerns. "I wish to speak to-day," the senator from Massachusetts declared, "not as a Massachusetts man, nor as a Northern man, but as an American." This patriotic prelude introduced Webster's statement of support for all the compromise's elements, including the Fugitive Slave Law. By the time the oration concluded, Webster had justified his support for slavery as an extension of the values extolled in the "Bunker Hill Monument Address," especially its central claim that the present generation's primary duty lay in preserving the tradition of the founders. "Never did there devolve on any generation of men higher trusts than now devolve upon us for the preservation of this Constitution and the harmony and peace of all who are destined to live under it," Webster told his Senate colleagues. Without any apparent sense of irony, he added a metaphor of national bondage to later published versions of what was a de facto defense of American slavery: "Let us make our generation one of the strongest and brightest links in that golden chain which is destined, I fondly believe, to grapple the people of all the States to this Constitution for ages to come." Thus did Webster forge a traditionalist chain to bind slave and free state to one great national past. Patriotic Americans could honor their country best by standing steadfast under the shadow of the fathers' tombs and preserving the Union at all costs.[12]

Not all Webster's listeners in the Senate, nor the readers who found descriptions and transcriptions of the speech in their papers the next day, were content to stay in that shadow. During earlier controversies over the Mexican War, Webster had opposed the extension of slavery into the territories. Now that he found himself compelled to support proslavery claims about the legality and even the religious morality of American bondage, northern antislavery correspondents and editors attacked him as a traitor to his principles. Some speculated that Webster had some selfish if not pecuniary interest in the compromise, perhaps related to his presidential ambitions, though the *Tribune* warned that he would find such promises mere "Judas kisses, given to mislead and betray."[13] Roger Sherman, Greeley's congressional correspondent, thought it "curious" that "Webster should suddenly become more tolerant toward the South, and distrustful of the free spirit of New-York and New-England antislavery men."[14] Walt Whitman, however, seems to have been preparing for such betrayal and was ready to dole out poetic retribution.

Less than a week before, his "Song for Certain Congressmen" had attacked suspected "Dough-faces," Webster presumably among them, as the tools of a phony American traditionalism that smacked of European monarchism, dismissing them as northern servants of "the dashing southern lords." Published in William Cullen Bryant's *Evening Post,* the poem lampooned northern collaborators as feudal underlings content to rest under the thumb of a southern aristocracy in exchange for the "good fat place" of patronage.[15] Webster's Speech of March 7 would have only confirmed Whitman's suspicions about this strain of northern duplicity, infirmity, and Old World backwardness. Indeed, it seems likely that the widespread news reports of Webster's oration, which continued for weeks, inspired the religious tone and content of Whitman's subsequent *Tribune* poems.

Tellingly, Webster's address not only defended the biblical basis of slavery but followed Calhoun and other southerners in linking Free Soil agitation to the recent sectional schisms that had divided American Protestantism. As Mark Noll observes, these religious bodies "had divided against themselves" at a time when they "enjoyed an influence over public life greater than any other religious tradition has ever enjoyed at any other time."[16] In rhetorically sanctifying the union of states by connecting it to church as the body of Christ, Webster was implicitly charging those opposed to the compromise as heretics and blasphemers.[17] Whitman's first poetic rejoinder to the speech, provocatively titled "Blood-Money," also referenced scripture and the ecclesiological belief that the community of believers represented the body of Christ on earth. Yet though he would prove a staunch unionist, Whitman did not allude as Webster had to the danger of schismatic betrayals of traditional unity. The poet presented Webster and his allies not as guardians of church and country but as traditionalist facsimiles of Judas Iscariot, dutifully repeating an ancient ritual of selling out the body and blood of Christ.[18]

"Blood-Money": The Betrayal of Divine Youth

Whitman was a better interpreter of Christianity than his reputation as a worldly poet might suggest, and (like Emerson) he recognized that the faith contained more nuanced conceptions of sacred history than Webster's traditionalism indicated. Basic beliefs in the resurrected Jesus, various sacraments, and the Holy Spirit placed God in an ongoing human history; this gave the faith of Christians of many sects a radical, presentist edge.[19] As previously suggested, this element of Christian temporality is sometimes overlooked in casual appraisals of religious tradition, which in fact are often interpreted and practiced by believers as radical rejections of certain understandings of traditionalist authority. Indeed, the *Tribune* had become the venue for an understanding of sacred history as a going concern, a belief that linked radicals emerging from various religious backgrounds in a "single conversation." As Dan McKanan puts it, "Neither the theological differences between Forty-Eighters and revivalists, nor the constitutional debate between abolitionists and the Liberty Party, nor the mutual distrust between abolitionists and artisans could keep radicals apart when all turned to the same newspaper for news of the day."[20]

That newspaper, of course, was the *Tribune,* and Whitman's first poetic offering to this antitraditionalist organ of sacred history was perfectly calibrated for its audience. Although it harshly repudiates Webster's recommended form of religiosity, Whitman's first news poem after the Speech of March 7 invokes Christian understandings of sacred presence. "Blood-Money" not only recalls the biblical story of Jesus's betrayal following the Last Supper but also connects that ancient story directly to the present political scene, the American battle over slavery, and the conflict between presentist and traditionalist memory. In the process the poem offers a profound reflection on the key theological issue involved in the interpretation of the Lord's Supper and the sense of spiritual continuity that the ritualized remembrance of that supper anchored: the Christian belief in divine immanence, the notion that the eternal divine could be paradoxically but authentically located in the present earthly moment.

Emerson had turned this form of sacred history toward his own cultural ends, and it also remained a potent belief in many more orthodox *Tribune* readers. As the previous chapter argued, notions of divine immanence animated various aspects of nineteenth-century American Protestantism, from interpretations of scriptural prophecy to sacramental worship. But in a more universal sense, the belief in divine immanence was what Christians since the first century had meant by their gospel, the prophetic "good news" that the God of ancient Israel had become personally involved and even embodied in the recent past in order to redeem the sinful world. Thus references in "Blood-Money" to that ancient time actually highlighted a powerful religious argument for nineteenth-century American presentism by reminding readers that their nation's dominant religious tradition did not depend on any father's tomb but rather on an empty one and on a risen lord.[21]

Grasping the poem's scriptural resonances demands a level of biblical literacy more common in the nineteenth century than today, for the speaker assumes a reader familiar enough with Christian scripture and practice to engage with the meaning of Christian remembrance and sacred history. In his retelling of the central narrative of the Judas story, Whitman draws on several distinct episodes from multiple books of the New Testament: Jesus's Last Supper at the Passover, his promise of a continuing personal connection to earthly sufferers, and Paul's adjudication of an early-church controversy in which the present suffering of the poor was ignored in deference to a traditionalist commemoration. All these scriptural references work together to provide a biblical basis for the presentist perspective the poem ultimately superimposes upon American slavery.[22]

While much of the poem's dramatic action concerns Judas's treachery in the passion story, Whitman also reminds readers of the Eucharistic rite first established at Jesus's Last Supper, the Passover meal that frames Judas's betrayal in the biblical narratives. In smaller letters just below the title Whitman printed a phrase that denotes both the betrayed Jesus and the meal he instituted for his remembrance: "Guilty of the Body and the Blood of Christ."[23] The line actually derives not directly from Christ's passion story but rather from St. Paul's warning to first-century Christians about the spiritual results of sharing the commemorative communion meal without proper self-examination. The famous passage had become especially problematic in New England in the eighteenth century, where it sometimes created divisions in Puritan churches that made communion a test of saintliness and sometimes full church membership. Hardly a minor theological point, the controversy over self-examination and the potential to incur guilt through the "tokens of his presence whereby Christ may be said to be present" in communion had helped end the pastorate of the greatest early American theologian, Jonathan Edwards.[24]

Thus Whitman's repetition of Paul's words recall not only the Judas story but also a ritualized act of early Christian commemoration based on Christ's actions at the Last Supper. The epigraph's significance has been overlooked even though the poem's central concern involves the association between sacred memory and political unity, as well as the associations of Christ's crucifixion with slaves' suffering. When they mention its content at all, commentators typically describe the poem's use of Judas to highlight more recent political betrayals; however, the poem borrows far more than a stereotypical villain from its biblical sources, for it uses scripture to reflect deeply on the high stakes of collective remembrance for both church and state.[25] Moreover, Whitman is clearly interested in how the power of memory to bind a community can be perverted, how what Webster might describe as a "golden chain" of constitutional traditionalism could become an instrument of mass enslavement rather than unity.

Paul was similarly concerned with a dispute over the proper form of collective remembrance when he sent the words Whitman cites to an ancient church in Corinth. In the passages surrounding the lines, Paul issues instructions about how these early Christians ought to properly remember Jesus through the common meal they shared in response to Christ's "words of institution." Tellingly, Paul is forced to intervene in order to arrest the Corinthians' habit of employing the communion ritual to cloak real divisions behind a pious patina of false unity. The young church's show of togetherness through Eucharistic observance was, Paul insisted, a mere spectacle rendered heretical by the inequality between members and the humiliation of the poor. In the King James version of Paul's letter, which Whitman knew well, the apostle rebukes his church's superficial gestures of unity without concern for propriety or justice: "Now in this that I declare unto you I praise you not, that ye come together not for the better but for the worse. . . . Despise ye the church of God, and shame them that have not? What shall I say to you? Shall I praise you in this? I praise you not."[26]

By referring to this controversy in Paul's church in a newspaper poem intended for a biblically literate audience, Whitman retools Paul's warning to misguided first-century Christians for the needs of nineteenth-century America. The initial biblical allusion suggests what the following poetic lines will confirm: that in Senator Webster's heyday as in Saint Paul's, appealing to sacred memory to achieve unity in the absence of justice leaves a community guilty; further, it leads to a violation of precisely what was nominally honored in the commemoration: the body of Christ for St. Paul, the American nation for Webster.

For Paul this paradox of guilty memory involved not only the unintentional mockery of a ritual observance but also a violation of the body of Christ and the church community; for Whitman, Webster's speech involved a similar abomination based on the mistaken appeal to a hallowed national tradition in the name of false unity. Thus before the poem even begins, Whitman has conveyed through his epigraph a biblical rejection of Webster's central tenet that the appearance of "schism," whether in church or nation, was the ultimate evil. Ceremonies of unity without a true commitment to all the community's members in reality sullied precisely what they pretended to praise. Remembrance of the founders, whether Jesus and Paul or Washington and Jefferson, became a sham when it was enacted in a way that refused to acknowledge the plight of the poorest members of either a heretical ancient church or similarly heretical modern nation.

The words of institution, echoed first by Paul and then by Whitman, were originally invoked to reinforce Christian communion through the sacred unity of the recent past, but they subsequently proved as divisive as any in the Bible.[27] Churches recited these verses in communion rituals intended to solidify coherence among their members, but Christian sects had been quarreling over the meaning for both the words and accompanying rituals for almost as long. Nor was the irony of this schismatic history obscure to American literati. Emerson's farewell sermon noted that "in the history of the Church no subject has been more fruitful of controversy than the Lord's Supper."[28] Yet he also had offered his own alternative understanding of authentic nationalist remembrance among the disciples. At the crux of these divisions lay the question of what it meant to remember together: In what way was the sacred past meant to be present and what sort of unity could that memory inspire? In dividing from his church based on his personal conviction that the ritual held no meaning, and in seeking an "original relation to the universe" rather than the tomb of a sacred tradition, Emerson was enacting the sort of schism that the ancient rite had been inspiring since its first-century inception.[29]

Yet from a historical perspective, the gospel accounts of the Lord's Supper had themselves appeared to inaugurate a presentist ritual. Within the larger biblical narrative, both Judas's betrayal and the meal occur during the celebration of the Passover, when Jews recalled how as slaves in Egypt they had sacrificed a lamb and been delivered from God's avenging angel. The supper, which would become a central rite of Christian remembrance, began as a paschal feast, a ritualized recollection of an ancient sacred history that Jesus insisted his coming and imminent death would fulfill and supersede. The paschal lamb of sacred memory, the disciples in John's gospel are informed, was now none other than Jesus himself, standing among them awaiting the sacrifice on the cross that Judas's betrayal would make possible.[30] This ritual of remembrance, which predated the establishment of the New Testament as authoritative Christian scripture, also arose from a presentist impulse.[31]

As I have already suggested, this essential Christian movement away from a primary identification with a distant sacred history, undertaken in the name of a recent manifestation of divine presence, exerted a powerful influence on antebellum America. Nineteenth-century American Protestants had different explanations of the Last Supper, and all nominally rejected Roman Catholic explanations, but most recognized that the institution of the elements reflected a reliable promise of divine involvement in the present moment of a faithful community's ritualized remembrance. In other words, it was a reminder that the shared history of that community remained, paradoxically, an immanent reality. Denominations might cast doubt on the literal truth of Jesus's biblical statement that the bread and wine shared in common remembrance by his followers were his body and blood, but they generally still believed that the elements signified God's continuing connection to his earthly church. Calvin's partial denial of Jesus's "real presence" in the elements "paradoxically led him to develop a dynamic reflection on the present but indescribably divine reality that underlies all materiality."[32] Three hundred years later, Emerson's repudiation of traditionalist understandings of the same rite consummated the same presentist trajectory, and *Nature* carried it to a political conclusion in its originating quarrel with Daniel Webster.

Whitman's "Blood-Money" makes the overlapping logic of that connection between presentist modes of Christian and national memory even more explicit by linking Webster's betrayal of revolutionary memory to Judas's betrayal of Jesus. Both Webster and Judas become dark traditionalist ministers, as the treasonous duplicity of Webster's ploy stands guilty by association with Judas's presence at the original Last Supper. This is all to say that, although Whitman was neither a Christian nor a theologian, his poetic vision corresponded with many Christian beliefs about divine immanence.[33] While "Blood-Money" focuses on Judas's sale of Jesus (in the Gospel of Matthew the price is thirty pieces of silver), the poem also grounds itself in the everlasting promise of divine presence that underlay Christian accounts of Jesus's betrayal and death. As represented in the passion narratives, Pauline epistles, and Eucharistic practices, sacred memory recalled Christ's presence as body and blood within a gathered community, and Whitman's poem similarly seeks to center divine presence in contemporary communal experience. Rather than situating Christ in bread and wine, however, the poet determines to seek him in the antislavery news and in the ongoing war against traditionalism.

In the first verse paragraph, Whitman sets the ancient scene in a way that highlights two different perspectives of time and history, one of which Christ embodies and one to which he falls victim. "Of olden time, when it came to pass / That the Beautiful God, Jesus, should finish his work on earth," the poem begins, "Then went Judas, and sold the Divine youth, / And took pay for his body." Readers often interpret Whitman's 1850 news poems' stodgy diction as a sign of the traditionalism and conventionality that marred Whitman's poetry prior to the publication of *Leaves of Grass* in 1855. But "Blood-Money," Whitman's first publication in free verse, is neither conventional nor traditional; on the contrary, it highlights the moral hypocrisy of the traditionalism of its time. To Whitman, traditionalists seemed intent on overlooking divinity within a contemporary community out of misplaced and superficial fidelity to the past.

"Blood-Money" refuses to admit this view of safely entombed sacred history. It seems to tell an old story, but the poem's language feels forced partly because it describes that story's temporal setting in an unsettling way. Rather than relying on the simple past tense, Whitman's first line ties itself in knots to suspend the reader between past, present, and future; while the tale is "of" olden time, it is not exactly in it, for the past evoked is fluid, a history coming "to pass," and the narrator leaves it unclear whether the "work" of Christ has been accomplished or is yet to be finished.[34]

The unusual characterization of "the Beautiful God, Jesus" as a "youth" further underscores Whitman's push toward the present. According to Whitman's narrator, the old sin of Judas lies chiefly in his selling of "Divine youth." This seems an odd way to describe a mature Christ approaching his final day, unless Whitman is suggesting not a youth but rather youth itself as the divine principle that Christ had embodied as the sign of a new creation and the broker of a new covenant. Similarly, falling as it does under the epigraph, "his body" cannot be seen apart from that body's role in making the new covenant present in the communion meal. The American heresy of traditionalism, the popular appeal of which also characterizes his other 1850 news poems, becomes a lens to interpret Judas's crime.

Judas's punishment also supports Whitman's Emersonian thesis that the betrayal of youth amounts to a self-defeating refusal of earthly life. Having taken pay for one divinely youthful body, Judas's subjective guilt punctuates the second verse paragraph with a dramatic image of his own corpse. The self-contradictory nature of his crime is confirmed when Judas hangs himself: "as though Earth lifted her breast to throw him from her, and Heaven refused him, / He hung in the air, self-slaughtered." Consistent with the broader concern with memory in "Blood-Money," Whitman's image of Judas as a suicide is a warning against traditionalist remembrance that demands one's refusal of self, life, and a divinity that remains ever present rather than past. Just as neither heaven nor earth can comfort the betrayer of youth, no hallowed tomb or regenerative grave will grace the retrospective age. The only reward for denying the present in the name of the past is eternal stasis.

The absolute isolation of this "self-slaughter" presents a dismal countersign to Emersonian self-reliance founded on the communion of nature and the soul. Yet Judas's guilty end had not prevented the betrayal of divine youth from becoming its own tradition in a purportedly Christian nation. Moving forebodingly from the biblical history to the present, through "cycles with their long shadows" that have "stalked silently forward / Since those ancient days," the poem draws its key equivalency between Judas's ancient betrayal of youth and Webster's only too recent one, which Whitman marks with a shift to the present tense: "Again goes one saying, / What will ye give me, and I will deliver this man unto you?" Judas had agreed in advance to betray Jesus in the gospel stories to the priestly caretakers of their shared nation and religion. In the nineteenth century, too, the compromise of Christian principles proceeds, ironically, as a pledge upheld with the high priests of a sacred national faith; the poem suggests that those traditionalists who uphold a compromised Constitution with a strengthened Fugitive Slave Law also "make the covenant and pay the pieces of silver." The poem exposes the sham faithfulness that, like Judas's dutiful adherence to an agreement shaped by mortal calculation rather than divine wisdom, left one honor bound to a diabolical covenant, one that made a mockery of Jesus's biblical blessing of the wine as a new "covenant in my blood."[35]

These scriptural references would have resonated with many of Whitman's original news readers. Greeley's audience knew their Bibles and also knew that the 1850 compromisers' sellout of divine young bodies was hardly metaphorical. Those who honored and perpetuated the old covenant ensured real bodies and souls would be changing hands for money; the real results of congressional perfidy would become sad chapters of America's enslaved history, carried in the pages of the northern newspapers.

That spring, antislavery voices in Congress and in the press had bludgeoned slavery's traditionalist Christian defenders with news of African American Christians recently abandoned to captivity. Unlike many of slavery's defenders, antislavery Christians cared little about whether slavery had existed in ancient Palestine, but they were increasingly concerned with sins they saw in the recent past and what such news required of them as Americans. During the debate over the Fugitive Slave Law, this ethical question was posed alongside graphic examples of slaves seeking shelter from slave catchers. Only two days before Whitman's poem appeared, Greeley's paper contained several such references, including a reminder of a controversy from the previous year in which two beautiful young fugitive girls had been captured with their mother in the national capital, caged, and nearly sold as concubines.[36]

That a northern senator like Webster should defend such abominations, occurring in this case within sight of the capitol where he spoke, proved shocking to many who might otherwise overlook the sin of slavery in the South. Roger Sherman's *Tribune* reports on Webster's speech also tied the northern senator to proslavery southern papers, politicians, and priestly advocates. Noting with chagrin that the *Charleston Mercury* had been unable to respond to Webster's speech "with any other than admiration and delight," Sherman then recounted how North Carolina senator George Edmund Badger, "echoing Webster's specious fallacies," argued that the Christian tradition was entirely compatible with "American serfdom."[37]

Refusing to admit the point, Sherman observed, as he had in previous letters from Washington, that slavery violated Christianity's central demand to do to others only what one would have done to oneself. To counter the hypocrisy of those who claimed to uphold the Bible's ancient blessing on slavery, Sherman revealed evils done in the present and witnessed in the press. Of slaveholders, the reporter wondered whether in "dragging them to sugar plantations and rice swamps—selling their children for gain, like cattle—whipping them as brute animals are whipped—denying them the sacred rite of legal marriage—keeping them in misery and bondage forever—going to war for new Territory in which they may fetch a better price—punishing with fine and imprisonment those godly men and charitable women who offer to teach them to read the Bible—and attempting to rule the United States and dispense its patronage in perpetuity.... *Is this doing by the slaves South as we would be done by?*" Though legal under the current Constitution, Sherman pointedly asked whether such actions were "fulfilling Christ's law?"[38] The week before, Sherman had made similar criticisms of Webster's speech, asking, "Did Jesus lay down his life for the slave, and shall a Calhoun or a Webster advocate his perpetual bondage, and treating him like a brute?"[39]

The constant battles in Congress and the popular press over the proper

Christian response to an all-too-present experience of slavery in the news helps explain the remarkable closing of "Blood-Money." Here Whitman moves from a veiled allegory of Webster's betrayal to more realistic depictions of human trafficking that culminate in demand for a messianic return of divine presence. The narrator calls upon the murdered and resurrected Christ, "First Born of the Dead," to "Look forth . . . over the tree-tops of Paradise" and "see thyself in yet continued bonds." Following this prophetic invocation are lines containing Whitman's frankest recorded descriptions of African American suffering, accompanied by the poet's no less dramatic insistence that slavery victimizes Christ himself. The poem ends by admonishing a heavenly Jesus, as the "Witness of Anguish—Brother of Slaves," to take his rightful place in the earthly present of March 22, 1850. "Not with thy price closed the price of thine image," a prophetic poet reminds the God who created African Americans in his image, before concluding with a final reminder of contemporary betrayals of body and blood: "And still Iscariot plies his trade."

Of course, Whitman was simultaneously addressing his imagined news reader along with Jesus as a "witness of anguish" and "brother of slaves." Whitman's first *Tribune* poem creatively relocated a magisterial Christ and the sovereign American reader—away from the passive distance of biblical traditionalism that could countenance slavery in theory and toward an earthly American present populated by actual suffering slaves, and by real sympathizing readers, a world of passionate national news that had already been mapped by the expanding antislavery press and the *Tribune*. Even as he launched this impetuous assault on the transcendent Christ in his heaven, Whitman also knew that many of his readers believed the Christ of church and communion had taken up residence in an embattled American present. As Frances Clarke argues, such examples of contemporary suffering and appeals to sympathetic responses characterized the liberalized currents of Protestantism to which Whitman was appealing through the *Tribune*.[40] Nineteenth-century believers were increasingly seeking Christ's redeeming presence not only in the communion practices surrounding the bread and wine as body and blood but also in the blood of enslaved persons and the body of sympathetic believers who responded to them. Those traditionalist hypocrites who commemorated Christ without a warmhearted commitment to the downtrodden earned only the guilt for both Jesus's murder and their own spiritual suicides.

"Out of Its State and Drowsy Air"

"Blood-Money" appeared in the *Tribune* on March 22, 1850. Early that summer, as Webster and other congressional leaders hammered out the details of the compromise, Whitman would once again cast them as venal traditionalists out only for gain, for whom "a dollar [was] dearer . . . than Christ's blessing." Published in the *Daily Tribune* on June 14, Whitman's "The House of Friends" castigates the nation's elder statesmen, as "Doughfaces, crawlers, lice of humanity," and closes with a call for action from a new generation: "Arise, young North! / Our elder blood flows in the veins of cowards—/ the gray-haired sneak, the blanched poltroon, / . . . / Are they to be our tokens always?" On the surface the poem seems merely partisan boilerplate, but in the context of Whitman's other news poems of 1850 and the wider debate Webster had helped spark on the North's position on slavery and constitutional authority, "The House of Friends" extends a somewhat more profound theme amid its sneering insults. Just as "Blood-Money" had, it begins with a scriptural epigraph, this time from Zechariah 13:6, and once again the poem would draw on the prophetic strain within Christianity to authorize a presentist reconfiguring of the nation's relationship to traditionalist authority. In addition to rebuking Webster and the other gray-headed traitors to the spirit of young America, the poem repudiates Webster's appeals to blood, in the Speech of March 7, as signs of pure ethnic heritage and race as a guarantor of American freedom and future national greatness. Webster had explained the need for compromise with southern states by insisting that such measures would save a nation that, despite its traditionalism, possessed "yet youthful veins . . . full of enterprising courage."[41] From Whitman's perspective, Webster's attempt to put old blood in new veins merely confirmed traditionalism's determination to sell out the divine blood of an eternally young nation. By transforming Webster's courage-filled veins into the veins of cowards, "The House of Friends" registers both scorn for traditionalism's "elder blood" and resistance to traditionalism's phony blood tie to the past. In its place the poet calls for a renewal of revolution, an arising "young North" built on the presentist premise of a generational break with the elders.[42]

Whitman would again celebrate the revolutionary potential of youth the following week in "Resurgemus," a poem that would have seemed like a flight into foreign territory only for those who had never before read the *Tribune*. Despite its international theme, this last *Tribune* poem was the final installment in the series of linked poetic interventions in the national crisis over the Compromise of 1850, and Whitman was not the only observer to connect those recent events to the international workingman's movement. Most significantly for the poet, Greeley's paper had effectively linked news of revolutionary events in Europe to American slavery debates, thereby blazing a trail for Whitman's appropriation of such foreign news for a similarly American purpose in "Resurgemus."[43]

In fact, the poem's positive account of this foreign history could not have emerged in the United States without the benefit of American journalistic initiative. Frustrated with the British press's conservative filter, Greeley eventually hired independent correspondents and finally sent two of his most trusted and talented writers, Charles Dana and Margaret Fuller, to cover the story themselves. Dana and Fuller sent back glowing reports of continental radicalism, and the *Tribune* angrily condemned the cynical brutality with which traditionalist forces violently repressed it.[44] Thus Whitman's poem originated in the *Tribune*'s circumvention of the conservative British press and its special correspondents' success in bringing the true history home to its Anglophone audience.

Coverage of 1848 demonstrated how thoroughly the spirit of presentism had invested the *Tribune*, and not merely because a major paper catering to the United States' historically conservative Whig Party publicly supported revolutionary European socialists. The paper also expressed the early enthusiasm for the revolts in the presentist terms of a new age no longer bound to the stale traditions of old Europe. The *Tribune* notably carried this zeal for "new vistas" further than other mainstream newspapers, even after it became clear that many of the revolutions' specific goals were too socialistic to be palatable to more conservative Americans.[45]

Thus the *Tribune* proved that America, unlike the dynastic European states, possessed the journalistic capacity to give the revolutionaries a fair hearing. In this sense it absorbed the new revolutions into a broader national narrative about America's unique connection to the recent past. As Andrew Delbanco suggests, to *Tribune* readers and other Americans, "What was happening in the Old World seemed a kind of backdraft from the New World."[46] By the same token, Europe's failure to accurately represent these nationalistic revolutionary movements in the press appeared as a prelude to its violent rejection of all revolutionary national claims. Thus, from the point of view of frustrated and interested American readers, Old Europe's repression of revolutionary news worked hand in glove with its repression of actual revolutionaries at home and abroad. By contrast, Greeley and his correspondents, in covering the European revolutions as newsworthy international events, also commended them as compatible with a reformist zeal that lay nearer to American homes and hearts. Fuller's role as an empowered correspondent in the same year as the Seneca Falls Convention was particularly important in this respect, for her foreign assignment was only the latest sign of the *Tribune*'s association with one of the Anglo-American world's most outspoken feminists.

As a well-known proselytizer of reform and an energetic Americanizer of radical European ideas, the *Tribune* contributed as vital a context to "Resurgemus" as any of the foreign episodes the poem describes only in the most general terms. Greeley, virtually from his paper's founding, had helped to domesticate European radicalism for an audience of American Whigs, and the *Tribune* "stood alone among major American newspapers in celebrating the social as well as the political dimension of 1848."[47] When Whitman's poem appeared at the top of the back page of Greeley's *Daily Tribune* on July 21, 1850, it was to carry on such work by interpreting foreign revolutions poetically for a distinctly national purpose.[48]

That purpose by 1850 was nearly synonymous with the antislavery movement. Throughout the spring of 1850, Greeley's paper ran foreign correspondence criticizing the continuing forces of European reaction side by side on the page with telegraphic reports on the political tumult in Washington and around the country. Thus Whitman's poetic reflection on 1848 mirrored the *Tribune*'s ongoing coverage of the European repression of radicalism alongside the national crisis of 1850 in a transatlantic pattern that would have been familiar to any *Tribune* reader. In a poem that considered democracy's prospects abroad, Whitman sought to bolster his democratic news readers' confidence in the cultural power of presentist memory to change the course of history at home.

At the fateful point that Webster's compromised traditionalist position was about to become national law, "Resurgemus" recalls a European liberation movement to shame the senator's bald hypocrisy and to expose the sham of his concluding appeal to American exceptionalism. Although conservatives in both the established parties were busy crushing rebellious Free Soilers in backroom deals, Webster had still claimed that "no monarchical throne presses these States together"; although the government was about to pass its strongest Fugitive Slave Law, that government had, according to Webster "in all its history . . . been beneficent [and] . . . trodden down no man's liberty." That all depended, of course, on whether a black fugitive had any claim on liberty, let alone on the image of Christ that Whitman's news poem had granted. In "Blood-Money" Whitman remembers those whom Webster forgets, following Jesus's damnation of the forgetful in the Gospel of Matthew in suggesting that the "Divine youth," once betrayed, still resides among the hounded: "I was a stranger, and ye took me not in . . . inasmuch as ye did it not to one of the least of these, ye did it not to me."[49] Similarly "Resurgemus" recalls the democratic masses that aristocratic Europe had literally buried without a tomb.

Under a Latin invocation of the resurrection, the first lines of Whitman's 1850 celebration of the Revolutions of 1848 counter Webster's traditionalist blindness toward the resurgent power of instantaneous, electrifying insight. "Suddenly, out of its state and drowsy air, the air of slaves, / Like lightning Europe le'pt forth, / Sombre, superb and terrible." The opening assumes the perspective of American news readers with all their exceptionalist prejudices about the "drowsy" European continent. Rendered in the past tense, it captures the surprise many Americans felt when they first heard the news that ordinary Europeans had somehow stood up against the powers of their long-honored rulers. But using the word "slaves," rather than "peasants" or "serfs," indicates that Whitman's version of European history also inhabits the American present of 1850. Other *Tribune* writers had drawn similar parallels between European agitation and the controversies over slavery in the territories both during and after 1848's revolutions. Readers were therefore well prepared to follow Whitman's linkage between the repression of 1848's challenge to aristocratic privilege and the servile American scene in 1850, in which the liberty of northern states as well as African Americans seemed threatened by "Southern lords" and their own aristocratic Slave Power.[50]

Having described slavery as a European phenomenon, the poem then turns explicitly to the situation of its contemporary American readers with a shift to the present tense. Now Whitman seems to address some version of the dough-faced targets of his previous news poems. "You liars paid to defile the People, / Mark you now," Whitman tells a global klatch of Judases, before predicting that the spirit of the dead "in new-made graves, / Bloody corpses of young men" will "bear fruits, and they are good." As in "Blood-Money," the poet anticipates a material resurrection to follow this sacrifice of youth, and even the borders of nation and continent will not restrain the risen spirit of crucified liberty in the prophesied future. "Not a grave of those slaughtered ones, / But is growing its seed of freedom, / In its turn to bear seed, / Which the winds shall carry afar and resow." "Not a disembodied spirit," the poet promises, "can the weapons of tyrants let loose, / But it shall stalk invisibly over the earth, / Whispering, counseling, cautioning."

Whitman's move from the safe distance of the past tense to a present full of dangerous life and a future of prophetic hope mirrors the movement of "Blood-Money" from biblical times to the latest news, and the final lines of "Resurgemus" draw on that same Christian message of divine presence, clearly paraphrasing Jesus's prediction of his own second coming from the gospels: "Is the house shut? Is the master away? / Nevertheless, be ready, be not weary of watching, / He will surely return; his messengers come anon."[51] From one perspective, then, the prophecy of "Resurgemus" was in its title, which offers a mystical vision that would resonate with the typical *Tribune* reader's Christian hopes for an ultimate victory of freedom and justice. Like "Blood-Money" it shows how Whitman was able to combine the strength of Christian and revolutionary memory for the *Tribune*'s press war against slavery, waged in urgent defense of the presentist soul of America.[52]

Yet in a far more concrete way, the poem describes the social power of news itself, a modern phenomenon for which its American authorship and readership supplies the amplest evidence. The dead men Whitman summons in imagination have already lived on in history through a new sort of "good news." An information revolution that coincided with the dead's political one had helped speed the spirit of revolt across national borders with the help of writers and publishers like Horace Greeley, Margaret Fuller, and Charles Dana. Whitman had not seen Europe for himself as a correspondent, but he had helped spread the word by clipping and republishing revolutionary stories as an exchange editor in New Orleans. By the time he composed "Resurgemus," such news of revolutionary struggles in one country had helped inspire similar revolts in others, and European leaders had already become the folk heroes of New York papers and parlors.

Recalling the unique power of these news stories, Whitman's last 1850 news poem invoked the sort of history and offered the sort of response that only an emergent information age could have produced. The corpses "Resurgemus" describes are those Whitman had first seen sympathetically described in foreign correspondence written for newspapers like the *Tribune*. As an editor he had himself sent the spirit of the dead out through issues of the *New Orleans Crescent*. They were the "seeds" that had traveled from afar—as Whitman had "predicted"—and in directly addressing the liars, who he knew could "mark" his words through the same news network, he was speaking not only to European reactionaries but to an audience closer to home: the defilers of "the People" who in passing a stronger Fugitive Slave Act had buried the spirit of the Revolution beneath the letter of their traditionalist law.

"The Air of Slaves"

Read in context as Whitman's last *Tribune* poem of that fateful spring, "Resurgemus" sought to strengthen American news readers' connections to their own sacred national history more than to any international community, and to promote a form of memory fundamentally opposed to Webster's traditionalist alternative. The poem borrows from the European storyline of 1848 to rebuke northern defenders of America's southern aristocracy in 1850. More broadly, its account of Europe's stunning social innovations contradicts the exceptionalist claims of American traditionalists such as Webster, much like the Judas comparison in "Blood-Money" had challenged their legitimacy as Christians. No advocate for slavery could be truly Christian, just as no devotee of traditionalism could be a true American. As a whole, the 1850 cycle denies traditionalists the right to ignore the plight of slaves and America's revolutionary potential while still claiming to be either authentically Christian or American. The ironies inherent in traditionalist nationalism, rather than the legitimacy of American nationalism per se, provide the political targets of all Whitman's 1850 news poems, including "Resurgemus." Whitman celebrates those same Old World revolutions in late June of 1850 to counter traditionalist claims to America's New World revolution as a restrictive heritage rather than a spur to further revolutionary action.

Reading the *Tribune* that spring and summer, many Americans might have wondered why their own professed New World leaders seemed so intent on dousing liberty's flame at home with the politics of the past. Webster at Bunker Hill had upheld the first revolution against European tradition while seeking to forestall all future revolutions. But he only completed the conversion to traditionalism in his Speech of March 7, where he sought to stifle senators' whispering of secession by invoking European authorities. Such talk was damaging because it threatened "to astonish Europe with an act of folly such as Europe for two centuries has never beheld in any government or any people!" "No, Sir! No, Sir!" Webster had exclaimed. "There will be no secession! Gentlemen are not serious when they talk of secession."[53]

No *Tribune* reader encountering the speech would have any doubt about what class of observers represented the "Europe" Webster feared offending. The appeal to the American "gentlemen" of the Senate took for granted their anxious desire for the good opinion of aristocratic but well-ordered European states. Yet ordinary *Tribune* readers had also witnessed another side of Europe, one that many would have regarded as more dedicated to America's revolutionary principles than their own "gentle" rulers. Webster's apparent inability to recognize the recently rebellious element in contemporary Europe, in the context of the 1850 debates, merely underscored his inability to acknowledge the fugitive slave, or to hear the still beating heart of the American Revolution that Whitman invoked when he called upon the young North to arise.

Greeley's news network had nourished the spirit of 1848 among the many thousands of American readers who formed the first audience for "Resurgemus," far more than would encounter the poem in *Leaves of Grass* five years later. Greeley's issues had pierced their own "state and drowsy air, the air of slaves" with bulletins from Europe, applying them to the crisis brewing at home. "Resurgemus" and the other *Tribune* poems had exposed a mass audience to Whitman's free-verse poetics, a liberated form that corresponded to the news's globalizing capacity to involve the masses in revolutionary changes of all sorts.

Yet despite its internationalism, the poem's barely suppressed violence, framed in the pages of a great national newspaper, seems in retrospect to turn inexorably toward an American target. Clearly Whitman is warning American "liars paid to defile the People" that the spirit of revolt might once again find purchase on American soil, rising again to battle a slave system Whitman tended to equate with European aristocracy and Old World traditionalism. Years later, when American compromises with liberty gave way to massive northern resistance to "Southern lords,"[54] to state-sanctioned slave power, and to traditionalism, the result would be Webster's worst nightmare: "war," as the senator had put it bluntly on March 7, "and such a war as I will not describe."[55]

PART II

WAR STORIES AND MEMORY CIRCUITS

Hypernationalism and the Transatlantic Time Lag

America, curious toward foreign characters, stands sternly by its own,
Stands removed, spacious, composite, sound.

—Walt Whitman, *Leaves of Grass*, 1856

The Atlantic Telegraph has half undone the declaration of 1776, and has gone far to make us once again, in spite of ourselves, one people.

—*Times* of London, 1858

National news at midcentury was never merely a domestic phenomenon, as Horace Greeley's 1851 visit to the Palace of Westminster demonstrated. Britain's internal debate over a national "tax on knowledge" also concerned the potentially disruptive social effects of America's alternative news model and the presentist spirit behind it. Similarly, traditionalist control over British news compelled the American news business to become even more independent, and overcoming the British suppression of revolutionary news in 1848 became a point of nationalist pride. Thus the midcentury Anglophone news business broke along a stark nationalist division, with each side seeing the other in oppositional terms. This book's early chapters addressed how a sense of sacred history developed around the "national style" of American news that Greeley pioneered in the 1840s and that presentist writers like Emerson and Whitman reinforced; by the end of 1850 a more militant presentism had taken shape in opposition to a British-style American traditionalism that the antislavery movement helped brand an American heresy.

Cosmopolitan observers assumed that such nationalist differences would erode under the increasing flow of international news and that the burgeoning midcentury communication network would facilitate shared international agendas. Marx, a Prussian who found himself in Britain writing for an American newspaper in the 1850s, thought that the rise of global mass communication would diminish local nationalist distinctions and that the march of global history would ultimately bury them.[1] Yet presentists and traditionalists, though they would deploy modern international communication, would continue to cleave the masses into separate islands of shared national history. In fact, Anglo-American nationalisms would gain strength during the 1850s, becoming more forceful and violent throughout an era when global communication was improving. Many American presentists, despite their progressive tendencies, would react violently against not merely traditionalism but also the apparent catholicity of Anglophone news.[2]

They would find a powerful ally in the transatlantic time lag. Throughout the 1850s, as newspapers crossed the Atlantic for an audience of foreign readers, they converted Atlantic space into national time, fostering nationalist fixations on news by providing a firm counterpoint to increasingly integrated transatlantic networks of culture, trade, and information. The Atlantic barrier maintained a fundamental division in the sharing of Anglophone news, linking national territory with the distinctively nationalist experience of news sharing. Meanwhile, as domestic news networks improved, these partisan audiences for news became increasingly apparent within the papers themselves. Thus the exchange of transatlantic news forged and exhibited discrete national memory circuits within the larger international arena. By materially manifesting the transatlantic time lag, national newspapers projected a clear geographical limit on news sharing and gave presentist memory a tangible place to settle.

Yet the transatlantic time lag was set to expire, as entrepreneurs worked furiously to lay the first transatlantic cable by the end of the 1850s. Part II examines how the prospect of such international communion and the uneven expansion of domestic memory circuits contributed to hypernationalist agitation among American news readers in the last decade before the war. Antebellum Americans became increasingly conscious of an impending political collapse. As Susan-Mary Grant suggests, they began to realize that they had failed to live up to the revolutionary ideal of an independent nationality, that "the Union that they created was built on sand," and that "as time passed the difference [between northern and southern outlooks] was becoming more, not less, pronounced."[3] By middecade, as northern newspapers fueled the long-running crisis over slavery's westward expansion, they projected a "fragmenting of [the nation's] ideological geography" even as they maintained (for at least the time being) the nation's transatlantic distinctiveness.[4]

The resulting nationalist anxiety and confusion, and the popularity of news from an as-yet undefined western territory, catalyzed the development of regionally organized memory circuits during the so-called civil war in Kansas. While the transatlantic background of this sectionalist struggle facilitated partisan identifications in important ways, it also shaped the production and promotion of Whitman's greatest work of nationalist literature. Indeed, I ultimately argue that, taken together, the first two editions of *Leaves of Grass* embodied a powerful presentist memory circuit, which the poet organized as a self-conscious response to the likely prospect of intersectional war. I begin, however, by analyzing a grand vision of international progress and peace, the Great Exhibition of the Works and Industry of All Nations. Exhibition coverage previewed a more violent stage of American presentism in a decade that would become mired in national crises and that would end in the Civil War. In particular, the exhibition demonstrated how conflict narratives in the popular press could foster a sense of place and thus bolster nationalist histories under threat of dissolution. Northerners' presentist struggle with traditionalism previously had possessed the character of a heresy trial. As the divisions of the 1850s intensified, the South would come to appear as "a zone to be invaded and subdued rather than fended off . . . through efforts at Northern ideological self-purification."[5] Thus the memory war would become a full-fledged crusade to recover the common ground of home and secure a holy land that American presentists could feel slipping away.

4

Palaces of Memory

Global Information and the Specter of Catholicity

A visit to the Crystal Palace is, in truth, a sort of figurative voyage of circumnavigation, by which . . . you traverse successively the various quarters of the globe, and see before you the productions, the arts, the riches, and in some degree the perspective national manners and customs of them all.

—Hon. C. V. Rives, *New-York Times*, 1851

The favored classes in Great Britain do and must . . . dread the contagion of our example.

—*New-York Tribune*, 1851

Throughout his early career as a publisher, Horace Greeley had learned that a successful national newspaper needed to provide more than reliable information. Using democratized news as a vehicle, the *Log Cabin* and the *Tribune* became powerful conduits of sacred history and symbols of national identity, elevating the masses and including them viscerally in the high moral standards and cultural refinement of the elite Whig Party. In the midst of an intensifying battle against traditionalist heresies, these ventures had actively projected a sense of sacred presentist community that transcended shared language, access to information, or superficial political affiliation. Greeley's 1851 tour of Britain would not only underscore a habitual transatlantic resistance to this American model of news and nation. It would ultimately demonstrate how Anglo-American commonalities could produce and perpetuate violent communal conflicts between dueling nationalist histories and how more efficient Anglo-American exchanges of information could push populations further apart and into more virulently nationalist camps.

This outcome seems to run counter to some descriptions of modern nationalism's foundations. Scholarship that traces nationalism's growth to the binding power of popular vernacular print must also account for situations in which the spread of such language failed to create national unity and even fostered increasing discord. Yet if we assume vernacular newsprint fueled nationalism largely by facilitating simultaneous access to information in a common language, then any absence of unity only seems explicable as a failure to communicate.[1] Similarly, it can be hard to see why nationalist divisions would actually intensify when international communication was becoming more efficient.

The seeming contradiction becomes more understandable once we acknowledge that, as Greeley clearly understood, nineteenth-century newspapers did not just communicate information. Rather, they provided a venue for shared history that popular audiences experienced as a form of national memory. Such a turn to memory helps explain why stark nationalist divisions tend so often to bisect the landscape of shared vernaculars. If shared history rather than shared language forms the primary basis for mass belief in a national identity, then under certain circumstances shared language might actually intensify nationalist divisions. Perhaps especially for populations experiencing anxiety over their national status, distinctions in shared history might become more important to maintain whenever a common tongue threatens to undercut the social relevance of nationality.

Policing those distinctions, actively and even violently, was especially crucial because the respective mode of memory associated with either side of the Atlantic divide seemed open to potential appropriation. Indeed, although they had become the basis for nationalist divisions, both traditionalism and presentism appeared to contain a universalist potential. British traditionalists, for example, might trace British identity to Gothic roots. Yet to do so they drew connections that were contradictory as well as ahistorical, for their supposedly distinctive "national" style inevitably intersected with a much more broadly relevant medieval heritage. The same ancient legacy they cherished could descend with few changes to virtually any individual within the historical boundaries of western Christendom. After all, neither medieval history nor Gothic architecture resided solely in Britain.[2]

Moreover, the revivalists' pre-Reformation ideals formed a contemporary link with the traditionally Catholic nations of the continent, for they recalled Britain's spiritual allegiance to the pope. Britain had only passed the Catholic Emancipation Act in 1829, and the Catholic conversions of

Pugin and other revivalists troubled many otherwise agreeable Protestant traditionalists who still hoped the Church of England would remain the bedrock of British nationalism. Prominent Anglican revivalists, including John Henry Newman, the leader of the Oxford Movement, had joined Pugin in embracing a faith historically regarded as a foreign threat. Their common spiritual trajectory suggested that traveling to the religious core of Britain's national identity might paradoxically lead one to Rome.[3]

By the same token, American presentists were packaging an inherently imperial doctrine as a more limited nationalist product. After all, the presentist view of sacred history might easily apply far beyond the western lands into which the *Tribune*'s readers were moving, and there might be no limit to what and who "America" and its shared history could eventually contain. The news, like the very ancient past, was anything but exceptional: it belonged to everyone. Bound only by the latest information, an American presentist might forfeit any claim to nationalist exclusivity by transcending all physical borders for an international utopia. Thus the temporal focal points of revivalist plans and revolutionary projects tended to destabilize their own nationalist assertions. Pushed to their limits, the unifying powers of both traditionalism and presentism created common histories that could be shared everywhere—and nowhere in particular.[4]

As the previous discussion of the memory war has suggested, each side sustained its nationalist claims partly through the ready opposition it found epitomized on the other side of the pond. As long as the British nation offered an emblem of the traditionalist heresy, American presentists could stake a distinctively nationalist claim; Tories found nearer to home merely needed to be sent packing for the true nation to reveal itself in all its glory. Meanwhile, British traditionalists could define their nation against a presentist threat they identified with the corrupted American system and spend their energies dispensing with treasonous revolutionaries at home.

Yet this stark division could not entirely obscure commonalities that continued to bind Anglo-American English speakers. Beneath longstanding transatlantic hostility lay the thought that nations separated by the Revolution of 1776 were converging, the possibility that the ongoing revolution and counterrevolution was actually a civil war, and the increasing probability that such a war must inevitably end. Once transatlantic distance ceased to obstruct a fuller communion, a traditionalist might wonder how ancient bloodlines and traditions could be impaired by less than a century of official separation. Similarly, a presentist might wonder why, rather than merely racing to publish European news in Wisconsin or sending a

European edition to England, the *Tribune* might not merge its operations with the *Times* of London or simply become indistinguishable from it.

This was not an idle question in 1851, for tensions between international involvement and national identity permeated the midcentury atmosphere. Generated by the news's international expansion, they hung over Greeley's parliamentary hearings on newspaper taxation. But Greeley would also find them suffusing London's exuberant streets that same summer. Indeed, he would witness the season's most dramatic indications of Britain's conflicted interest in the democratization of knowledge issuing not from the Palace of Westminster but rather from an equally remarkable palace that had provided the true focus of his London visit.[5] In the Crystal Palace in Hyde Park, Greeley would find a partial answer to the question of why national news would thrive in the coming years, drawing energy from the international information network that the building so powerfully symbolized.

This chapter analyzes an Anglo-American battle over news coverage of the Great Exhibition of All Nations, held in the Crystal Palace. It highlights how the mechanics of Anglophone news coverage inevitably created separate and distinct memory circuits within the broad frame of transatlantic news. These memory circuits arose from technological, political, and psychological factors. Improvements in technologies of immediacy—such as telegraphy, steam presses, and modern railroads—enabled national news gathering and dissemination in tighter domestic news cycles. Meanwhile, the transatlantic time lag remained a barrier to transatlantic news sharing and therefore the full integration of Anglophone news publics.

At the same time, American politics were becoming more open to popular involvements that went well beyond the franchise. News came to provide, especially in northern portions of the United States, an experience of political call and response; government leaders shaped the rhetoric and policy that made up one part of the news content around the anticipated popular responses that made up another.[6] Thus the news cycle bound mass publics together in a great national circuit of political consciousness and activity. Just as important, that circuit was grounded in the most recent shared history, which alienated transatlantic Anglophones could not share. The same newspapers that activated domestic memory circuits simultaneously projected anachronistic transatlantic reports of international events, foreign policy, and public opinion.

Public anxieties related to the increasingly global flow of information in the 1850s, combined with the apparent distinctiveness of domestic news cycles, precipitated various strains of hypernationalist extremism.

Nationalist anxieties and hypernationalist reactions sometimes explicitly appealed to ethnic or religious identities and anti-immigrant or anti-Catholic prejudices. Yet they were always first and foremost anti-catholic, in that they resisted the potential expansion of shared history to the universal plane. Hypernationalism's chauvinistic attachments to the nation also did not preclude criticism of the state; in fact, as a reaction to the state's global legitimacy and communal coherence, it was concerned with the perceived incapacities of standing nation-states to adequately represent national realities in the face of both international and internal pressures. Such anxieties would prove especially potent in the United States, where nationalists would struggle with the status of a twice-divided nation facing deep social divisions and the communal pressures of a global field of communication.[7]

Spectacles like the Great Exhibition sought to expand that field of neutral information, at least in theory, and so became targets for all manner of nationalist backlash. Some British Protestants whose prejudice had been primed by Westminster's reinstatement as a Catholic archdiocese in 1850, now regarded the foreign hordes who responded to England's "Invitation to all Nations" as an "invasion by Rome."[8] But many more, even those who supported the internationalist theory behind the exhibition, would succumb to a more fundamental anti-catholic paranoia, cowed by the specter of a universal but virtual connection. Popular newspapers covering the exhibition, because they engaged patriotic publics that were even larger than the crowds that visited in person, offered a clear indication of how this sort of catholicity would interact with nationalism in the coming years. This chapter uncovers their anti-catholic bias by examining how they profitably projected combative visions of a shared national history against an internationalist background. In their effort to concoct nationalist histories for their home audiences from the raw material of internationalist news, they helped convert an exhibition organized to facilitate peace among nations into a battlefield in the memory war.

From Palace to Palace: The Great Exhibition and the Technologies of Immediacy

Traveling to testify before the world's most powerful legislative body had amounted to a diversion from a far more important stop on Horace Greeley's itinerary. His parliamentary detour required only a short walk. But in returning from it Greeley would have traced a vast continuum of mid-nineteenth-century attitudes toward the sharing of history, with towering architectural symbols at either pole. Leaving the Palace of Westminster, he would pass Westminster Abbey, Buckingham Palace, and the Wellington Arch to find himself suddenly absorbed in a great crowd surging west on its way to a landmark raised to challenge all that had come before.[9]

For just two miles due west of Parliament was an informational display of unheard-of scope, housed inside a massive glass and iron warehouse that differed in nearly every way from the faux medieval walls that sheltered Greeley during the hearings. Inside the gates of this marvelous "Crystal Palace," sprawled across the southern edge of Hyde Park, the same modernity that A. W. N. Pugin so abhorred had been putting on a show before the eyes of the world.[10] America would soon see it too, through the eyes of Horace Greeley.

While the Palace of Westminster channeled the architectural spirit of a bygone era into a nationally exclusive form, the Crystal Palace, an innovative prefabricated structure and harbinger of the modern skyscraper, showed what faith in the open exchange of the most recent information might accomplish. Envisioned as a perfect home for the Great Exhibition of the Works and Industry of All Nations, it was as impressive an attraction as anything it contained. Composed of just under a million square feet of brilliant glass, put up quickly and against the odds, the palace was the largest enclosed building in the world, a temple of glittering power. As a temporary structure to be seen through as much as looked up to, it both distinguished itself from its Gothic neighbor and perfectly expressed the intent of the spectacle it was designed to stage. Like an edition of a modern newspaper, and unlike Pugin's monument in stone, its focus on the most recent past implied its own impending obsolescence. Nominally the Palace was merely a delivery system for information, a launching point for progress. But it, like the exhibition it staged, was much more than that.

The first of many World's Fairs, the Great Exhibition was organized to encourage technological development by highlighting new products and processes sent by forty participating nations—a necessary remedy for British insularity in the judgment of the nation's modernizers, but one that conservative critics tried to block as a threat to the literal and cultural health of the nation.[11] The exhibition's emphasis on information sharing paralleled the goals of modern news publishers: both sought to convey the latest developments from around the world to the largest possible audience. And like the ultramodern Crystal Palace, the news's aspirational potential could not have been fulfilled in an earlier time.

Global news had been available on a limited basis in prior eras, but the essential features we take for granted in our news today—the synchronicity and relative uniformity that allow it to provide huge populations with nearly simultaneous access to the same historical information—only became legitimate public expectations in the middle of the nineteenth century.[12] These new capacities allowed the news to establish a cultural position it would fill in the coming century as the starting point in the history of an interconnected globe, the same history to which the Great Exhibition appealed. When the Crystal Palace and its wonders became one of the great news stories of the era, the news media that covered it were in a sense holding up a mirror to themselves: both papers and palace manifested the common ideal of connecting the world through information.

The institutional structures undergirding this vision of global history rose from several complementary developments, all of which allowed ordinary Anglophones in the decades around midcentury to participate in forms of public life that extended well beyond the local scene. Telegraphy, photography, and steam-powered transportation and publication, along with the establishment of the early wire services, converged to create powerful information networks that were opened for the first time to popular audiences in the 1840s and 1850s. Enabled by steam, new cylinder presses began printing news at speeds that allowed nearly simultaneous consumption by readerships numbering in the hundreds of thousands while steam-driven rail systems delivered that news far and wide. New techniques also set the stage for the mass production and dissemination of billions of paper photographs.[13]

These were nineteenth-century versions of information technologies, but (then as now) information was only part of the point: their real power was social, for they had the capacity to put global history in the hands of the masses and thus, in theory, to tie the world together. Furthermore, the unprecedented speed with which they delivered information meant that shared history arrived with fewer layers of social and cultural mediation.[14] In this sense too, these were technologies of immediacy: the aura of democratic openness that adhered to this early iteration of the mass media proved as striking to many observers as the numbers such technology allowed it to reach. Bringing history within arm's length, they also lifted the masses in a pattern that, as Liah Greenfeld has suggested, was modern nationalism's sine qua non.[15]

The Spiritual Telegraph and the Universal Republic

As accelerating improvements increased the scope of these technologies of immediacy, news would begin to affect transatlantic relations in new ways. On the surface, those effects seemed to indicate a stronger Anglo-American bond, for news was traveling between Britain and its former colonies much more rapidly. Fast and reliable oceangoing mail ships powered newspapers across the seas, and greater things were on the horizon. Even before the opening of the Great Exhibition, the submarine telegraph cable from England to France was being laid, and Samuel Morse was confidently predicting the instantaneous transmission of news across the Atlantic. In 1858 Morse's prophecy would be fulfilled when the first transatlantic telegram between the queen of England and the president of the United States signaled an era in which oceans of distance would no longer preclude the nearly instantaneous sharing of information between the hemispheres.[16]

This technological achievement sparked great outbursts of political excitement. The *Times* of London went so far as to herald the transatlantic cable as the conqueror of Anglo-American antagonisms, proclaiming that "the Atlantic Telegraph has half undone the declaration of 1776, and has gone far to make us once again, in spite of ourselves, one people." Although the paper overstated its case (and shared in the general despondency when the cable began to fail just days later), its reference to an undone American Revolution revealed an underlying assumption that modern communities, and even powerful nations, could be built and rebuilt through shared information and improved communication.[17]

Indeed, the *Times*'s celebratory pronouncement was a steam-powered precursor to the electric communication it foresaw, a newspaper column stretched out like an olive branch from one domestic news network to another. Though they could not access the unreliable new cable, the *Times*'s publishers knew that steam already carried their paper to New World audiences; their words were read eagerly by New York editors who clipped, quoted, and reprinted articles and editorials from the major British papers and who conveyed foreign news to smaller communities via the rail-bound editions and the Associated Press wire. Even at the beginning of the 1850s the *Times* was already consciously, if often somewhat indifferently, reaching communities throughout the United States and indirectly addressing an American as well as a British public. Thus transatlantic readers could already be regarded as secondhand consumers of British news; seeing them as potential subjects of a vast Anglophonic empire constituted, for the *Times* at least, a relatively short leap.[18]

Nevertheless, despite massive improvements in midcentury communication, there were still clear limits on global exchange. Time as well as space had previously distinguished Anglophone audiences, and still did to a great extent, for they could not actually share the same history as news in any meaningful sense. The better ships of the eighteenth century had taken nearly a month to complete an Atlantic crossing; faster nineteenth-century steam ships still typically took ten days to bring a New Yorker news from London.

Never quite new until after the Civil War, transatlantic news's anachronistic inaccuracies made decoding it difficult and responding to it politically problematic. In previous generations it had contributed to several Anglo-American conflicts, the American Revolution and the War of 1812 most prominent among them. Such bad information presented the flip side of the *Times*'s high hopes for the potentially unifying benefits of the transatlantic cable.[19]

Yet the transatlantic telegraph and other globalizing developments actually raised an even more dramatic prospect than Anglo-American rapprochement. The real question was whether transatlantic news readers could belong to the sort of international community to which the Crystal Palace aspired or whether their sociability would restrict itself to imagined fortresses within the common terrain of international information. To this question could be added a corollary: Would the modern world of increasingly shared information lead to world peace or intensification of nationalist conflict?

Both questions preoccupied Richard Cobden, the great British advocate for world peace, free trade, and global news, who was one of the most sympathetic listeners to Horace Greeley's parliamentary testimony on the political benefits of the American newspaper system. Cobden believed that a freer, more widely circulating press was crucial to the democratization of knowledge and the advance of modern civilization.[20] Not surprisingly he also thrilled to the ideals of the Great Exhibition, and shortly before Greeley's arrival, he had memorialized the event in advance. In an oration that anticipated the mark the exhibition would make on the future, Cobden also demonstrated his faith in the power of a common global history to bind the world together. Speaking to an audience in Birmingham, Cobden heralded the exhibition's opening as a chance not merely to display the benefits of technology but also to "break down the barriers that have separated the people of different nations, and witness the universal republic." In Cobden's vision, the spectacle of an imperial Roman triumph would be reversed, making 1851

> a memorable [year], indeed: it will witness a triumph of industry instead of a triumph of arms. We shall not witness the reception of the allied sovereigns after some fearful conflict, men bowing their heads in submission; but, instead, thousands and tens of thousands will cross the channel . . . with the fullest conviction that war, rather than a national aggrandizement, has been the curse, and the evil which has retarded progress of liberty and of virtue, and we shall show to them that the people of England . . . are ready to sign a treaty of amity with all the nations on the face of the earth.[21]

Although his hopes for the exhibition had yet to be tested, Cobden based his precipitate commemoration of it on a seemingly self-evident assumption. A world of shared information would eventually eliminate local distinctions and therefore the need for national wars, which would finally become nonsensical once ultimate power was vested in a universal community to which all belonged.

Peace advocates who supported the exhibition often drew on Christianity for inspiration, especially the prophetic vision of a world without war.[22] Yet even for the less religiously committed, a spiritual aura of humanistic zeal surrounded visions of perfect (and peaceful) information sharing; as Paul Gilmore has observed, many midcentury moderns could imagine the era's "apparent dispersal of universal reason and a common language, as mirroring a spiritual telegraph permeating the universe and enabling the union of all souls."[23] Moreover, at the time that Cobden articulated his vision of a cosmopolitan millennium, the English-language news network might have appeared its announcing angel, the bearer of a common intercontinental history and a broader way to belong. The great papers of London and New York appeared in a common tongue, after all, and their content was conveyed to transatlantic Anglophones still at least partially bound by a sense of common heritage.

This transmission often relied on editors such as Greeley, who eagerly sought copies of British papers like the *Times* and often competed with other American publishers to secure them even before the mail ships docked. American interest in news from Britain was so intense that agents for the papers secretly booked special ships and trains in an all-out effort to be the first to print the latest news from London, and celebrated races between New York publishers to snatch British newspapers from ships approaching the eastern seaboard dramatically publicized the growing news network.[24] Efforts to publish international news concerned more than profit margins and editors' egos, for the difference between a paper that could provide the latest intelligence from Europe and one constrained to more pedestrian arenas was not merely superficial. Access to global news characterized modern life. Indeed, the concept of modernity becomes difficult to define without reference to the expanded international view—and the corresponding diminishment of local environments and traditions—that both the mid-century news revolution and the Great Exhibition epitomized.[25]

Yet American interest in the latest London news did not a transatlantic community make. In the same years in which Americans were clamoring for news from England, they were filling the news at home with Anglophobic vitriol and threats of war over Oregon, Cuba, and nearly everything in between. The celebrated competition for foreign news between the *Tribune* and the *Herald*, for example, corresponded with rising Anglo-American tensions over the Oregon border in 1846. If, as Elisa Tamarkin has convincingly argued, Americans' fascination with Britain in the antebellum era did not contradict so much as index the reality of American power, that reality could and did also register in hostile acts and threats of full-blown war.[26]

To suppose that both American Anglophilia and Anglophobia might be modes of expressing American nationalism is to suggest a deeper paradox, one that extends both to the larger global sphere and to our own era. This is the simple fact that nationalist assumptions do not necessarily run counter to internationalism. Rather, as Thomas Peyser puts it: "The very idea of modern . . . nationalism is unthinkable without a highly developed sense of internationalism [because] only when an acute consciousness of different cultures has arisen will one feel impelled to catalogue or cultivate from all the others." The mid-nineteenth-century internationalist impulse almost always reflected a world filled with nations whose internal cohesiveness it largely supported. Jeffrey Auerbach has shown how the Great Exhibition's international display of national commodities and communities showcased this national-international linkage; so too did the organizational structures of mid-nineteenth-century newspapers.[27]

Though it has always been essential, this bond between national and international identifications remains counterintuitive. Rather than recognizing that international and national communities emerged in lockstep, the most common views of internationalism regard it as an extension of the forms of political and cultural consensus that supposedly fueled nationalism. As communal boundaries expand in size and scope, the typical theory goes, they pass from local to national and finally to transnational associations as stages in an evolutionary process. As Peyser explains, "Globalization seems to build on the earlier development of nationalization, amalgamating nations just as nations had earlier gathered to themselves politically, culturally, and even linguistically distinct regions."[28]

This was the rough logic of the vision Cobden articulated in 1851. Both national and global communities depended on ideas of shared understanding and mutual benefit; thus their prospects seemed to rise in concert with modern technologies that increased the range over which goods and especially information could be exchanged. Nineteenth-century British and American national systems were pushing aside prior affiliations and erecting national identity upon new common ground made possible by the same developments that facilitated the advent of the popular newspaper: industrialization; urbanization; and improved technologies of transit, communication, and publication. Many foresaw a transnational conclusion in the trajectory of the shrinking and increasingly shared world, which in the Anglo-American sphere had allowed nationalism to supplant more localized identifications and the local memories that supported them. As the channels of international understanding proliferated, the thinking went (and often still goes), the borders of modern belonging would expand beyond the nation and toward the universalist ideal of Christian prophecy and Cobden's dearest dreams.

Instead, the expanding information network at midcentury produced an age of nationalist conflict and laid the groundwork for the powerful modern nations that would dominate the following century.[29] The decade Cobden looked to as a turning point toward greater international unity and away from national divisions and war brought precisely the opposite of his hopes. For Anglophones on both sides of the Atlantic, the 1850s would ring with violent expressions of nationalism and hypernationalism that challenged not only the international order but also the political consolidation of standing nation-states with threats of further fracture.[30]

An "Imperfectly Occupied" Space: Exhibiting the Transatlantic Time Lag

At Parliament, Greeley had been called as an expert witness. When he arrived at the Great Exhibition, he came as judge and jury, serving as an official member of one of the groups charged with awarding prizes and as the critical correspondent for a huge home audience of curious *Tribune* readers. In these juridical capacities, Greeley's nationality seemed destined to clash with the expectation for objectivity and the internationalist ideals of the event. As a juror and a reporter Greeley was to apply an unbiased and universally relevant standard to all the exhibits. That task aligned perfectly with the organizers' beliefs that the power of new information transcended partiality or nationality, but it contradicted the distinctions that identified exhibits according to national origin, as if nationality was the single a priori designation unifying a staggering variety of productions.[31] Similarly, although Greeley's reportage might claim to deliver merely the facts on the ground, those facts were powerfully structured by that ground's location in the heart of England and the *Tribune* audience's location thirty-five hundred miles away.[32] While he might have managed to maintain more than a modicum of fairness as a juror, as an adjudicator of exhibition news, Greeley would abandon objectivity completely in the name of national defense, taking up a position on embattled American turf within the shared terrain of Anglophone print. In this nationalist positioning he was far from alone among the internationalist supporters of the exhibition. For although the Great Exhibition had been conceived as a celebration of peaceful dialog between nations, Greeley arrived to find a media war already under way inside the Crystal Palace and his own nation up to its neck in it.

As in so many Anglophone disputes, the conflict raged over chasms of time as well as space. From the start, reporters had largely followed nationalist parameters that literally divided the exhibition halls; thus even as they spread information across national boundaries, they simultaneously made comparisons and judgments linking that information to national origins and situating it in relationship to their own national audiences. This general tendency to frame information according to national spaces was exacerbated by the Atlantic distance that governed the speed at which both information and material goods could travel from the United States to Great Britain. The American contributions to the exhibition initially had been underwhelming, partly because many of the exhibits did not arrive until after the Crystal Palace doors had opened and partly because the United States had been awarded a particularly large exhibition area that made the scantiness of its first offerings more glaring. As the *Illustrated London News* commented, "The United States make a very imposing outside show, with a space second only to France in extent, but unfortunately the performance does not come up to the promise."[33]

The requirements of transatlantic travel meant that the situation could not be quickly remedied, for it would be at least ten days before Americans would even feel the embarrassment of the discrepancy as it was conveyed by the transatlantic press. That foreign coverage stung more because American newspapers had predicted a much different opening. In fact, the home press had raised hopes that the exhibition would show Europe how far the United States had progressed during its relatively brief life span, and many had assumed a great national success. Their published prognostications had preceded Greeley across the Atlantic by mail steamer. The British press and public had read them against a compelling physical backdrop of a largely empty department, "as imperfectly occupied," the *Times* observed, as America's "vast continent."[34]

This material manifestation of empty national promise would have been damaging enough, had it not corresponded so perfectly to assumptions of international difference based on the United States' identification with the New World and the engines of presentist memory—especially the cheap mass-marketed newspaper. In British press accounts, the US failure to fill its allotted section quickly became a damning metaphor for the young nation's supposed tendency to overreach and a golden opportunity for John Bull to take "Brother Jonathan" to task for his adolescent boasting.[35] The abundance of agricultural products that occupied most of the small space the United States had managed to fill also became in British eyes a sign of a rude colonial economy.[36] But perhaps most revealing of all was how the initial story of American failure confirmed the folly of the US dependence on modern mass-marketed newspapers and on an unreliable and partisan history of the recent past. The *Illustrated London News* pointed out that, in the advance publicity for the exhibition, the American press "according to its custom" had "so bewildered parties about to exhibit with indiscriminating praise, that the greater number were filled with most unhappy notions as to the value of the Transatlantic part of the Great Exhibition." In describing this effect, the paper famous for its engraved pictures sketched American culture as a chamber of mirrors fabricated by unscrupulous news editors. "According to popular opinion, as taught by their newspapers, the United States were to carry off the chief glories of the 'World's Fair.' The spread of this opinion was not extraordinary, when we consider that it was re-echoed by the journals of every city, every town, every township, every village.... Now, as in the United States every one reads the newspapers, and many read nothing else, it was ... natural that the people should fancy they were going 'to lick old worn-out Europe.'"[37]

Though based to some degree on a real difference between British and American approaches to journalism, the irony of a journalist condemning news readers for the sin of reading too much news illustrated the strength of nationalist prejudices. In contrast to the caricature of a rustic national culture raised on the flimsy scaffold of an irresponsible national news network, the *Illustrated London News* provided detailed evidence of impressive British exhibits. Although the exhibition encouraged its forty nations to learn from each other's advancements, it simultaneously advertised the host country's power, publicizing British submissions that eventually claimed 78 of 170 prestigious Council Medals. While some commentators coveted even more, the home audience for such British triumphs was growing by the day, as excitement over the exhibits swelled the London papers' circulations. Britain's supercilious press as much as its superior exhibits prompted Greeley's sardonic observation that "John Bull, whatever else he may learn, will not be taught meekness by this Exhibition."[38]

The transatlantic time lag formed the unstated background for the British press's superiority and Greeley's embittered responses to it. Until recently British papers, especially the *Times* of London, would have had few significant American naysayers with whom to contend. Their pronouncements might inspire rebuttals once they appeared in the pages of American papers, but by then Americans would know they had already spent more than a week becoming conventional wisdom in Europe. Thus the time lag tended to magnify all British judgments about matters of international import, for it gave them the quality of settled law by the time Americans encountered them. This left American readers incapacitated in the face of criticism and thus offered one the surest signs of the asymmetrical power exerted by British news and opinion over their understanding of themselves as well as European events.

This overwhelming advantage in casting judgments helps explain the zeal with which Greeley undertook his response to British attacks on American exhibits. For in this case, the *Tribune* had a correspondent on site, one with clout who knew his own reports would appear contemporaneously with those from London, in a paper that boasted one hundred thousand subscribers. In short, Greeley gave US nationalists a champion able as well as willing to take the British bull by the horns.

In correspondence to the *Tribune* Greeley attacked the British for misrepresenting a strong American showing. The real scandal, the editor professed, was that negative British reports had blinded even some American attendees to the significance of their home country's contributions. These present-day Benedict Arnolds, "without knowing anything more about [our exhibitions] than they have gleaned from *The Times* [of London] and *Punch*, aided by a hurried walk through the department, are busily proclaiming that this show makes them ashamed of their country," the scandalized editor complained.[39] These actual American visitors, who had surrendered the right to judge their own culture to the authority of the British press, clearly were standing in for Greeley's imagined American readers; his own eyewitness account served to displace the *Times*'s privileged position among Anglophones and thus its capacity to make *Tribune* readers "ashamed of their country." While Greeley did not dispute the fact that the United States might have presented itself in a more flattering light, he found much to admire among the American offerings.[40]

Greeley certainly had a point. The supposedly paltry American exhibits eventually included a version of Cyrus McCormick's revolutionary reaper that was swelling the world's food supply and speeding westward expansion. A Colt revolver and a Singer sewing machine represented the groundbreaking mechanization and rationalization of American industry. In the arts the American sculptor Hiram Powers's naked figure *Greek Slave* formed one of the palace's central (and most controversial) attractions.

Yet it was the presence of the *Tribune* and the person of Greeley that represented perhaps the most important American development. Even as he battled the British press to spin public opinion in favor of the American exhibitors, he was revealing as much about the modern era as any machine or artifact he observed. Beauty at the exhibition was in the eye of the beholder, and newspapers were the eyes of the nineteenth-century world. Greeley could determine what many of those eyes saw, and he worked tirelessly to overcome the London press's haughty dismissals with what he later admitted were overly positive and heartily nationalistic assessments of his own.[41]

Thus, rather than disputing the derisive British description of American cultural dependence on news, Greeley would use that dependence to his advantage. Both American and British correspondents, like Greeley's parliamentary questioners, agreed that the press shaped America's identity and sense of history; Greeley understood that with a total circulation that exceeded that of the *Times* of London, he could use his elevated position in the *Tribune*'s bully pulpit to deliver an alternative history of the exhibition that would refute British challenges as they were made.[42] In actively and patriotically shaping the historical vision of his readers, Greeley actually reinforced his journalistic foes' chief criticism: that the United States was a nation lacking any real culture and possessing a brief history that amounted to an accumulation of unreliable newspaper reports. But he also showed how national identity could shape itself effectively around even such a shallow version of history and highlighted the nationalism that underlay the supposedly neutral sites of both the exhibition and the British press.

This outcome would have been less surprising had Greeley been a simple-minded chauvinist rather than the internationalist his résumé indicated: an advocate for labor rights and the common man, popularizer of Fourierist theories and supporter of Utopian communities in the United States, eager publisher of international correspondence, and champion of republican causes the world over.[43] Supporters of the international exhibition on both sides of the Atlantic recognized Greeley as a natural ally; in addition to chairing a jury, he was asked to grace official banquets honoring the exhibition's British organizers. Yet Greeley rarely commented on the Great Exhibition in his paper without adding a fair dose of nationalist sentiment. Like some of his British peers, he used the greatest of international extravaganzas as an excuse for nationalistic posturing. Greeley's example suggests that such nationalist tendencies did not originate solely from the personal partisan rancor of journalists but rather from the structural correspondence between the event they were covering and the media in which they worked.

Transatlantic Contagions and Hypernationalist Agitation

Greeley had an explanation for the anti-Americanism he saw in British exhibition coverage, and it arose from his understanding of the memory war. This new spate of British hostility did not represent, Greeley claimed, the undying hatred of a former foe. Rather, it arose as a new British concern that the American national system would ultimately triumph over the British nation's traditionalist attachment to aristocratic privilege. If both models were judged fairly, according to the ideals rather than the realities of the Crystal Palace, Greeley had no doubt that America's democratic institutions would win out.

Some scholars of nineteenth-century American culture have pointed to a definite anxiety of influence at the heart of antebellum culture, suggesting an almost pathological American need to differentiate the United States from Britain by inoculating it from the mother country's influence.[44] Yet according to Greeley's letters home, it was British anxiety that formed a more significant obstacle to future transatlantic combinations, and he thought he had located its source in the specter of an infectiously democratic culture. In some ways, this was the flip side of a Puritan impulse among American Protestants, which had led them to see the United States' peculiar role in "moral persuasion with evangelical piety and democratic institutions offering a contagious example" to the world.⁴⁵ The British press and political class had targeted America's democratic print culture along with its exhibits. This suggested to Greeley that British worries were rising in proportion to the growing global network of shared information. Exhibition boosters had celebrated the transformational potential of dissolving national divisions in a single informational pool of recent global history. Yet the potential to actually realize that hope would require a dramatic reorganization of society.

Not surprisingly, that prospect had already spurred a backlash in Britain, especially among the anxious traditionalists with the greatest stake in the status quo. Some Britons still regarded the exhibition's most important promoter, Prince Albert, as a foreigner simply because he was an ethnic German, and managed to maintain the prejudice despite Albert's happy marriage to Queen Victoria. These defenders of racist-tinged traditionalism were hardly thrilled to host an event that would draw thousands of aliens from distant lands in order to revel in an orgy of modern developments in the heart of London. As Jeffrey Auerbach notes, "Popular writers published tracts whipping up anti-foreigner hysteria by raising the specter of plagues and epidemics as well."⁴⁶

Many others saw the Crystal Palace's physical presence in Hyde Park as an invasive violation of the traditionalist national order and expressed this opinion in various ways. William Morris, ever the opponent of industrialized modernity, dismissed the wonders of the exhibition as "wonderfully ugly," while a parliamentary defender of the national past protested prior to the palace's construction that a stand of ten elms in the park was being cut down to make room for a modern monstrosity. A. W. N. Pugin's followers complained that Britain's modern industry had made the palace a temple for tasteless objects and art, while pamphleteers warned it would become a cradle of disease, exposing an unsuspecting British public to new plagues from abroad. The Duke of Wellington, hero of the Napoleonic wars, worried that the British working classes, under pressure from foreign agitators and the excitement of the exhibition, would devolve into a mob.⁴⁷ To such critics the American style of popular newspaper—with its cheap price, wide-open subscription lists and mass audience—also suggested a radical sting concealed in the exhibition's ethos of openness. Sensing this, Greeley encapsulated the problem with a typically pithy metaphor in his May 27 letter home, warning American readers that "the favored classes in Great Britain do and must ... *dread the contagion of our example.*"⁴⁸

Greeley penned the letter the day after the first so-called shilling day. The exhibition had opened at the beginning of the month and had already drawn many thousands of season ticket buyers and five-shilling day passes. On May 26 the price of admission at the Palace dropped to a shilling, a cost the working classes could more easily afford. As critics noted at the time, the Royal Commission behind the exhibition had set ticket prices using the same logic of social control that set the tax rates for newspapers.[49] Thus it was hardly surprising that Greeley would see British fear of working-class crowds and support for upper- and middle-class privilege as connected to their attitude toward America's popular press and democratic culture.

Unlike many Anglo-American conflicts of the past, the new form of anti-Americanism Greeley identified was not based on any failure to communicate. On the contrary, it resulted from communication's wildest successes. The transatlantic news's relative proximity and the prospect of the transatlantic cable had brought the germ of democracy perilously close to Britain's vitals. Greeley explained, "This contagion was not imminent and did not seriously alarm" in earlier decades, when the United States was "some sixty days distant, and heard of mainly in connection with Indian fights or massacres, fatal steamboat explosions or insolvent banks." In a new era, though, in which "New-York is but ten days from London and New Orleans (by Telegraph) scarcely more, the case is bravely altered, and it becomes daily more and more palpable that the United States and Great Britain cannot both remain as they are." Here, then, Greeley revealed the shadow lurking behind the later celebrations of Anglo-American telegraphic communion: a traditionalist nightmare of a democratic disease spreading from across the sea in the form of transatlantic news. The spread of ideas combined with meritocratic judgments meant, Greeley thought, that everything from Britain's bloated traditional bureaucracy to its national church might be moved to reform by their new proximity to American models. The growing information network had become a social paradox that reinforced nationalist antagonisms precisely because it seemed capable of surmounting them.[50]

This was viral data indeed, for it posed a potent threat to the ruling class's entrenched interests. British traditionalists who maintained a connection between the nation and its ancient past through their titled personage and their inherited privilege observed the creep of Americanization within their own information system with an increasing sense of unease. Although the British government's antiradicalism had severely restricted the growth of the penny press, the circulations of the major London papers were nevertheless expanding to include more and more of the middle class, many thousands of whom had paid to attend the exhibition even when the prices were elevated.

The sharp spike in newspaper sales during the Great Exhibition also indicated an untapped popular market eager not only for news but for inclusion within the community the national paper sought to serve. At midcentury, the *Times*, with its network of foreign correspondents and unchallenged domestic reputation, stood "unequaled in the breadth and depth of its reporting, the gravity of its tone, the grandeur of its pretensions and its sheer physical bulk."[51] Moving into the 1850s its circulation was increasing and, especially in moments of national crisis or interest, the *Times* was the paper huge numbers of Britons turned to. Yet such influence would cut both ways, and the *Times*'s growing readership raised the destabilizing possibility that a larger cross-section of the British public would require a shift in the paper's basic political stance. Thus the major cultural bellwethers in Britain, including the chief editorial voices in the mainstream London press, often found themselves struggling for control of a network that was already threatening to transcend class lines.

Greeley implied that the *Times*'s anti-Americanism at the exhibition expressed nervousness toward shared information's unpredictable political pull. The American editor assumed that powerful resistance to cultural contagions would bend historical facts to the claims of class and party, in a process with major implications for Anglo-American relations. Greeley predicted that more closely knit transatlantic populations would only provoke those who had been privileged by Britain's national system into demanding the "suppression of the truth with regard to America—with regard especially to the prevalence of order, justice and tranquility within her borders." The exhibition coverage was about more than the exhibition. For elite interests to remain secure, republics must be proven effective only "for a time in a rude and semi-barbarous community of scattered grain-growers and herdsman."[52]

Greeley therefore believed British observers would condemn American-style republican institutions as "utterly incompatible with a dense population, with general refinement, the upbuilding of Manufactures and the prevalence of the arts of civilized life"—in short, all that the exhibition displayed and advanced as indications of national strength. Democracy would be dismissed as incapable of balancing the cultural refinement and industrial progress that a true national culture demanded. While British elites might sympathize with their American cousins as individuals, for them the democratic threat was now close at hand and must be met—even, said Greeley, if that meant unfairly lampooning perfectly respectable exhibits. The American editor insisted that British anxieties, intensified in proportion to their increasing proximity to political alternatives from across the Atlantic, had raised the cry "so often and invidiously renewed by the London daily press, of surprise at the meagerness of our country's share in the Great Exhibition."[53]

Greeley's analysis of the political tension between the British and the American press helps explain his own war of words over exhibition coverage. Greeley was not merely ashamed that his nation (betrayed by the state's incompetent administration) had failed to prove itself to the world but was also concerned about whether that nation could be said to exist at all when British newspapers held sway over a nominally American public. Greeley's initial contributions to the controversy and his later analysis of it suggests that more than simple nationalism lay behind his news narrative and the British narratives he battled against; in fact, they were "hypernationalist" in two senses. First, they drew energy from the peculiar distress that exposure to the international scene created, the fear that one's own nationality was suspect and vulnerable to internationalist alternatives. Second, they expressed doubts about the connections between one's nation-state and the national identity to which it attached itself. The hypernationalist response arose partly from an unsettling belief that the state's institutional representatives and those who maintained society's status quo could not sufficiently support the real nation with which they were identified.

As a popular movement hypernationalist memory thus did not appear as an invented tradition that required state control, nor was it an internationalist alternative of the sort Marx would have recommended. It also did not arise naturally from traditional ethnicity, kinship, and culture; although its perpetrators often coveted and projected precisely this sort of national authenticity, maintaining it required active construction. Hypernationalism was anxious rather than confident, because national realities had been seriously called into question. In the Crystal Palace controversy as elsewhere, hypernationalist memory advanced to support what was tangibly lacking. Without such support, Greeley worried American readers might be enticed to follow the *Times* of London's lead straight to Queen Victoria and Prince Albert's dynastic feet. On the other hand, he identified a corresponding British concern that American newspapers might infiltrate the carefully managed elitism of the British market for knowledge and thus unleash Britain's revolutionary masses.

Such fears help explain the violently nationalist oppositions arising within the Crystal Palace. As Auerbach's analysis indicates, internationalism laid out a context by which the supposedly peaceful exhibition might become "emphatically a war—of products and values." News inevitably carried that conflict along with information about exhibits, but it also intensified it. Thus on either side of the Anglo-American news battle, the maintenance of national identity seemed to require militantly defending the Atlantic border precisely because the lines of communication between the hemispheres—especially between the United States and Britain—were becoming clearer, swifter, and more reliable. And even as newspapers facilitated that communication, they also played a large role in the new militancy, in part because the home audience seemed to crave it.[54]

Oppositional narratives may have been especially important for two nations who shared much in common, including a reliance on English as their dominant language, and who thus had much to fear from cultural "contagions." Much as Britain and the United States sought to underline their national distinctiveness, their mutual antagonism owed almost nothing to xenophobia. They knew each other all too well. British anti-Americanism largely stemmed from worries about a threat of Americanization that seemed credible precisely because the two nations already shared so much. American nationalists also had reason to fear a shrinking Atlantic world, not because they perceived a barbarous Other on the opposite shore but because the face of their transatlantic cousin was still too familiar. Americans still relied on the artistic, economic, and technological output of the Anglophone world's purported mother country to a great degree; culturally, they still looked to Europe for models, still made best sellers of cheaply reprinted British books and waited breathlessly for the latest chapter of whatever British serialization they found occupying the pages of their periodicals.[55] This sea of shared transatlantic culture contained innumerable threats to their nationalist autonomy, and Anglophones seemed to require constant reminders of perceived cultural disagreements in order to maintain notions of national distinctiveness. The exhibition's newsmakers therefore could profit by enhancing transatlantic rivalries with overblown conflict narratives, for nationalist distinctions, precisely because they were somewhat dubious, helped make the Anglophone news marketable.

Prior to the late 1860s, the transatlantic time lag and the common English language organized American and British news exchange and provided an important structural element to the allure of shared nationalist histories in the news. It was not merely that these two nations in particular came into sharper focus through exaggerated opposition to the other. Nor was it that continuing shared access to transatlantic news tended to project a reflection of each national culture as the "Other's Other."[56] It was that the transatlantic time lag created relatively authentic experiences of shared history within the larger Anglo-American cultural frame and thus imposed the authority of a territorial identity onto recent history that could not be shared on the other side of the Atlantic.

Pulp and Place

For major British papers, nationalist narratives helped alleviate a peculiar political tension that accompanied the modern media's growing popularity. In an era during which many saw popular news as an agent of Americanization, anti-American rhetoric would prove especially tempting, and Greeley rightly guessed that British insults arose as reactions against neither American newspaper editors nor their working-class publics. In criticizing America, papers like the *Times* were recoiling from the uncertain future they saw for themselves and for the memory of the British nation. Similarly, combative American newsmen like Greeley were responding not merely to the power of the *Times* but also to a traditionalist mode of national memory that threatened the foundations of their nation as well as their business.

Yet the exhibition coverage also suggested that the real existential threat to either side came not from any particular foreign contagion but rather from the fetid modern swamp that made such contagions inevitable. The fundamental problem was paper itself or, rather, the fact that the modern world seemed to be made of such indiscriminate pulp. The trajectory of global news suggested that historical experiences everywhere were relevant to everyone, but a history common to all could have no special relevance to any particular community. The threat the British press feared most, and what many of its readers feared as well, was not actually America. Rather, it was a world in which individuals would have nothing to cling to, no durable bond to tie them together. While the universality and immediacy of information might inspire utopian prophecies and dreams, it could do little business among human groups accustomed to topos: a sense of place mediated by those particularities that made communities distinct and desirable.

Little business, that is, without the modification national memory provided. Attending to nationalism's reliance on collective memory as well as circulating print suggests why shared language could become the victim of its own success. Modern communication networks created the necessity as well as the opportunity for national memory to function as a stabilizing force.[57] While international mass publics might be bound by information provided by newspapers in a common tongue, that link also suggested mnemonic losses: memory of shared land exchanged for a networked world of kin for global associations, of special providence for universal progress.

National memory emerged in the news, then, to address the same gaps in modern belonging exposed by transatlantic media coverage of an international exhibition of universally relevant knowledge. The idea of the nation as the provider of a distinctive past within the international context became attractive as an imagined limit on a globally available Anglophone history.[58] This helps explain why, rendered in English language news that was fundamentally structured by its potential and actual transatlantic availability, the Crystal Palace became a hothouse of national memory.

In the exhibition, America's original sin had lain in its failure to fill the space allotted to it, and in a way this is precisely what Greeley's presentist mode of memory sought to remedy. By reinforcing the national borders within the Crystal Palace, exploiting his access to the national memory circuit shared by *Tribune* readers, and highlighting the British press's reaction against an American contagion of presentist memory, he gave concrete shape to the nation he served. Into the mostly empty space of an imagined nation he poured more than images of plows and sewing machines; he actualized the Atlantic division in the form of news and made America tangible to itself in space and time.

Thus Greeley's coverage of the Great Exhibition of 1851 showed how nineteenth-century news could meet the challenge of filling the spaces of its readers' national imaginations while operating within a field of increasingly global information. The threat of contagion was real. Nevertheless, the national histories Greeley doggedly championed received validation from publicized news cycles that, by distinguishing a public of domestic from foreign readers, manifested a nationalist memory circuit. Physical limits, the Atlantic span most important among them, established these cycles by imposing spatial boundaries on how the news could be produced and consumed.

Throughout the 1850s, the presentist memory circuit could define itself against a relatively traditionalist British alternative created by the American publication of transatlantic news. Structurally, how such news appeared underscored the most significant nationalist division within global Anglo-American language and culture. In dominant northern papers especially, this transatlantic rift furthered the nationalist association between the western homeland and the publicized practices of domestic news sharing. Nevertheless, focusing on the nationalistic potential of such practices could also magnify internal divisions that hinged on how domestic news was shared as well as interpreted. This in turn could make disputes over current events and diverging sectional responses to them appear as existential threats to a unified American nation bound to a common sacred history of the recent past. A few short years after Greeley returned from Europe, regionally organized memory circuits began to provide alternatives to the authoritative shared history previously defined by the Atlantic divide. Not surprisingly given the stakes of the earlier memory war, these alternative histories became targets of new hypernationalist crusades to recover control of America's sacred past and the geographical integrity of an imagined holy land.

5

Wars and Rumors of Wars

Kansas and the Presentist Crusade

We may say again, what God said long ago, "Woe unto them that decree unrighteous decrees," and the people to whom we speak can convert this prophecy into history, as it has so often been converted before, in the condemnation and disgrace to those who are guilty of this great transgression.

—Rev. R. H. Richardson, quoted in *New-York Tribune*, 1854

Is there a North?

—Horace Greeley, *New-York Tribune*, 1856

The middle of the 1850s was a heady but confusing time for American presentists. During these years, stories of violent national conflicts at home and abroad dominated the news. Like the *Tribune*, British papers such as the *Times* of London and the *Illustrated London News* grew rapidly to keep pace with popular interest. A change of state, both for national newspapers and national governments, accompanied these increasing circulations. Papers stopped merely covering national conflicts and began to contribute to them, becoming "protagonists" in essential struggles over national definition and defense, in far flung places like Kansas and the Crimea as well as national capitals and news centers.[1] Thus major newspapers were expanding dramatically even as the national histories they perpetuated became increasingly fraught and convoluted.

At the same time, the popular press was transcending the religious and political institutions on which it had depended and taking a more prominent position within national life. As major papers like the *Tribune* and the *Times* became their own power bases, their popularity helped destroy venerable political parties, depose governments, and divide churches. Thus the expanding press in these years contributed to widespread concerns about the stability of national foundations. Yet it also provided a spiritually potent means for mass readerships to participate in the recent past as embattled national audiences within the broader transatlantic sphere. The mid-1850s were the years in which presentist memory came of age.

This chapter explores the northern experience of reading transatlantic news during the so-called civil war in Kansas. It shows how the conflict in that territory, though a long-running domestic news story, was also merely the latest chapter in a larger narrative that concerned America's place in the world. Accounts from "Bleeding Kansas" nationalized and sacralized a regional audience's involvements in the presentist memory of a sectional conflict but operated against a backdrop of nationalist anxiety arising from shared transatlantic news. This broader international background helped make a territorial dispute over slavery's expansion appear as a struggle for national existence and a presentist crusade to recover an American holy land.[2]

As Christopher Hanlon has argued, transatlantic connections shaped understandings of antebellum sectional divisions in ways that were sometimes surprisingly complex.[3] The transatlantic connection in the press was more straightforward, and for that reason tends to be underestimated. It might seem merely coincidental, for example, that a mass audience of American readers encountered the charge of the Light Brigade in the same issue that reported the advance of proslavery forces across the Missouri-Kansas line. Nevertheless, such stories, and the corresponding accounts of popular and elite responses to them, raised similar questions about national definition and division. Printed on the same paper, they might mutually inform their readers' beliefs about their own nations and nations in general.[4] Reliant on the ever-present news, the northern self-consciousness that developed in opposition to the South never stopped looking east.

Yet such northern news readers were also gazing west. The conclusion of the Mexican War in 1848 had set the table for territorial disputes by opening vast western lands into which slavery might conceivably expand. The Compromise of 1850 had answered some questions of settlement definitively but without settling the fundamental problem that this new territory had raised in the national imagination: Was the United States one country or two? Slavery's primary southern advocates saw their region gaining national consciousness in direct proportion to perceived northern slights. Paradoxically, efforts to exclude slavery from the West helped southern whites imagine the South as a distinctive national territory, grounded in a well-established homeland and the conservative traditions of the republic's founders, and in opposition to northern innovations that were becoming apparent in the press. Around the time of the compromise, John C. Calhoun was already complaining that the federal government "claims the right to resort to force to maintain whatever power it claims against all opposition.... Indeed it is apparent from what we daily hear, that this has become the prevailing and fixed opinion of a great majority of the [northern] community.... The character of the Government has been changed in consequence, from a federal republic, as it originally came from the hands of its framers, into a great national consolidated democracy." Yet the South, Calhoun suggested, literally had no place in such a nation; describing the new western lands, he insisted, "The North is making the most strenuous efforts to appropriate the whole to herself by excluding the South from every foot of it." Moreover, as to "the social organization of the South" under slavery, those northerners who are "most opposed and hostile, regard it as a sin . . . [and] themselves as implicated in the sin and responsible for not suppressing it by the use of all and every means." At the opposite end of northern opinion, "those least opposed and hostile, regard it as a blot and a stain on the character of what they call the Nation."⁵

Thus Calhoun mapped the territorial question according to sectional geographies and insisted that determined northern resistance to slavery's expansion amounted to a nationalist incursion on southern society as well as state sovereignty. Clearly this was more than merely a political dispute. Calhoun was also describing a memory crisis and geographical chasm; in denying slavery a place in the West, a unified North was denying the South's right to exist within "what they call the Nation." The compromisers were already debunking Calhoun's notion that relatively little divided northern opinion, but as Liah Greenfeld observes, though the idea of a universally antagonistic North was "patently untrue," that did not mean it did not possess symbolic power; rather, "the South and the North, which were but names of geographical sectors, the borders between which were established by convention and could be recharted, in the Southern consciousness became reified concepts, collective bodies possessed of antagonistic souls and pitted against each other as might be two warring persons."⁶ Furthermore, as Calhoun correctly guessed, a common spirit of intensifying presentist resistance animated many northern opponents, and a common focus on western geography was eliding the political nuances that separated them. Despite northern leaders' appetite for compromise and the northern public's willingness to bend on some matters, northern opposition rallied against the

South when slavery's traditionalist defenders sought to advance a claim on the future as well as the past. In the context of northerners' Eurocentric visions of their transatlantic heritage, that future was what the battle over western lands symbolized. Slavery's expansion there would mean that "the Nation," as Calhoun implied, could only exist in name, for the American homeland would then be destined, like its public opinion and political culture, to become permanently divided along a northern/southern border.[7]

Those divisions emerged most powerfully in Kansas, but the civil war fought over it in the mid-1850s was influenced by stories from many places—the Crimean Peninsula, the Houses of Parliament, and the streets of Washington, DC, as well as the Kansas Territory. Just as important, distant events in the West appeared within northern news cycles as anachronistic fodder for popular and well-publicized partisan responses. As a new global force on the local scene, middecade Anglophone news tended to undercut traditionalist nationalism and the fundamental connection to land that gave a particular people their place in the world. In their international as well as domestic content, American popular newspapers projected images of national homelands challenged by internal strife and clouded by nationalist anxieties arising in the transatlantic news. Yet as engines of hypernationalist agitation they also facilitated novel political associations grounded in the presentist memory of newspaper readerships. As new nationalist lines between North and South solidified in the pages of the *Tribune,* they would refract the divisions at the heart of the Anglo-American information network and the transatlantic memory war.

Foreign Affairs: To "Gain Great and Solid Things of the Future"

It has always been difficult to explain the Crimean War (1853–1856), let alone justify it as a British war of choice. Partly this was because the official first draft of its history had to compete against a far more negative version arising from a newly energized mainstream British press led by the *Times*. American readers, who received British war news indirectly through papers like the *Tribune,* were surprised to see poor planning and callous leadership shake the British public's faith in aristocratic and religious pretensions. The British government under Lord Aberdeen had launched the war in 1853 with great patriotic ceremony in the name of the "national interest" and the Christian religion. Nevertheless, the war itself contradicted any number of the traditionalist tenets of British nationalism, including the virulent antipathy toward Catholic and revolutionary France that had fueled previous religious wars and defined British identity for centuries.[8] British leaders set aside their suspicions of Bonaparte's nephew, Emperor Napoleon III, to forge a French alliance against Russia, a former friend that was nominally fighting to support Christians living under an Islamic empire. Moreover, political and military leaders mismanaged the conflict to an appalling degree, and their questionable conduct eventually devolved into a national crisis. When the controversy ultimately brought down Lord Aberdeen's ministry, the now highly popular and critical British press took credit and blame. Thus, despite Russia's eventual defeat, Britain appeared weakened in victory and confused about its government's relationship to its population. In part because the Crimean War was also the first to be extensively covered by the British press, American readers had secondhand access to every debacle and many damning editorials through their own papers.

Transatlantic war news portrayed a badly overextended British nation-state whose traditionalist foundations had eroded, perhaps beyond repair. Even put in the generous terms of the foreign secretary, Lord Clarendon, the Crimean adventure was a great bloviating muddle of mind-numbing abstractions: "It was a war for the independence of Europe, a battle for civilization against barbarism, a war to liberate mankind, advance civilization, and at the same time 'gain great and solid things of the future' for Britain."[9] The Crimean Peninsula itself bore no geographical connection to the British homeland, and Aberdeen's successor, Lord Palmerston, hoped to offer it to the Turks as part of a complicated division of territory among the continental powers. Partly for this reason, the war also proved highly dubious as a defense of national religion. Religious controversies involving orthodox Christians had helped generate the initial conflict among Turkey, Russia, and local powers, and these provided an excuse for many observers to attach religious trappings to the conflict—including a surprising number of British Protestants. But for others, in particular traditionalist Anglicans who were less constitutionally opposed to Orthodox piety, appealing to religious affiliations raised as many problems as they solved in terms of British national memory. Significant disagreements separated the dominant faiths of Britain and its French and Turkish allies, and a Turkish defeat at Russian hands might raise the prospects for Christian emancipation and self-rule within a weakened Ottoman Empire.[10]

As the war dragged on, as the costs rose, and as the military's mismanagement became apparent, the obscure justifications for the fighting cast a pall of national uncertainty over the mainstream British press. The *Times*'s war correspondents, especially William Howard Russell, became famous as the war's most important critics. Through them American editors and readers learned that Britain's army, heir of a glittering heritage, was hopelessly mired in the past. The few aging veterans of the Napoleonic wars, such as the British commander, Lord Raglan, had not seen serious combat in a generation, and the ranks of younger officers had almost no battlefield experience. Moreover, the army's aristocratic leaders managed to sink to the level of the worst American stereotypes, proving the utter insufficiency of noble blood and parading both their decadence and incompetence within the first few months of operations.[11] Their failure to achieve a decisive military victory unsettled the public's confidence not only in British arms but also in aristocratic stewardship of the nation, and by the end of the war even Lord Clarendon would admit that, were the war to continue, "there is still so much that is radically defective in our military administration that the chance of failure would be quite as great as that of success."[12]

Prime Minister Palmerston was slow to grasp this new reality. He had authored the doctrines of national interest that had helped inspire the recent war and had not only taken for granted that the British nation was secure enough to project its interest on the shores of the Black Sea but had boasted that British strength could be extended anywhere in the world where an Englishman was threatened. That same nation now found itself on unstable ground not only in the Crimea but in its own newspapers.[13] News from the front did not merely indicate failures to achieve discrete war aims. Despite its patriotic impulses, the news seemed to expose Britain's nationalist assumptions as moribund or fraudulent. At the Paris peace talks, it fell to Clarendon to convey the widespread perception he found among Britain's allies as well as its enemies: namely that foreign audiences had seen beneath the bluster and grasped the weakness of the British nation-state and of Palmerston as well. Foreign diplomats assumed Britain might seek a continuation of the war merely to prop up Palmerston's sagging popularity, and they had no fear about resisting British pressure. "Whatever Palmerston in his jaunty mood may say," Clarendon told the Liberal leader, "we could not have made war alone, for we would have had all of Europe against us at once, and the United States would soon have followed in the train."[14] Clarendon's own counterparts abroad regarded the foreign secretary as a "slave of the English newspapers."[15]

All of this suggested that a struggle launched as a patriotic holy war and fought in the national interest had run aground upon larger questions of what would define the nation in the international sphere. For American readers, the confusion of British aims was underscored by the asymmetry of its alliances: with Napoleon III, whom the *New-York Times* disparaged as "a parvenu Emperor, a usurper" and "an imperial coward," but also with the Ottoman Empire. The *Tribune*'s London correspondent, Karl Marx, would report the "doubt, mistrust and hostility" that Turks felt toward their western allies early in the war and their fear that France and Britain "are going to dethrone the Sultan, and divide the land," while making Muslims "slaves to the Christian population." Indeed, the *New-York Times* would dismiss Turkey as a "sham" nation, "old and outworn" and incapable of holding the line against Russian aggression, and would argue that any British success in the Crimea would require casting aside the Turks in favor of a "New Christian State on the Bosphorus, the Danube, and the Black Sea" that would unify "local municipalities among the Christian population." To "the question as to whom the country belongs," the *Times* responded that "there is in European Turkey a [Christian] population who have stood their ground during four long weary centuries of misrule and oppression."[16]

The *Times*'s fantasy of an ancient and spiritually pure Christian nation—freed from Turkish oppression, bound naturalistically to the land, and arising from the ashes of global conflict—concealed a deeper doubt. Great Exhibition coverage had inadvertently displayed the same unease, and Marx had featured it in his famous manifesto. That underlying worry was that international communication and commerce was exposing modern nations as political shams. War news seemed to confirm that fear, revealing British national weakness to the world, troubling readers, unseating governments, and projecting transatlantic visions of national deconstruction across the Atlantic. Thus the *New-York Times* would prophesy that once the unfolding "masquerade of war shall have passed over," ordinary Britons "will inquire into the amount of profit, in glory, freedom and material welfare which it was promised, from that crusade of Civilization against Barbarism, Justice against Wrong, &c., &c."[17] Carried to American news readers witnessing their own national union unraveling in Kansas, Crimean War news portrayed venerable nations shaken to their core and left the idea of the nation itself tottering in an Anglo-American world awash in war news.

Rocky Relations: Cuban Annexation and the Recruitment Affair

The sense of nationalist uncertainty that suffused American Crimean War coverage also characterized two major news controversies involving Anglo-American diplomatic conflicts. The first of these arose directly from British challenges in the Crimea. So many British soldiers were dying, in mismanaged camps and hospitals as well as on battlefields, that the army was having difficulty replacing them with fresh bodies from the British mainland. This shortage of homegrown troops led to the so-called recruitment affair.

As a news story, the affair revolved around unstable nationalities, and even its minor details muddied the nationalist connections between people and place that the period's transatlantic news tended to obscure. The conflict hinged on whether the foreign-born population residing in America could be recruited for British regiments at the front and, if so, whether they could be surreptitiously transported to Canada for enlistment. The British recruitment effort had foundered when expatriated Irish nationalists living in the United States had vehemently opposed their efforts, and it concluded with the exiling of British diplomats from America. Thus news narratives of the recruitment affair inevitably evoked a swirling mix of dubious and shifting nationalities, none of which seemed to provide a firm and lasting place in the transatlantic world.[18]

At the most basic level, the news controversies over recruitment involved legal questions about how bodies could be marked, moved, and organized; the Anglo-American disputes concerned the tenuous bonds of sovereignty that delineated an individual's relative attachments to various national homelands and home governments. Another set of major transatlantic news stories, which concerned potential American expansions into Cuba, similarly complicated the nationalist relationship between land and people. Though prosperous, Cuba had long been ruled uncomfortably by Spain as a slave colony, and its history churned with suppressed revolts, racial oppression, and class conflict. It also had been a consistent target for both British and American interference, all of which complicated any sense of independent national definition or even firm colonial affiliation within a particular imperial agenda. Throughout the 1850s, partly through the machinations of the future president, James Buchanan, the United States would promote various Cuban annexation schemes. Buchanan's addendum to 1854's notorious Ostend Manifesto argued that America might justifiably seize Cuba from Spain based on "the great law of self-preservation." Buchanan's metaphor for this rationalization betrayed the precariousness of his own nation's edifice, as well as the negligible rights of Spain or Cuba. "The very same principle ... would justify an individual in tearing down the burning house of his neighbor, if there were no other means of preventing the flames from destroying his own home."[19]

Merging with resentments surrounding British recruitment, annexation plots aroused fervid resistance in Britain, where the United States' internal divisions did not go unnoticed. Responding to both stories in an 1856 editorial, the *Illustrated London News* insincerely apologized on behalf of the British government and people for having presumed "too much upon a kindly sympathy" in signing up Americans for service in the Crimean War. The paper shared the widespread British surprise at the hostility the recruitment scheme had provoked, while charging the United States with national inconsistency and republican hypocrisy. "We all live to learn—nations as well as individuals; the British people now see that there is more sympathy between Russia and the United States than they had imagined." Despite Americans' democratic pretensions, it was a common commitment to slavery, the British illustrated paper insisted, that had birthed this monstrous international union. "Extremes meet. The most stringent autocracy and the most unbounded democracy in the world have sentiments and passions in common. The serfs of Russia and the negro slaves of America prove, in more senses than one, that there are bonds which united the policy of the two great empires."[20]

Yet the *Illustrated London News* also concluded that for all its imperialist bluster, the United States did not have as robust a national constitution as it assumed. While Mexico had proved "a tempting morsel" for the United States, it could never be "wholly possessed," and though Britain continued to hear rumblings of filibusterism and official plans to seize Cuba, any such "attempt would array against them not only Spain, with England and France, but the antislavery States of their own Confederation. Filibusterism may try it, and the filibusteros will be hanged; but the United States will not attempt it, for if they did they would dissolve the Union."[21]

British lack of confidence in American national unity was hardly unusual. Nevertheless, in 1856 such British doubts drew upon news stories that underscored the weakness of standing nation-states even as they descended into the midcentury nadir of Anglo-American diplomatic relations. Such stories troubled the national categories that identified territories and populations, challenging national unity and implying that nationality itself was an arbitrary designation with little reality behind it. Thus Anglo-American clashes over sovereignty in Cuba and recruitment in the United States compounded the trials of traditionalist nationalism apparent in Crimean War news. Meanwhile a similar sense of ambiguous nationalities and dissolving political unions arose within the central domestic news story of the mid 1850s, the battle between pro- and antislavery forces in Bleeding Kansas.

Kansas-Nebraska: Unpopular Sovereignty

Buchanan and other American leaders sought to annex Cuba as part of a larger movement to expand the American slave system. One thrust of the proslavery plan sought the acquisition of new territory in the Caribbean and as far away as Central America. But another involved organizing new slave states within established US territory. The push to bring slavery to Kansas, a sparsely settled western region where it had been tacitly banned since 1820, would radically alter the American political landscape and create a new focal point for nationalist anxieties that were also fermenting throughout the transatlantic news.

The crisis began with the passage of the Kansas-Nebraska Act, legislation that laid out the terms under which the new territory would achieve statehood. Like Britain's original war strategy, the act emerged from expansionist agendas pursued in the name of national interest. Yet, like the Crimean adventure, it inaugurated a period of national division and threw national politics into turmoil. Thus an expression of America's continental ambitions ensured that its territorial destiny would be anything but manifest.

Introduced by Senator Stephen A. Douglas, one of the Compromise of 1850's architects, the new act extended the southwestern territories' right to decide the slavery question to the as-yet unorganized territories ceded to the United States in the Louisiana Purchase. In essence Kansas-Nebraska revoked the already weakened Missouri Compromise by rescinding the Free Soil status of the land immediately west of Missouri. This dubious alteration of a long-standing agreement arrived cloaked in the democratic-sounding mantle of "popular sovereignty" but was neither democratic nor popular. Interpreted in different ways by different factions, it inspired little support and much anxiety among the northern public, and its application caused one of the more bizarre parodies of self-government in US history.[22]

By allowing recent settlers to decide Kansas's slavery question, the law divided the territory into two distinct camps, each with its own version of Kansas's place in national history and each with contradictory visions of its future. Pro- and antislavery groups raced to Kansas, many of them less interested in settling than in settling the slavery issue, and they brought weapons to complement their respective arguments. Some Missouri border jumpers only stayed long enough to vote proslavery candidates into office and roust their opponents from their land if not their convictions. Northerners following the news from afar, and harkening to the many sermons, speeches, and editorials delivered by powerful antislavery advocates, funded

Free Soil settlements and sent guns to defend them. While the transcendentalist minister Theodore Parker insisted that Kansas had finalized a deep national division and that "no moral union makes the two one," the *Tribune* called for more guns, bodies, and blood to ensure Kansas entered the Union as a free state.[23] Pro- and antislavery governments sent dueling constitutions to Washington for approval, forcing their consideration not just by politicians but also by all who followed the news. As it played out in the papers, Kansas's divided history exacerbated conflicts between and within national political parties, breaking the two-party system and splitting the branches of government.

As the symbolic center of national news stories, the Kansas Territory formed a hospitable environment for these divisions to germinate. Its indeterminate relationship to the nation-state tended to complicate the centralizing claims of national sovereignty as well as popular sovereignty. While the federal project, as Trish Loughran suggests, helped to contain the republic's unruly sprawl within an imperial logic of national time and space, Kansas became federalism's Waterloo.[24] For years, the news pouring out of the territory tested the geographical foundations of an already fluid national imagination. Kansas's physical territory existed within the national border. Yet it had no corresponding political viability and few actual residents prior to the law that marked it out for premature statehood.[25] The settlers who would soon arrive, northern papers predicted, would enjoy less sovereignty under Douglas's system than European nations "under the Ottoman empire."[26]

Such invidious transatlantic comparisons proved accurate, as settlers' mixed motives and brief residencies disrupted the communal links between place, people, and political will. Lincoln would observe "the different expectations for popular sovereignty possessed by northern and southern migrants," while proslavery leaders would find confirmation that abolitionist zeal subverted "the good order of the community."[27] Yet before long even ordinary readers realized that something was going very wrong in Kansas. Charles Taylor has suggested that "the legitimacy principle of popular sovereignty" is closely tied to the memory of "an antecedent unity, of culture, history, or . . . language" and to the broad inclusion of minorities within the body politic.[28] In Kansas, Douglas's version of this principle failed so spectacularly as to call into question all antecedent unities and the national system that relied on them.

As legends derived from recent incursions into Kansas, tales of "border-jumping" ruffians and "crusading" abolitionists made for effective propaganda in part because their temporary residency undercut the crucial connection between the land and its population. Northerners saw Missourians as "border ruffians"; Missourians regarded northern emigrant aid societies as "an intermeddling... by foreigners."²⁹ Yet because both sides were similarly vulnerable to the charge of transience, the territorial struggle delegitimized both Kansas and the national union associated with it. Missourians might regard Kansas as their backyard while northerners might call it "free soil," but regardless of what side one took in the long debate over its political status, no one really seemed to belong in Kansas. At the same time, Kansas's dueling constitutions, by aping the pretensions of popular government, challenged the essential relationship between national representation and local facts on the ground. There had been fewer than eight hundred white settlers in Kansas when Douglas passed his bill, a mere tenth of the vehemently divided population that would be counted less than a year later.³⁰ Lacking in recognizable history, long-settled land, or even a minimally unified political structure, Kansas was missing the raw material upon which national integrity depended.

As a developing *Tribune* story, Bleeding Kansas projected an increasing deficit of political legitimacy onto a fresh national canvass. It also reinforced older doubts about American nationality that had suffused Anglophone culture since the republic's founding, and in particular it lent support to British slights against the United States' recent provenance. These had been renewed in the same years the Kansas news story was taking shape during the recruitment and Cuban scandals. Mainstream British opinion, by assuming American residents could be easily absorbed into Britain's imperial agenda, had shown scant consideration for US sovereignty or American nationality. Furthermore, even as the British government was pursuing distant misguided adventures in the name of national interests, it both refused to countenance Buchanan's imperial adventures undertaken in the name of national survival and cast aspersions on the Union's capacity to contain increasingly violent struggles over slavery. Buchanan's presidential run ensured that these transatlantic controversies would fester, exacerbating old American worries that Britain considered the United States merely a troublesome pretender on the international scene rather than a real nation worthy of respect.³¹

Kansas bolstered these doubts about America's nationalist claims with seemingly undeniable evidence. Indeed, the Kansas-Nebraska Act appeared designed to produce a parody of American nation building: first in theory, by preemptively guaranteeing the sovereignty of a populace that existed only in the imagination, then in practice, by allowing a process under which no representation of the popular will could be taken seriously. If, as Taylor suggests, the doctrine of popular sovereignty is part of the fabric not only of modern nationalism but also of modern temporality, then Kansas news arose as a violation of national time as well as space.[32] The dueling histories spun around newspaper coverage of the crisis, especially in the increasingly popular and widespread *Weekly Tribune*, highlighted the weakness not merely of the federal system but also of the connections among a nation's people, land, and government.

In the process it eviscerated previous notions of America's common sacred history. The religious divisiveness of the Kansas struggle can be easy to overlook in retrospect, in part because proslavery forces were so clearly pursuing an immoral cause. Yet as Mark Noll has argued, the evangelical attachment both to a unified American nationalism and to scriptural authority were precisely what made the struggle over slavery a "theological crisis" as well as a political one. "The political standoff" that ultimately led to war, Noll observes, "was matched by an interpretive standoff" over slavery, for "no common meaning could be discovered in the Bible, which almost everyone in the United States professed to honor." Regardless of what position one held, slavery was the problem that American Christianity could not solve, and thus it challenged the core Protestant faith in the United States as a distinctively Christian nation. Yet this did not mean Christianity was silent, for whether one was fighting against slavery or abolitionism, the religion demanded action to free the nation from the scourge of "our national sins."[33] Both sides in the struggle assumed that the Bible and its God stood with their version of American history and that godlessness and treason stood on the other.

Moreover, both sides could see the armies of darkness and light emerging in Kansas coverage while, just a few columns away, a war Britain had launched in the name of God and country would end in a morass of aristocratic incompetence, damaging press reports, and immaterial gains. As national religions at home and abroad were being overtaken by news events and popular responses to them, Kansas took shape at the far corner of a global muddling of nationalist beliefs that were shaking traditionalism's foundations. Any resolution to the nationalist dilemma, it seemed, would have to harness the power of the same press that was undercutting national institutions, and the presentist mode of memory fit the bill. Nevertheless, as the following section will argue, the reality of Kansas could not actually be incorporated into the nationalist news cycle any more than Kansas could be incorporated into the Union as it was then constituted. Northerners would instead revive their faith in America's national reality through a hypernationalist reaction against the old status quo and would ground the nation in their own community of news readers. Rising to build what Horace Greeley later recalled as an "organization . . . resolved on, spontaneously and simultaneously, by a million Northern firesides," they would affirm the presentist spirit through commitments that spread conflict and violence well east of the Kansas-Missouri border.[34] In the mid-1850s, as readers daily imagined their distinctive sacred history at war on contested national turf, they sought to recapture an American holy land and their own embattled sense of home.

Bleeding Kansas Dry: Presentist Crisis and Response

Over the course of the 1850s, Kansas would send three separate constitutions to Congress but would not achieve statehood until after several southern states had seceded. Actions on the ground helped doom the attempt to integrate the Kansas Territory into the federal system, but so too did the firestorm of reported violence that effort prompted. Greeley and other newspapermen had not merely followed the political battles over the 1854 act. Rather, "The controversy they began fanning in response to the legislation made them greater forces than ever" as they became material beneficiaries of a protracted struggle over national interests.[35] Over the course of two years millions of readers were not allowed to take their eyes off Bleeding Kansas, though nearly all lived many hundreds of miles distant. Claiming that civil war had already broken out in the territory, the New York papers raised the prospect that full-blown intersectional violence might not be far behind.

This was clearly a sectional crisis, but the battle to secure Kansas also opened a new front in the transatlantic struggle to validate the American nation as a distinct fiefdom within a larger civilizing project of Anglo-American history. To justify its founding, the Republican Party's charter in one midwestern state cited "the necessity of battling . . . for republican government, and against the schemes of aristocracy" to enslave the North and thus the nation.[36] News publishers relied on territorial conflict narratives to distinguish their readers as a geographically grounded and embattled national public within this global field of vision. The papers rightly identified the fights between antislavery and proslavery interests as a single civil conflict, for it constituted a newly potent division within a nation-state that had only recently renewed its union vows. Yet it is equally important to understand the Kansas story as an intensification of the older memory war that allowed a mass audience to relocate their nationalist sentiments through a form of spiritual combat that arrived in their daily and weekly editions. The presentist crusade revolved around the Kansas story, inspired violent religious zeal, and tapped into Christian memory to protect and strengthen the nation. Advancing their visions of sacred history, northern newspapers sought to recover an ideal of territorial continuity, political unity, and national legitimacy.

Their campaign depended on both offensive and defensive components, and the tone of coverage swung from paranoid to triumphalist. Throughout the North, sensational stories from Kansas formed a microcosm of both sectional unrest and broader nationalist anxieties, permanently reopening the debate over American slavery and raising the prospect of national dissolution. Yet northern coverage also revealed clear signs of a nascent nationalism that was reorganizing mass belonging along presentist lines. After Kansas, the battle over slavery was no longer a matter of mere legislative maneuvering but involved real bullets, as the papers were happy to tell their publics.[37] Because the strife in Kansas implicitly demanded readers take sides on the basis of their attitude toward slavery, whatever their party affiliation, Greeley and other former Whigs saw the crisis there as the final nail in their old party's coffin.[38] Yet "the visions of violence that haunted Northern politics in the 1850s drove a political alignment," pushing moderates, radicals, and even northern Democrats to unite under a single banner.[39] Rather than bemoaning the fall of American Whiggery, Greeley would celebrate the advent of "the most gigantic, determined and overwhelming party for freedom the world has ever known."[40]

The Republican Party's ascendency reinforced what Kansas had already compelled many well-established institutions and politicians to recognize: namely, that political life now revolved around the nation's shared history of news. Howard Holzer describes it as a time when "politics and newspaper technology were changing rapidly, each in a sense because of the other."[41] Indeed, in these years Washington was becoming increasingly a political scene rather than merely an institutional hub as the newspapers swept the national capital and its eminent denizens into a dramatic nationwide cycle of reading, political action, and governmental response. An unprecedented upsurge of political reporting accompanied the antebellum expansion of popular newsprint and spiked in the 1850s, as political speeches filled the papers as well as best-selling pamphlets. The sheer pervasiveness of political news changed not just the way politics appeared but also the way it was practiced: popular print became the omnipresent venue for political opinion, compelling legislators to speak to their reading publics and about, rather than to, the politicians on the other side of the aisle. Officeholders responding to the territorial crisis in partisan fashion became colorful characters in the larger national news story, planets orbiting the new journalistic core of a modern nation's political life. As Thomas Leonard observes, "[It] was the political institutions that gave way. The reporting system that was completed in the 1850s helped to create . . . fresh channels for political action that swept away patch-work groups like the Whigs and even the most adept straddlers like Stephen Douglas."[42] Born of the modern press and the spirit of reform, these fresh channels promoted more responsive forms of shared history than the old federal system could provide and thus became the basis for more potent forms of presentist nationalism.

As this mode of memory gained power, the political leaders who had hoped to hold the country together with the Compromise of 1850 had lost an important measure of political control. The old guard might rail against "the slave power" or "Black Republicanism" as the sinister forces complicating the organization of Kansas and threatening the party structures that had undergirded the old Union. Yet their increasingly publicized and inflammatory rhetoric masked their more passive role. Framing the Kansas struggle within the confines of nominally intersectional party politics obscured the separate northern and southern histories that were raging within the inherently oppositional framework of the news itself. By 1856 the *Tribune* would be proclaiming that the presidential election "had to be carried by the cause, or not at all. Who the candidate is is a matter of small consequence. . . . In the North and in the South there is a strong and determined current of sentiment and opinion upon the great question of the day . . . not in any degree under the control of, or even subject to modification, by the power of any man in this election." The struggle in Kansas, the paper insisted, "must electrify the canvass till the North is in a blaze. The standard-bearer, the candidate of the campaign, will be measurably forgotten . . . compared with the influence and power of the idea which is to inspire the movement."[43]

Coupled with the sense that the national pretensions of popular sovereignty had been punctured, diverging histories in the news suggested that national authenticity could only reside in one or the other view of the struggle. In the face of daily evidence of sectional division, efforts to maintain intersectional coherence amounted to denials of the true Kansas story and also of the true nation taking shape around violent Kansas news. Thus, news from Kansas encouraged readers to overcome their sense of political and geographical dissolution through violent hypernationalist agitation, a response that ironically threatened the historical structure the nation-state.[44]

It was hard to remain a moderate northerner when news reports of outrageous attacks by proslavery thugs arrived with daily regularity and when papers like the *Weekly Tribune* energetically publicized extremist positions held by politicians on both sides. In an 1856 lead article titled "A New Civil War in Kansas," the *Tribune* reported that Georgia's governor "had recommended that if Kansas or any other Territory should be refused admission to the Union on the ground of having a Constitution that sanctioned Slavery, Georgia should thereupon instantly call a Convention and take steps for seceding from the Union." In the same issue a former Missouri senator was cited as having called for "arms, men and money to be instantly forwarded to the aid of the Border Ruffians."[45]

Such reporting, which connected violence in the territory to the potential for violent schism elsewhere, supports historian David Potter's contention that there were "two wars" in Kansas—the scuffles between settlers, which sometimes had as much to do with conflicting land claims as positions on slavery, and the epic struggle represented in the newspapers, which was always more politically important than what was happening in the West. Grasping this broader significance, Greeley "proved a true field marshal in the propaganda war" largely because he saw beyond the territorial dispute to the nationalist potential of the violent Kansas news story.[46]

Yet in important ways the first war in Kansas was always out of reach, since actual events in Kansas lay outside the news network's technical capacity to transmit immediately; thus those fighting and suffering in the territory remained the point of national interest but not of the sort of national substance accruing around the active sharing of news along a domestic memory circuit centered far to the east. Kansas's distance from news centers made it easy fodder for propaganda, but that was merely an accidental aspect of its more essential alienation. If the original problem of territoriality was that no one actually belonged in Kansas, then it soon became apparent that encountering Kansas in the newspaper did not actually bring anyone home, except inasmuch as it brought them together around an imperfectly shared history. The problem was not that territorial violence and suffering could not be conveyed through language, although scholars have written compellingly on this representational problem as a central element of the Civil War era.[47] Nor was it a matter merely of inaccurate representation caused by flaws and mishandling of information technology. The problem was that accounts of violence and suffering in the territories, despite their centrality to readers' sense of ongoing national history, lay beyond the range of what could be effectively included in the national news cycle. Even in 1856, at a time when telegraphic communication linked Washington and New York, it would often take more than ten days for news from the seat of the struggle in Kansas to be published in the *Tribune*. This was virtually the same distance that separated the memory circuit of domestic news from British papers that arrived via steamer.

It was largely this temporal distance between a Kansas battlefront and a closely networked home front that created a sense of two Kansas wars, one based on facts and one built on propaganda. Yet this kind of neat and somewhat sinister division can obscure something important: Kansas was never fully a place, because its early history arose from more than one place. Settlement there was driven by national political news, and that political news ran continuously alongside the territorial struggle playing out at the extremity of the nation's borders—a constant loop of shared history created by publicized responses to news events that inspired further events. This latter variety of Kansas history formed the home turf on which Greeley's propaganda war was fought, but propagandists did not invent it; it arose from the mechanics of modern news cycles.

Those cycles left the happenings in Lawrence or Lecompton as far removed as London from the New York–based memory circuit of reading and response. Thus the structure of the American information network could hardly help but present Kansas as a territorial enigma marked by real sectional violence, and in this sense, Kansas posed a challenge to presentist as well as traditionalist versions of American national memory. Revoking the Missouri Compromise had undercut traditionalist defenses of the constitutional union; Douglas's doctrine of popular sovereignty had staged a dramatic failure of nationalist expansion under federalism. Yet the newspapers' public failure to encompass the action in Kansas within the presentist exchange of news also helped make Kansas a flashpoint for public anxieties about the state of the Union and American national legitimacy. Thus the press's weakness as well as its power contributed to a northern memory circuit that stood anxiously between uncertain connections to both territorial West and transatlantic East, challenging nationalist assumptions about America's unified populace, contiguous territory, and common sacred history.

Meanwhile a southern version of the Kansas war appeared in northern papers and helped inspire a degree of northern hostility that the conflict there could never have achieved on its own. Indeed, northern resistance to slave power now nearly matched the level of Calhoun's most paranoid dreams. The spread of national news made sectional stratification palpable, displaying to northern readers what Trish Loughran aptly calls "the nightmare of national consolidation" under the slave system.[48] Even in the first stages of the Kansas-Nebraska bill, partisan visions of history became obvious to northern readers primed by the controversies over the 1850 Compromise to recognize "the Congressional propagandists of Slavery" among the ranks of northern as well as southern politicians.[49] In the eyes of the *Tribune*, political opportunists like Douglas were eagerly trafficking in a proslavery version of history.

Yet the most potent outrage for either side arose not only from the insidious attempt by the other to rewrite national history along partisan lines but also in the successful cultivation of regional audiences who appropriated it as their own. As the *Tribune* sarcastically remarked, southern politicians and papers assured their readers that "the Border Ruffians are quiet and excellent men . . . who have been ruthlessly set upon by a horde of Abolitionist invaders." Such proslavery accounts, the *Tribune* said, are "as rich as [they are] characteristic" of the southern view of Kansas's history.[50] The *Tribune*'s concern, increasingly, was not only proslavery propaganda or political partisanship but rather a separate and simultaneous cycle of shared southern history. It was not just that Kansas's territorial history was being written or read in two different ways but also that each version of that history was bringing two separate peoples into public consciousness. The same reciprocal sharing of history through which the *Tribune* impressed the sense of common nationality upon its far-flung audience seemed to be mirrored by a foreign culture armed with its own southern cycle of news and political response.[51] Thus while blatant partisanship in reporting meant that the true history of Kansas, for readers both North and South, remained enigmatic, the bifurcation of the news's cycle of shared history became compellingly concrete.

Here, too, geography seemed to underwrite the separate cycles of news. Bleeding Kansas, which the *Tribune* presented as a distant territory torn by violence, was in fact playing midwife to a different political landscape organized around the paper's northern readership and its alienation of the southern alternative. By the *Weekly Tribune*'s own late 1856 count, more than two-thirds of its audience resided outside New York State. More than ten thousand readers lived in each of five midwestern states, which all reported subscriptions increasing at least 50 percent during the Kansas war.[52] Although Greeley was perpetually hopeful that his paper might appeal to moderate southerners, the rapid and publicized spread of his increasingly antislavery organ through an almost exclusively northern readership suggested that the nation was dividing its own loyalties according to the regionally divergent histories of the Kansas Territory.

Week after week, as the paper highlighted the outrages of border ruffians and gradually made these creatures of Kansas synonymous with an increasingly alien southern culture, its published circulation figures would bear out the northern slant in readership in the starkest terms. In late 1856, from a staggering total of 278,280 subscriptions, the *Tribune* company was sending a paltry 1,219 to states that would later secede. Almost half of these went to Virginia, probably a fair number to what would later become West Virginia. The *Tribune* sent more papers to Africa than to Arkansas, more to South America than to all but three southern states. More residents of Europe than the cotton belt counted themselves as regular Greeley readers, and the paper had more subscribers in Canada than below the Mason-Dixon line. Moreover, the northward slant of the *Tribune's* readership was no secret; a geographical census was prominently featured right alongside election results, correspondence from Bleeding Kansas, editorials encouraging northerners to stand up against southern outrages, and nationalist responses to condescending British attacks. Thus the *Tribune*—through its regionalized readership as much as its editorial positioning—increasingly defined a new northern nationalism in opposition to challenges arriving from the transatlantic East, the territorial West, and the enslaved South.[53] From this perspective, through the publication of incompatible histories, divided geographies, and alienated memory circuits, the *Tribune* projected not merely an intranational division but also a hypernationalist response to a national memory crisis that was only nominally centered on Kansas.

Calling Out the Country

Resolving the crisis required the reestablishment not merely of a particular state or nation-state but rather of the belief that the modern nation could exist at all in any meaningful sense. And though modern news's failures of representation helped spark this memory crisis, it also suggested a way out of it. During the same years in which the Crimean War and the British press were combining to project a national crisis across the Atlantic, American newspapers, particularly the *Tribune*, would step into a breach that the news itself had opened and offer themselves as a new foundation for their audience's embattled nationality—despite the fact that they clearly represented the shared history of only the northern half of the nation-state.

Thus Greeley would, in the midst of the crisis, claim to be speaking for "the country" even as he was increasingly aware that his constituency was technically regional. A reprisal of the *Tribune*'s booming circulation throughout the North was featured in an 1856 article appropriately titled "Power of the Press" and ostensibly written to answer a failing Democratic paper's attempt to localize belligerent Kansas coverage as "a quintuple conspiracy" among the five daily journals "of New-York to rule the government." In answering, the *Tribune* blasted its journalistic antagonist, the *Union*, for being a treasonous agent of "slave-breeders and Border Ruffians." Rather than propagating a New York conspiracy to usurp governance from the politicians, Greeley insisted the city's papers were speaking as "journals of the country."[54]

In referencing this country, he was claiming to transcend New York, but he was clearly not speaking for the Constitution or even for a meaningful union between North and South. Whether such a "country" existed and which states it could still claim were both live questions in January of 1856 when Greeley wrote his defense of modern press power. Yet in speaking of country, he was not speaking of a specific government (which his democratic interlocutor had assumed was threatened by the power of the press) but rather claiming to speak for what lay behind any national government: the shared history, the contiguous geography, the embodied community—in short all that his own paper's reporting from Kansas had (intentionally or not) helped call into question. Greeley was, in other words, defending not just the power of the press but also the hypernationalist paradox of an authentic nation of news readers that superseded the authority of a troubled nation-state.

The key to establishing his northern memory circuit as an expression of national legitimacy lay in the news's capacity to both inspire and publicize popular responses to news events. This involved more than merely editorial influence or effective propaganda, for it absorbed a wider swath of cultural involvements, including religious identities. As Congress was considering a vote on Kansas-Nebraska, Greeley's *Tribune* would, on a single page, report on the congressional debate, insist that "there is a North that refuses to be trampled upon," call for "a Mass Meeting of the observers of plighted faith and the defenders of Freedom, to be held at Washington," and report on a religious controversy between ministers opposed to the act and Stephen Douglas, "who objected to [their] making the Sabbath an electioneering day, and the occasion for stump speeches." Douglas would instead assert that "the purity of the Christian Church, the purity of our holy religion and the preservation of our free institutions require that Church and State be separate, that the preacher on the Sabbath day shall find his text in the Bible, shall preach Jesus Christ and him crucified, shall preach from the Holy Scriptures, and not attempt to control political organizations and political parties of the day." But for the ministers in question and many of Greeley's readers, Douglas was recommending a traditionalist approach to Christian witness that amounted to apostasy. Instead they demanded prophetic action, as Douglas indicated while quoting the full-throated presentism of a sermon published in Chicago. "We may say again," the Reverend R. H. Richardson had preached, "what God said long ago, 'Woe unto them that decree unrighteous decrees,' and the people to whom we speak can convert this prophecy into history, as it has so often been converted before, in the condemnation and disgrace to those who are guilty of this great transgression." Most vexing to Douglas, the suggestion had already inspired an intense popular response. "The people take the hint," the paper reported, "and it was not long before some of them had him (Douglas) burning in effigy."[55]

From such violent beginnings, Kansas coverage would continue to operate as a mechanism for prophetic call and response, a means to recover a spiritually authentic nationality from the untenable experience of an anxiously severed history. While the papers presented a divided nation, and in the *Tribune*'s case seemed to exacerbate the sectional schism with revolutionary rhetoric, the reciprocal practices of news production, news reading, and news making through popular political action also suggested how that national reality could be recovered. Audiences could find evidence for the true nation in their own sharing of a history that developed in violent opposition to an enslaved alternative.[56]

Of course, northerners needed to maintain the illusion that their revolutionary adjustments represented some level of continuity with the old Union. This may help explain Greeley's almost delusional faith in a southern readership for the *Tribune*. At any rate, it strains credulity to suppose that anyone not holding some level of antislavery conviction could read the *Tribune* without revulsion during 1855 or 1856.[57] White southerners opposed to the presentist vision of sacred freedom refused to share in freedom's history and had in fact made participation in the *Tribune*'s readership a crime against the state.[58]

Giving as good as he got, Greeley prodded his northern readers to banish an intolerable division and to fight to free themselves from a status quo that bound them to a foreign element and an alien history. This was to be a war, he insisted in 1856, waged not in Kansas but anywhere the news from Kansas had spread, a civil war between freedom and slavery "to be ceaselessly waged until one or the other finally and absolutely triumphs."[59] It was to be, in other words, not the end of the nation but the end of national uncertainty. By the time Greeley made the editorial assertion that there was no middle ground between North and South, it amounted to little more than the capstone of the divergent histories of the Kansas war that had been running in northern papers for months and had made a mockery of the notion of the old constitutional unity. "We are not one people [but] two peoples," the *Tribune* had declared. Kansas demonstrated that "we are a people for Freedom and a people for Slavery. Between the two, conflict is inevitable."[60]

Greeley's American fighters for freedom became appreciable to themselves as "a people" by organizing around an oppositional Kansas history whose boundaries corresponded to the geographical regions where the *Tribune* was generally read. Greeley clearly hoped that his audience could empower the nationality already manifested through the news cycle by overwhelming a corrupted government apparatus. Thus in 1856 Greeley would ask the goading question "Is there a North?" during the run-up to the presidential election. His call also included a presumed response, for his own paper was grounding the reading experience of the *Tribune* in northern geography and placing it in opposition to the antagonistic history of an increasingly bellicose and imperial South.

In this sense the newspapers articulated a self-fulfilling prophecy when they reported on the civil war in Kansas. The underdetermined territory became a virtual space in which readers could witness their own sense of a shared past defined against its alternative. News from the territory and the larger conflict narrative it necessitated highlighted the communal failures of the established nation-state, stoking the desire for an authentic national community and relocating it in the active sharing of news as a suddenly combative form of memory.

The literal ground for this memory was not Kansas but everywhere such news was shared, a point Greeley skillfully articulated in his editorial by metaphorically linking politics to terrain.[61] "Year after year our public men have been giving up the ground under our feet," Greeley argued, "and all the time protesting that there was a point beyond which they could not be driven. If that point is not now reached, it never can be. If the North quails now, it will be generally understood that the slave power may do its will and that the North will submit." If Kansas had been organized and settled to gain both literal ground and figurative strength for the nation, it—and the whole northern populace with it—could also be lost through a failure of principle. To lose the war over Kansas, to submit to the southern vision of its history, meant Greeley's readership would also lose the ground beneath their feet, the ground on which all national memory was established. Greeley, turning away from a broader audience, began to call on "all in the North to show their colors."[62] Doing so meant making news, not merely reading it. Northerners harkened to the call, revolting against the Pierce administration's move to recognize an enslaved Kansas and taking matters into their own hands. Refusing to remain passive in their response to news, they addressed the Free Soilers' plight with social action, making themselves felt from the pulpit to the ballot box.

Whether the North called itself a nation or not, by the mid-1850s it was certainly beginning to look like one, especially in enormously popular newspapers that unabashedly denominated "two peoples" rather than two political parties or two positions on slavery. As Susan-Mary Grant observes, antebellum "northerners, no less than southerners, were engaged in a quest for self-definition that ultimately led to the development of an ideology predicated not on the American nation but on a Northern one."[63] Considering how northerners read the news from Kansas, it would be hard to dispute Grant's point. Yet the development of an embattled northern nationalism and the presentist holy war for America's soul were not necessarily as antithetical as they might seem. If Kansas arose in the news as a territory in search of definition, the other would-be states of the future American republic came to share its fate. The unified America of northern dreams, like Kansas, did not yet exist except in the prophetic promise of future freedom. It would require a new revolution, and a violent conquest led by the spirit of northern presentism, to secure that holy land.

Kansas Comes Home

The *Tribune*'s Kansas coverage helped enact a seismic shift that was actually centered on the home front, where the real news was read and made as memory. In the same years when an increasingly anxious home audience for Crimean War news had prompted a reshuffling of the British nation-state, the political ramifications of sharing the news from Kansas completely upended American politics and launched the Republican Party. Yet the *Tribune* described its own intimate relationship to the new northern politics as surprisingly passive: "With words of cheer," the paper related in an early 1856 self-assessment, "we have hailed the beginning and watched the progress of that mighty REPUBLICAN movement."[64] This might have accurately described Greeley's role as an editor; nevertheless, his paper had made the nationalization of sectional news visible by giving this mighty mass audience a way to belong. In this sense, launching a new party merely gave a name to a sacred shared history that the *Tribune* and the Kansas story had already propagated throughout the North.

Similarly, though it formed one of the pillars of Republicanism, the *Tribune* was not, strictly speaking, a party paper.[65] It might be just as accurate to say that Republicans constituted a paper party—one that began with reading, grew in concert with the sharing of a new kind of news, and reached a far-flung and unprecedented range that roughly corresponded to the geographical reach of the *Tribune's* growing circulation. Just as important, readers knew their numbers and geographical reach were growing. The 1850s saw a huge jump in news readers generally, with subscribers amounting to more than 40 percent of the total US population by the end of the decade.[66] The *Tribune* was at this surge's forefront, scoring its biggest gains during Bleeding Kansas's height. By 1856 the proprietors were able to boast that the *Tribune's* combined editions had gained more than one hundred thousand total readers in a mere eighteen months, an increase of 50 percent, and it flaunted its six-figure circulation in oversized black print on the same pages that contained news from Kansas and Greeley's antislavery editorials. Incubated by stories of "the perfidious violation of the Missouri Compact, and stimulated by the astounding outrages whereof the rights of the Free Settlers of Kansas have been the victims," Republicanism had sprung out of the news, reversing the earlier dynamic between political parties and their designated newspapers.[67]

Promising that the new movement would unite all those dedicated to containing slavery, the *Tribune* editors pledged their paper to the Republicans and advertised its potency with a tally of its massive circulation: two hundred thousand copies in all its editions, with a subscription list it claimed to be twice that of any newspaper in the world. Low cost had contributed to this astonishing growth, but the paper's real value was as a political barometer for northern sentiment and an index of shared history; "While its extreme cheapness ... has doubtless largely swelled its subscription list," the paper admitted, "it would be absurdity not to perceive in this unprecedented patronage some evidence of public approval and esteem" for its positions. For the *Tribune*, growing subscriptions measured the "progress of the mighty REPUBLICAN movement"; news of the party's rise chronicled the active response to news from Kansas.[68]

Some responses to newspapers were more active than others. Violence in Kansas generated fistfights on the congressional house floor.[69] Greeley himself recounted an attack on his person in the national capital in February when a Democratic representative from Arkansas, Albert C. Rust, assaulted him for a perceived slight in the *Tribune*. Far from assuaging such tensions, Greeley titled his published account "Border Ruffianism in Washington" and used the incident to agitate his northern readers further. Confronting Greeley in the street, Rust had asked his name and if he were a "non-combatant." Greeley replied that it depended on the circumstances, whereupon Rust landed several blows to Greeley's head and stalked off. Later that same day Greeley encountered Rust again and, when again accused of being a noncombatant, still refused to take "exception on that account." Rust responded even more violently, producing "a heavy cane, which [Greeley] had not seen before" and aimed a glancing blow at the editor's skull. Several onlookers then stopped the fight, even as Greeley gamely "was attempting to close with" his assailant.[70]

The account of the attempted caning of "Uncle Horace" offered a parable of the violence underlying intersectional relations. Greeley obviously intended his northern readers to take Rust's behavior as a typical example of the same sort of proslavery "ruffianism" his paper constantly reported from the territory. It raised the prospect that the distant political divisions evident in Kansas, drawn not merely with ballots but with blood, now defined the national community as a whole. As the physical target of violence, Greeley ceased to be an editorial voice and became undeniably embodied as a representative of this communal division. Greeley administered no blows of his own, but his refusal to be cowed led Rust to strike at him first with his fists and then with a cane, and he was certain that the southerner would have eventually pulled a gun. For this reason, a bruised Greeley avowed that "it certainly would have been a pleasure to me, had I been able, to perform the public duty of knocking [Rust] down."[71]

Greeley's language suggested his northern audience should be prepared to follow his example. Rust and by extension his fellow southerners were bullies who would interpret peaceable argument as dishonorable; northerners should be under no illusions about their brutal natures, Greeley advised, but neither should they be intimidated. Greeley's story dismisses passive responses to southern "ruffians" as tacit acceptance of the incipient threat of force the South always carried concealed like a cane. Yet what was most crucial about this transplanted Kansas story was how, even as it was carried from Washington throughout the North, Greeley's personal confrontation dramatically solidified an imagined nation through firm resistance; the national spirit felt by *Tribune* readers became embodied in Greeley as the physical site of intersectional violence.[72]

Whether through the destruction of the Whigs or of the Aberdeen government, the press's new capacity to develop a militantly national public had massive political consequences. The newspapers were not merely representing or even shaping public opinion. Rather, they were giving a nascent public access to a shared history defined by violent conflict, and the surge in circulations that accompanied such battles gave the presentist memory circuit a tangible form.

Greeley could not have known it at the time, but his self-consciously symbolic account of Rust's attacks would be followed by a far more infamous caning a few months later, in which Preston Brooks beat Charles Sumner till he was bloody and senseless on the Senate floor. Probably more than any other violent contribution to the Kansas news cycle, this famous incident brought the war home by convincing millions of northerners to adopt Greeley's stance of firmer resistance to southern violence. It did so partly because it integrated the two sides of the Kansas war story, bringing together the intersectional violence with the sharing of Kansas history on the home front. The cause of the attack was Sumner's speech, "The Crime against Kansas," which happened to insult Brooks's relative and fellow congressman Andrew Butler but was prepared in advance as a national press event as much as an oration. Politics followed the news as much as the news followed politics, and Sumner always intended his words to be spread as soon as possible through popular print.[73]

Despite Brooks's sense of family honor and grievance, Sumner's words were not really intended for his present auditors (Butler was not even physically present for the speech) but rather for the wider Kansas news audience. And though the violence seems to have caught Sumner by surprise, it too might be seen as part of the national news story's script. In their increasing advocacy for firmness and violence, Brooks and Sumner, like Rust and Greeley, were leveling the discrepancy between Kansas news and the home audience, following a prescription to actualize the struggle in the hinterlands as part of the news war at home.

Although Sumner would leave the public eye to recover from his trauma, he would continue to serve in the same government as his adversary, a new hero of the proslavery cause. But the nation behind that government increasingly appeared fragmented and illusory. A peculiar gap became apparent as the event of Sumner's caning took shape as yet another divisive news story. Notes of approval such as those struck in the *Richmond Enquirer* grated on northern ears: its editors argued that Sumner's breed of abolitionist had "been suffered to run too long without collars [and] must be lashed into submission."[74] Even northerners who would never consider themselves abolitionists were taken aback by "the tone of the Southern Press & approbation, apparently, of the whole Southern people," which seemed to confirm the South was "a lower civilization." Northerners voraciously consumed strident condemnations of southern brutality in their own papers and "perhaps a million copies of Sumner's speech," infuriating southerners. The *Tribune* memorialized Sumner by reproducing an engraved portrait in the ordinarily austere pages of its weekly edition.[75]

Even as middecade newspapers came to embody a violent breach between North and South, the modern news's transformation tracked a more fundamental division spreading throughout the transatlantic world. On one side stood national systems built on traditionalist assumptions of union, supposedly vested in venerable political offices and customs; on the other, a more visceral national reality was becoming apparent in media coverage of bodily and bloody clashes, the wars and rumors of wars that defined the period from 1853 to 1856. Like the Kansas narrative itself, the shift suggested a fundamental weakness not just in a particular government, or even the shortcomings of the federal system, but in the United States' failure to appear as an authentic national community on the global stage. If press reports of the period were to be believed, it was an affliction America shared with the "old and outworn" nation of Turkey, with France and its "parvenu" emperor, and with a Britain ringing with hollow boasts.[76] Everywhere the press seemed to be revealing national shams. Everywhere nationalist anxieties were crying out for redress, prompting popular audiences to recover the national community by violently defending their nationalist memory. During Bleeding Kansas, these recoveries sought to nationalize regional affiliations the news made evident among its readers, imperiling the standing nation-state in the process. Yet because British disparagement of American national legitimacy had mirrored anxieties raised by Kansas coverage, and because British news readers also appeared as a discrete community within northern newspapers, northerners might also seek transatlantic targets for their hypernationalist zeal and train their spiritual weapons East as well as South.

"Go Far to Light the Flame of Civil War"

As the northern papers' efforts to promote the civil war in Kansas crested and merged with Republican Party politics in 1856, their editors suddenly found themselves considering the real prospect of a shooting war with Britain. War fever, which had begun to rise during the controversies over recruitment, spiked just as the Paris peace negotiations between European powers were getting under way in February of 1856. Thus the *Times* reported on Horace Greeley's speech counseling moderation toward the South at the Republican Convention in Pittsburgh, while in an adjacent column it weighed the threats of war that it found in the *London Chronicle*.[77] On March 1, the *Tribune* informed its readers that Parliament as well as the major London papers were openly discussing the possibility of breaking the transatlantic peace. Intemperate politicians and a still habitually hostile press, believing "war is over with the [Russian] Autocrat . . . foam away at the [American] democrats on this side." Yet just as the British press had dismissed this prospect by jeering at the weakness of American national unity, so too Greeley predicted that any British attack on the United States would dissolve Britain's own national union. Economic "distress" in the event of war would decimate the working classes and "would go far to light the flame of civil war" in Britain. "The chain of Britain's Colonial possessions would snap under the strain. Canada and the lower provinces would fall into our hands." Even if initially successful, no British army could sustain a long-term invasion of North America. "Indeed the military strength of England," far from being battle tested, "has been demonstrated in the late war to be insignificant."[78]

Given that the Crimean and Kansas conflicts were not yet fully settled, the hunger for a transatlantic war in 1855 and 1856 seems hard to fathom. Yet internal and imperial conflicts were always projected abroad and interpreted as signs of national strength and legitimacy through transatlantic news. In this sense the wars in Kansas and the Crimea were also struggles against dubious transatlantic observers. The Anglo-American controversies of these years revived harsh foreign judgments that were never fully dormant but rather lay like a murky undercurrent of nationalist doubt just beneath the press's blustering chauvinism: the British knowledge that Americans had perceived Britain's national weakness from afar, the American knowledge that Britain had seen into their own domestic fragility. In a sense, all conflicts of the period appeared within the frame of a larger civil war that had never been settled, a cousins' war that, as Kevin Phillips has noted, was also a war of religion.[79] The desire to reenact an internecine struggle among Anglophones drew energy from the broader popular attraction to a crusade for national integrity, an appetite that motivated both internal strife and transatlantic belligerence. Thus Anglo-American war fantasies emerged on both sides of the Atlantic as alternative routes to the same destination, an alleviation of nationalist uncertainties born of the shared international scene of Anglophone news.

Reporting on these controversies created occasions for nationalists unsettled by recent news to weigh international identifications against domestic alternatives. Fresh from the territorial conflict of Kansas, American papers were eager to maintain their role as primary repositories and authenticators of the nation-state's common past. Yet their rise had simultaneously undercut their home audiences' traditionalist assumptions and created an image of divided national history. Fomenting transatlantic hostility may have provided a compelling solution to that problem for at least two reasons: first, because it obscured the experience of domestic turmoil by projecting it onto transatlantic cousins with clear divisions of their own; second, because it relied on newsprint as a venue of relatively limited transatlantic exchange whose mechanical features produced an image of relative unity on one's own side of the divide. Thus despite all his efforts to pry northerners away from their attachment to the enslaved South, Greeley would insist upon American unity in facing down British threats. Responding to British saber rattling, the antislavery *Tribune* even foreshadowed an argument from none other than King Cotton, insisting that the British working classes would revolt if a war with America halted trade; thus the *Tribune* highlighted the internal weakness of the British nation in order to maintain the imperviousness of Greely's own.[80]

For though he knew his British counterparts might read his paper, Greeley also knew they could not really share the history they might find there. The relative difficulty of responding quickly to transatlantic news, which became more acutely felt during any Anglo-American crisis, also created a comforting distinction in the sharing of history that corresponded to the raw physical span of the Atlantic. Any paper that carried both national and international news also constantly projected national legitimacy as a function of Atlantic distance. Thus the transatlantic threats of war that the *Tribune* ridiculed appeared in readers' experience from across a literal ocean of time. Their home paper's in-kind rejoinder to British insults sought an immediate response from Greeley's domestic audiences, a completed memory circuit that would demonstrate the national integrity and strength the

British press had questioned. The resulting image of a defiant news audience, communicated through a sea voyage of approximately ten days' time, then became transformed into *American* opinion: nationalist fodder for Britain's much-delayed and undoubtedly nationalistic reaction.

In the midst of internal turmoil fueled by hypernationalist agitation surrounding the Kansas conflict narrative, the traditionalist transatlantic other remained a crucial foil for the presentist crusade of the mid-1850s. Even as it bore witness to significant and intensifying internal divisions, Anglophone news would continue to organize itself around distinctive transatlantic memory circuits, reproducing the unavoidable geographical division that the transatlantic time lag imposed on the sharing of histories published in a common tongue. Greeley and his British counterparts, whatever their editorial stances, supported the nationalist exclusivity of news structurally in every edition of their papers and leant support to nationalist sentiments during the 1856 spike in Anglo-American hostilities. That both sides could point to the diminishing unity on the Atlantic's far shore only underscored the importance of the temporal horizon that limited their sharing of news as memory. This dynamic helps explain why Walt Whitman, a New York newsman turned poet, in these same years would draw on transatlantic hostility to introduce a nationalist memory circuit of his own: the shared history in free verse that encompassed the first two editions of *Leaves of Grass*.

6

"Transatlantic Latter-Day Poetry"

Nationalist Anxiety and the Memory Circuits of *Leaves of Grass*

> To the images from this twin source (of Christianity and art), the mind became fruitful as by the incubation of the Holy Ghost. The English mind flowered in every faculty.
>
> —Ralph Waldo Emerson, *English Traits*, 1856

> [America] Sees itself promulger of men and women, initiates the true use of precedents,
> Does not repel them or the past, or what they have produced under their forms, or amid other politics, or amid the idea of castes, or the old religions.
>
> —Walt Whitman, *Leaves of Grass*, 1856

In 1856, a few months after the *Tribune* had reported on the prospects for a transatlantic war with Britain, Ralph Waldo Emerson finally published *English Traits*. He based the book on his travels in the 1830s and 1840s, but it also reflected the vexed nationalism that marked the transatlantic world of the mid-1850s. Throughout his postclerical career, Emerson had dwelt extensively on American national culture and its strength relative to British precedents, but recent news had raised fresh challenges to his beliefs about literary nationalism and the poem he called America. Nevertheless, when he eventually took up the topic of literature in one of the last chapters of *English Traits*, he implicitly defended American literary prospects by criticizing British alternatives. Tellingly, Emerson placed these reflections between his critical appraisals of British journalism and religion and found that like these other elements of Britain's modern national culture, British literature was sunk in a traditionalist death trap.

Damningly, Emerson compared the mother country's literature to "stumps of vast trees in our exhausted soils"; just as we "have received traditions of their ancient fertility to tillage, so history reckons epochs in which the intellect of famed races became effete. So it fared with English genius" after the Elizabethan age. Meanwhile, contemporary English literary critics insisted that "all new thought must be cast in the old moulds. The expansive element which creates literature is steadily denied."[1]

By situating Britain's literature between its religion and journalism, Emerson was making a point about American literature as well. True national literature, wherever it established itself, Emerson insisted, must take up the mantle of sacred memory; it must reside between good news and divine presence, the space of an eternally "expansive" spirit revealed in contemporary elements. This was the spirit the glorious epochs of English literary creativity had embraced. In discussing the ecstatic origins of an English language that combined a commonsense focus on the materials close at hand with Platonic elevation, Emerson dramatized the emergence of Gothic elements from primeval shadow into the celestial light of a sacred national history. "When the Gothic nations came into Europe they found it lighted with the sun and moon of Hebrew and of Greek genius. The tablets of their brain, long kept in the dark, were finely sensible to the double glory. To the images from this twin source (of Christianity and art), the mind became fruitful as by the incubation of the Holy Ghost." The result was literature, though not in any narrow sense. Rather, "The English mind flowered in every faculty."[2]

Around the same time Emerson was tracing English literary authenticity to a primitive Gothic encounter, George Eliot, the future British novelist, was trying to make sense of her own barbarian. A strange book had been published in New York the year before, and a few copies had arrived in London with no indication of author or publisher. Eliot found that "the singularity of the author's mind—his utter disregard of ordinary forms and modes—appears in the very title-page and frontispiece of his work." It included only a stamp of "the English bookseller," leaving the author nameless. In place of a name she reported a portrait of "a bearded gentleman in his shift-sleeves and a Spanish hat, with an all-pervading atmosphere of Yankee-doodle about him," leaving the reader to "infer that this roystering blade is the author." The book's content proved similarly unusual, a rambling preface followed by a "poem written in wild, irregular, unrhymed, almost unmetrical 'lengths.'" Thus Eliot reported that the book's "external form . . . is startling, and by no means seductive, to English ears, accustomed to the sumptuous music of ordinary metres."[3]

Eliot was more familiar with both book and author than she indicated in the summer of 1856. Greeley's *Tribune* had published Emerson's glowing praise for *Leaves of Grass* the year before, and Eliot herself had previously reviewed it in April. In March, the *Saturday Review* had also received a copy, into which had been "pasted . . . a number of notices extracted with the scissors from American newspapers," including Emerson's own letter to Whitman congratulating him "at the beginning of a great career." The journal had reviewed *Leaves* three months before Eliot's review appeared in the *Leader*, and just prior to recommending that British readers throw the book "instantly . . . behind the fire," the *Review* had gone to the trouble of reprinting several lines that "embodied Mr. Whitman's theological creed": "Why should I wish to see God better than this day? / I see something of God each hour of the twenty-four, and each moment then, / . . . / I find letters from God dropped in the street, and every one is signed by God's name, / And I leave them where they are, for I know that others will punctually come for ever and ever."[4]

As Eliot surely knew, the *Saturday Review*'s proprietor was A. J. B. Beresford Hope, one of the Gothic Revival's strongest advocates and certainly no friend to Whitman's presentist creed. She also recognized that Whitman's lawless poetry, whatever its faults, was undertaking a form to match his nation, and her appraisal of Whitman's singularity as a writer hinged on his connection to a distinctly American land, society, and sense of history. Thus she began her own review in the *Leader* by explicitly describing Whitman's presentist spirit as an American contrast to Britain's Gothic-style revivalism. "'Latter-day poetry' in America is of a very different character from the same manifestation in the old country," Eliot averred. "Here it is occupied for the most part with dreams of the middle ages, of the old knightly and religious times . . . as if Heaven were perpetually betraying the earth with a show of progress that is really a regression." By contrast, "in America, it is employed chiefly with the present. . . . The minstrels of the stars and stripes blow a loud note of exultation before the grand new epoch, and think the Greeks and Romans . . . and the later men of the middle centuries, of small account before the onward tramping of these present generations."[5]

For Eliot, as for the *Saturday Review*, *Leaves of Grass* arrived in London packaged as the launching point for a presentist cycle of nationalist reading to which it bore witness. Framed in the context of its previous critical responses, including Emerson's, the book exhibited itself in British eyes as a distinctly American memory circuit that practiced the presentist gospel it preached by linking an unquestionably American author to his nationalized readership. The *Saturday Review* abhorred this circuit of American reading nearly as much as the book that initiated it, exhibiting a palpably nationalistic distaste at Whitman's placement of earlier reviews on his first edition's title page. The clippings "pasted" and "extracted with the scissors from American newspapers" were part and parcel to a despised "theology" of scraps and the name of God Whitman claimed to find in the transient experiences of the American street, coming again for ever and ever like the daily news. Whitman's literature stood between religion and journalism, just as British literature had in *English Traits*. Yet Whitman channeled these elements in a presentist mode and thus gained what no contemporary British writer had managed to earn from Emerson: recognition as the author of an authentic and spiritually potent national literature.

Cheap modern news had connected Whitman to Emerson and his other American readers; its capacity to serve as a conduit of sacred history as well as literature was central to the poet's point, as was the disdainful reaction the clippings from "American newspapers" raised in Britain—a reaction the poet was careful to include in the second edition of his masterpiece. This chapter shows how, in the face of nationalist anxieties pervading the transatlantic scene of middecade, Whitman's 1855 and 1856 editions worked together to celebrate and embody the nationalist memory circuit that modern news made possible. Moving from an important self-review to a poetic reflection on antislavery news and finally to the 1856 edition's deployment of traditionalist objections to the first edition, it demonstrates how Whitman re-created the modern news's transatlantic background. Taking the familiar form of the presentist memory circuit as a model, Whitman subverted the divisions within the suddenly less United States by recovering a more substantial transatlantic division in common sacred history and offering the body of his circulating text as the common ground of a more stable nationalist identification. Recommending himself in the first edition as the bard whose "spirit responds to his country's spirit" and who "incarnates its geography," in the second he would close the national memory circuit to

> dispense with other lands, incarnating this land,
> Attracting it body and soul to himself, hanging on its neck with incomparable love,
> Plunging his semitic muscle into its merits and demerits,
> Making its geography, cities, beginnings, events, glories, defections, diversities, vocal in him.

Thus Whitman would attempt to claim the prophetic mantle of "The Poet" that Emerson had set before him more than a decade earlier and simultaneously earn his place behind the British reviewer's fire.[6]

"An American Freeman"

In October 1855, Whitman anonymously published a review of his own *Leaves of Grass* and Tennyson's *Maud* in the *American Phrenological Journal*. Appearing under the title "An English and an American Poet," the piece offers a defense of poetry as an expression of national spirit and national blood but draws a hard line between the American and English races. "The poetry of England, by the many rich geniuses of that wonderful little island, has grown out of the facts of the English race, the monarchy and aristocracy prominent over the rest, and conforms to the spirit of them. No nation ever did or ever will receive with national affection any poets except those born of its national blood.... Thus what very properly fits a subject of the British crown may fit very ill an American freeman."[7]

The notion that American and British literatures were destined to diverge had been advanced by American literary nationalists before.[8] Yet Whitman's argument was in many ways designed for his times in particular, and Tennyson's prominence as a British poet laureate who could boast a large American following explained why it was necessary. At a time when the weakness of nationalist arguments was being exposed in the transatlantic world, Tennyson's continuing popularity on both sides of the Atlantic suggested either that imaginative literature had no deep relation to nationality or that America's separate national status was itself imaginary, a variety of Anglophone fiction. Moreover, in claiming the right to review both poets, and in presenting Tennyson as "the best of the school of poets at present received in Great Britain and America," Whitman readily admits the transatlantic portability of English-language verse.

Yet Whitman's reviewer speaks as an uncomfortably global Anglophone, intentionally straddling the spatial and temporal vectors of the transatlantic divide only to point out that such an awkward pose is doomed to collapse under the weight of national realities. In the middle of a decade rife with dubious nationalist claims, the review composes an argument not merely for American literary nationalism but also for the legitimacy of nationalism as a whole: that "national blood" that would bind native poet to an affectionate reader. Furthermore, rather than merely attempting to legitimize a separate American branch of Anglophone culture, the reviewer appeals to

British nationality to make a more radical argument for entirely separate literary trees, for literatures rooted in the solid ground of national memory rather than the relative swamp of shared language. Thus the puff piece cleverly supports Whitman's propagation of distinctively American literature by first presenting Britain's traditionalist version of national memory as the source of all properly English poetry.

The review's compact second paragraph performs an exercise in rhetorical alchemy, drawing together central metaphors of both collective memory and nationality—of an ancient land, race, tradition, blood, and spirit—in order to ground British literature in what it presents as national "facts."[9] It begins by linking literary genius to national geography, though in doing so it takes some creative license with obvious political divisions. By shifting its focus to the poetry "of England," it follows common practice in immediately reducing the entirety of the "wonderful little island" of Great Britain—including Scotland and Wales—into that smaller political unit of England, transferring the potentially fractious divisions within British nationalism onto a single unifying body of firm geography bounded by the sea. Thus the review ties a slippery tradition of poetry in English, which continually crossed that oceanic boundary with nearly as much ease as it crossed Hadrian's Wall, to the terra firma of a neatly circumscribed geographical fact.

The author then subtly shifts his factual reference point to a racialized discourse. Yet once again he dodges the potential problem of an Anglo-Saxon category that might elide the Atlantic border while colliding with Celtic obstacles. The race that matters to this reviewer is simply "English" and seems as firm in the reviewer's imagination as the island from which it literally springs, in part because, like the land, the race embodies history. It houses the hereditary "facts," the "monarchy and aristocracy" that do not here represent merely ordinary hierarchy but more importantly the means of vesting the authority of present British identity in the distant past through inherited privilege. The British class system is thus transformed from mere social institutions and practices into the source of a national "spirit" that is thoroughly traditionalist.

In this brief passage, Whitman uses the language of memory to summon a power beyond language, a power that is very nearly the opposite of language: his vision evokes a materially grounded poetry that "conforms" to the national spirit and grows out of national bodies—bodies of land, racialized bodies, bodies full of "national blood." Yet in all of it, the reviewer is not really concerned with Britain any more than he is actually interested in reviewing *Maud*, which he does not bother to excerpt. Rather, by establishing a foundation for contemporary British poetry in an exclusive memory of land, blood, and race, the review simultaneously denies the communal legitimacy of Britain's literature anywhere beyond its literal shores. In particular, Whitman's America, as much by virtue of its geographical distance as because of its democratic institutions, stood beyond the effective range of Britain's imperial verse. Thus Tennyson, for all his poetic mastery of a shared English language, was excluded based on physical principles that stood beyond and beneath language and upon which national identities as well as national literature were established. Subject to such a crown, his verse could not prove "fit" for "an American freeman."

So original that at first blush it seemed aggressively unpoetic, Whitman's book of poems impresses the reviewer as a nationalist revelation and a literary revolution. It sought to emancipate the American reader from a distant land and feudal legacy that Tennyson, as royalty's pet and a purveyor of well-disciplined poetry, could not help but uphold. Truly American readers could not maintain the royalist pose such poetry assumed for long, unsupported as they were by the underlying structures of British national memory; thus the chief attraction of any literature temporarily shared with British peers was also bound to fade in time, under the influence of a more spacious New World culture. In literature as well as politics, Britain's national spirit appeared as a "gentleman of the first degree," as the reviewer put it later, a character perfectly fitted to the limited scope and social constraints of a small island nation with a long and august history. To modern Americans drawn to their country's expansive vistas and wide-open future, that same British literature must feel both "wonderful" and as "little" as the place that had birthed it.

Not surprisingly, given his true identity, the anonymous reviewer had accurately characterized the method behind a book that many readers regarded as obscene madness cast in awkwardly broken lines: Whitman was aiming at something other and greater than a place at the British laureate's table. As "one of the roughs," the poetic persona behind *Leaves of Grass* laid claim to a more commanding title as bard of a new nation, a new era, and a new world.[10] To fulfill such a purpose it would not be enough to be acknowledged as a good poet; on the contrary, according to the standard set by Tennyson, Whitman would have to be judged bad enough to stand outside the generally accepted criteria of poetic excellence in English. Exchanging conventional aesthetic values for an independent national literature, Whitman had in his first book willfully abandoned the well-worn terrain of British precedents and started fresh with a spiritualized free verse he had first adopted in his 1850s news poems.

As George Eliot and other British readers were quick to note, Whitman had avoided conventional rhyme and meter with a purpose—namely, to suit an American freeman who was freed first and foremost from the Old World's shackles.[11] The unorthodox expressions of *Leaves of Grass* were English only in name; more fundamentally they were the hints and indications of a wholly different form of national memory emerging from a new continent. Just as a conforming "spirit" corresponded with an England conformed to monarchical and aristocratic traditionalism, so the review associates American freedom from aesthetic conformity with adherence to a presentist spirit. That spirit was the only real "law," the basis for the only true religion and the literature of a land Whitman now understood as free soil.

Because *Leaves of Grass* enacted an ambitiously nationalist memory project, "An English and an American Poet" toiled to increase the aesthetic distance separating the work of free verse that it described from the best poetry that preceded it and surrounded it, rejecting Shakespeare as a forebear and Tennyson as a peer. Not that there was any choice; the strange rhythms and unrhymed lines that characterized *Leaves of Grass* could hardly be more different from the regularly ordered constructions of Tennyson and other English poets. As the reviewer admitted, "Lovers and readers of poetry as hitherto written, may well be excused the chilly and unpleasant shudders which will assuredly run through them, to their very blood and bones, when they first read Walt Whitman's poems." Competing with Tennyson's readers on Tennyson's turf, Whitman was doomed to fail—but only, he anonymously insisted, because that turf was as indelibly English as England itself, even when it had been imported to an American parlor.[12]

The nature of true American turf, and the presentist form of national memory in which an authentic poetry could germinate, proved more difficult for the reviewer to describe than the traditionalist alternative. It is not merely the case that the forms of English memory had been established in a land that happened to be distant from America but rather that the lands themselves were different. All aspects of English memory would have to be transfigured in an America that refused to bow to precedents, British or otherwise. As Whitman's reviewer puts it, "Not a borrower from other lands, but a prodigal user of his own land is Walt Whitman." While he regarded Britons' conservation of their ancient island's past as proper for their national identity and a form of memory perfected for "the present phases of high-life in Great Britain," that model of land use no longer fit the United States. Mid-nineteenth-century America, prodigal with its own inheritance and its own land, offered a presentist mode of national memory that the reviewer implicitly recognized as the source of Whitman's new poetry. In *Leaves of Grass* Whitman had identified that new mode of memory closely with a model of news sharing still defined by Atlantic distance.[13]

Whitman's argument for independent and coherent national literatures seems out of keeping with the mid-1850s news environment dominated by national crisis. England, which the reviewer presented as a geographically and racially unified island country, had seen its interests thwarted in a distant land and had lost so many British troops in the Crimean War that it had resorted to soliciting American volunteers to fight for the crown under a foreign enlistment act.[14] Meanwhile *Leaves of Grass* first appeared during a summer when slavery and states' rights were dividing the same nation-state that Whitman's poetry celebrated, when rumblings of southern secessionists were growing from a whisper to a roar. Whitman therefore was hoping, with almost ludicrous optimism, to be a "prodigal user" of land that was being pulled apart by intensifying sectional conflict. In the midst of the battle raging over Kansas, his imagined American "freeman" might as easily invoke the division between northern and southern regions as the one between the Atlantic's eastern and western shore. Considering Kansas, the Crimea, Cuba, and the national confusions of the recruitment affair, Whitman's confidence in the nationalist unity of American and English readerships seems remarkably naïve.

Nevertheless, as chapter 3 demonstrated, this was not Whitman's first encounter with sectional strife nor his first attempt to address it by appealing to the international scene in his poetry. As he launched his poetic career in earnest in 1855 and 1856, he clearly understood that the United States' internal divisions, effected powerfully through popular print, might obstruct the development of national poetry. Yet he refused to recognize a significant division between slave and free states. This might have seemed nonsensical had it not reprised a conscious strategy Whitman had developed in his earlier news poems of 1850. Once again, he was reframing sectionalist tension as an international concern and uniting an American nationality he associated with presentism against British precedents and British-style American traditionalists.

Under acute domestic pressures, Whitman would seek international contrasts and conflicts, sharpening his poetic persona as the national bard on the wet stone of the international scene. Faced with the prospect of internal schism, he would attack sectionalism and transatlantic influence by treating them as parts of the same memory problem. Thus he sought to build his reputation as an authentically American writer through a strategic conflation of sectionalist and transatlantic pressures, casting both as similarly misguided refusals of an authentically presentist American nation. This strategy began to take early shape in poetic engagements with antislavery news in the years prior to the initial publication of *Leaves of Grass* in 1855, and it would shape the first two editions of Whitman's masterwork.

Furthermore, Whitman's approach was not as naïve as it seemed. If the splintering American nation and the possibility of a militarized Mason-Dixon line posed an obstacle to Whitman's quest to become the singer of a single unified nation, he nevertheless had some reason to look for hope from abroad. As widespread reports of British war fever indicated, transatlantic news registered intranational divisions on both sides of the ocean. Nevertheless, news of the controversies of 1855 and 1856 also showed Whitman and any other news reader that British anti-Americanism and the prospect of transatlantic war could still raise a nationalistic response at home. Thus Whitman could plausibly assume American readers might still regard the Atlantic as the most relevant national border and rally to a "union always surrounded by blatherers and always calm and impregnable."[15] Both 1855's *Leaves of Grass* and his careful promotion and repackaging of that material in subsequent months demonstrated this belief. Perhaps the same transatlantic division of shared history that structured the presentist memory of the news also could support a new national poetry, designed for the American freeman by a national bard.

American News and the 1855 Edition's Transatlantic Scene

As "An English and an American Poet" suggested, the first edition of *Leaves of Grass* framed its literary offering as an intervention into transatlantic memory. The opening paragraph of the book's long prose preface proclaimed to the Anglophonic globe that while "America does not repel the past," that past was no longer binding. The old life of Europe, having "served its requirements has passed into the new life of the new forms," relinquishing its proud place to "the stalwart and wellshaped heir who approaches." This heir, of course, was an independent American nation that claimed as a birthright the best of all that preceded it.[16]

Yet the approaching heir will always be approaching. Though commanding the past's legacies, Whitman's America will refuse to strike the bargain of begotten blood and will refuse to allow the past to prescribe its present movements. *Leaves of Grass* converted presentism to poetry, forging a tight connection between its chosen mode of memory, the distinctly American nation, and the form of its art. To the preface's author, the dawning modernity of the mid-nineteenth century belonged by rights to the New World and to a new sort of nation defined by its present diversity rather than an ancient heritage, "not merely a nation but a teeming nation of nations."[17]

Affirming the past only on the present's terms amounted to a wholesale denial of traditionalism as well as British authority: the American nation was not identified with the British heritage that most of its inhabitants claimed; it did not deny the past, but it did deny the call of transatlantic blood. As Kenneth Price has noted, many antebellum poets excused American writers' present deficiencies by heralding a future greatness vouchsafed by, in Whittier's phrase, "the proud blood of England's mightiest [coursing] through their veins." Price points out that while other American writers "might reassure themselves with thoughts of their English blood, Whitman scorned the very idea" as yet another sign of American dependency.[18]

Whitman's refusal to submit to an authoritative British past created an opening for the novelty of his free verse, but it served other purposes as well. By focusing on the British threat, Whitman engaged the America that Kansas had revealed, addressing the struggle over slavery and section without allowing it to overwhelm his devotion to a union that included the South. Whitman encouraged his early readers to meet such apparent internal division not with compromise between the sections but rather through an intersectional reprise of "the haughty defiance of '76" in every arena of American life at the expense of British authority and the past it safeguarded.[19] He located the avenue for achieving this feat in the presentist memory of modern news and his own modern verse.

Not surprisingly, this transatlantic strategy reveals itself most clearly in the 1855 edition's two news poems, both of which in different ways reflect upon transatlantic influence on the American scene. The first, "Resurgemus," already discussed as an early *Tribune* poem in chapter 3, reappears as the first edition's untitled eighth poem. The second is a typically overlooked poem that Whitman would ultimately title "A Boston Ballad," which immediately followed "Resurgemus." This latter poem memorialized the recent case of Anthony Burns, who gained national fame as a captured runaway a year before the publication of *Leaves*. When Burns was arrested and tried in Boston in 1854, he quickly became a cause célèbre. Compliance with the Fugitive Slave Law forced the court to return Burns to Virginia under federal pressure, and newspapers detailed the fugitive's procession under guard past a mortified Boston populace. The poignancy of this sad parade arose from Boston's coerced complicity in slavery's sudden appearance. The dramatic confrontation horrified northern witnesses far and wide, because it confirmed that slavery could stain the streets of any town in the free states.

The Burns affair echoed other celebrated instances of recently recaptured fugitive slaves, including that of Thomas Sims in Boston, whose removal had prompted Emerson to take a strong public stand against slavery. The Sims rendition, which took place in April 1851, served as an important backdrop to Whitman's poem. It shared several obvious details with the Burns case, and Emerson and other abolitionists had periodically commemorated it as a mark of shame within the antislavery movement.[20] Like the Sims rendition, the Burns affair confirmed Whitman's earlier certainty that the Compromise of 1850 had saved the Union only by sacrificing the national spirit, even as it ceded local control of northern communities to the "Southern lords."[21] Rendition cases underscored the North's subservience to slavery as a national institution, and the price of the traditionalist nationalism on which slavery's authority was based. Little wonder then that many northern observers saw the Burns case as an ominous incursion by the South with its slave power.

Whitman saw things somewhat differently. Whereas other northerners identified Boston's enforcement of the Fugitive Slave Act as a sign of insidious southern power, Whitman saw the hand of transatlantic influence and a set of villains similar to those he identified in "Resurgemus" as the reactionary killers of revolutionary young men. Much like the Kansas-Nebraska Act, which President Pierce signed into law within a week of Burns's capture, publicity surrounding the case enflamed northern fury against the South, converting the abstractions of sectional strife into a specific shared concern among legions of northern news readers.[22] As a dedicated unionist, Whitman sought to redirect those passions away from southerners and toward an English antagonist who was at once more distant and more intimate than the southern slave power.

Strange as it seems, Whitman interpreted the Burns sentence as evidence that many northerners were still losing the old battle against the same British aristocratic and monarchical traditions that he would also argue typified British poetry and compromised American literature. Thus *Leaves of Grass* frames the Burns incident as an international struggle against British power and memory rather than as a conflict with the South. "A Boston Ballad" expresses Whitman's yearning for a transatlantic struggle to replace the civil conflict that was dividing the same national readership *Leaves of Grass* hoped to cultivate.[23]

Jerome Loving, whose biography mines Whitman's early newspaper poems for insights into his antislavery beliefs, points out that much like the Revolutions of 1848 the sensational account of the Burns case had become such a familiar news story by the time "A Boston Ballad" appeared that Whitman did not have to mention the case's details.[24] Yet Whitman's refusal to name the subject did not merely reflect a national audience's familiarity with a news event; it also reflected upon how such news functioned as shared history to create that audience and bring it to self-consciousness. The story's familiarity allowed Whitman to discuss the event without noting the primary cause of its notoriety: namely, an abusive southern power and northern reaction to it. For Whitman, that sort of familiarity presented a major threat to the Union, and his poem attempted to redirect his audience's powerful anti-southern response toward a British-styled traditionalism. Ironically, the most relevant racial category in the poem is neither white nor black but rather British. The enemy in the poem is not the South but rather what Whitman would call in his later self-review "the facts of the English race, the monarchy and aristocracy prominent over the rest" and the political and literary orientation "that conforms to the spirit of them."[25] In today's parlance, "A Boston Ballad" was a striking exhibition of political "spin"; faced with a sensationalized media event that widened the sectional divide, the poem reinterprets that news item as a call to renew America's independence from British values and traditions.

Bones of King George: Whitman Internationalizes the National Crisis

This transatlantic objective helps explain why Whitman chose to include the poem in the first edition of *Leaves of Grass*. Hoping to serve as a national bard of both North and South, Whitman had little reason to once again raise this threatening specter of sectional conflict in 1855. But rather than avoid the Burns affair, he crafted a poem that resurrected the old revolutionary struggle with Britain as an alternative to sectionalism. "A Boston Ballad" replaces the doughface congressmen and pusillanimous northern politicians of Whitman's early antislavery poems with a fresh slate of American Tories—shills for British values of monarchical rule and traditionalist social order. "A Boston Ballad" made the implicitly Anglophobic slant of Whitman's earlier antislavery poetry explicit by dramatically refiguring the peculiar American institution as a cadaverous heirloom of Europe's moldering vaults.

The poem's first lines initiate this transatlantic perspective by addressing "Jonathan," the character who personified the United States in its relation to

John Bull.²⁶ "Clear the way there Jonathan! / Way for the President's marshal! Way for the government cannon!" the narrator commands.²⁷ By issuing this command to move, Whitman's narrator maintains his own ironic positioning, which depends largely on his critical capacity to stand temporarily apart from an American "Jonathan" and other national icons in the poem, such as the Stars and Stripes and Yankee Doodle. Thus he can derisively measure the distance between such showy nationalistic displays and the apparent lack of American commitment to the spirit they represented.

As he had in "Resurgemus," Whitman in "A Boston Ballad" links a monarchical and repressive Old World to American slavery. Now, though, that foreign element appeared at the heart of Boston in the town's tacit support of government-sanctioned slave catchers. Alluding obliquely to the crowds gathered to watch Burns's forced extradition, the poem's narrator initially seems to support the government action with his own commands. Yet the domineering tone only underscores the uneasy subservience of a citizenry who had failed to uphold not only the antislavery cause but also the spirit of presentist freedom. Thus when the grief-stricken ghosts of America's revolutionary heroes appear, the narrator directs these "Yankee phantoms" "back to the hills" around Boston.²⁸ As nearly all of his readers would have been aware, these were the very hills that Daniel Webster, traditionalist broker of the 1850 Compromise, had identified as sacred pillars supporting the union of slave and free states in his "Bunker Hill Monument Address." It was this same union that Webster sought to maintain in his notorious speech of March 7, 1850, and its defense of the strengthened Fugitive Slave Law that now sent Burns back to his southern masters.²⁹

As chapter 3 demonstrated, Whitman had followed Emerson in attacking Webster for deploying revolutionary memory as a traditionalist hedge against fresh outbreaks of revolutionary spirit. Whitman's figurative description of the ghostly train also traces this Emersonian vein by creatively identifying the fatal flaw in Webster's unionist rhetoric: namely, the senator's assumption that America's revolutionary legacy could accommodate itself to any contemporary political position short of disunion. Burns became a test case for this theory, for his rendition introduced into the streets of Boston an American Toryism every bit as conservative as the regime the American Revolutionaries had bled to overthrow. By locating the only true patriots among the phantoms of the revolutionary generation, Whitman hoists Webster on his own petard: by sacrificing liberty for expediency, the compromisers had secured a nominal and moribund union and abandoned a republic founded on vivid principle.

Whitman's narrator steadily builds a bitterly sardonic critique of such shortsighted unionism. Throughout the poem, the narrator increasingly alienates the contemporary Boston scene from its close connection to the revolutionary heritage, culminating in a climactic ironic endorsement for the dead British king's coronation—an act that symbolically repudiates the patriots' goals and sacrifices by resurrecting tyrannical monarchs in America. His final assessment of "Boston town" suggests that the patriots' old foe, King George III, would have been perfectly comfortable among liberty's compromisers, those American contemporaries who had betrayed the revolutionary spirit during the Burns affair.

Thus the narrator declares that the tearful revolutionaries forced to bring up the parade line at Burns's extradition no longer "belong" in the streets of Boston. For a true representative of the town's unnaturally retrograde spirit, the people will have to "send a committee to England, / They shall get a grant from the Parliament, and go with a cart to the royal vault, / Dig out King George's coffin—unwrap him quick from the graveclothes—box up his bones for a journey."[30] Having identified Westminster Abbey as the sepulcher of present-day compromisers' true fathers, Whitman ends the poem with a derisive image of the skeleton of George III reigning over a suddenly monarchical Boston, a once-proud community that a few generations before had fired the shot heard round the world.

The poem transforms Burns's expulsion from Massachusetts into a royal mandate as well as federal order, and Jonathan's failure to resist such coercion in the final lines offers more than a symbol of ethical impotence coupled with greed. "Stick your hands in your pockets Jonathan," Whitman's narrator concludes, for "you are a made man from this day, / You are mighty cute—and here is one of your bargains."[31] Like those who resolved the 1850 crisis, and those who sent Thomas Sims back to Georgia, the appeasers of the Burns affair commended moral compromise for the sake of commerce and peace. But the poem also equates that avaricious flexibility with a failure to recognize the gift of a liberated present as the true legacy of the revolutionary separation from Britain and its king.

"A Boston Ballad" follows "Resurgemus" in the first edition, and like the earlier news poem, it both seeks out transatlantic reference points to criticize national faithlessness and also aligns monarchical regimes with American slavery. Stripped of all specific reference to the Burns case, the poem locates its sole subject in the evils of British influence. It contains no mention of slavery or, more to the point, the South. Yet by including the poem within the 1855 volume in which it first appeared, Whitman also tied the American rejection of a slave system fit for a king—George III, in this case—to his larger effort to liberate American poetry from its British antecedents. The poem's framing of revolutionary memory reveals that Whitman is less interested in standing up to the South than in reinforcing American democracy's antagonistic relationship to traditionalism, to the Old World, and especially to Britain. To the extent that Boston's return of a fugitive to his master mitigated the essential transatlantic distinction upon which the United States had been founded, the Burns affair appears in *Leaves of Grass* as a repudiation of the American Revolution and America's democratic identity.

Thus the transatlantic world—"England" and "Parliament" as well as "King George's coffin"—hangs as a looming specter over a distinctly American liberty. In both poems, Europe's ghostly presence takes shape in an America haunted less by the past than by a traditionalist threat. Similarly, while Whitman had at least alluded to the "slave-breeders" in "Song for a Certain Congressman," "A Boston Ballad" ironically decries American hypocrisy without explicitly citing the southern slave power.

Ignoring this aspect of intersectional politics represents a significant elision. Whitman obviously knew that since 1850 northern fury had been growing in response to similar intrusions by southern interests into local environments. The poem, moreover, is perfectly willing to identify features of the Boston locale and to vilify federal power under the Fugitive Slave Law. Indeed, from its opening line the poem evokes the town's local spaces and population by ordering them to make "way" for the symbols of a compromised national power: "the President's marshal," "government cannon!" and "the federal foot and dragoons."[32] This sort of coercion, which requires Jonathan to vacate his natural place in his city, obliterates precisely the sort of particularized local experience that the greatest poems in *Leaves of Grass* celebrate.

Yet Whitman's oddly placed speaker mitigates an otherwise negative appraisal of a hobbled American nation-state by casting it as a pale imitation of an utterly moribund British model of monarchy and deference. He holds a position both within and apart from Boston, and in his ironic criticism he maintains the potential for an alternative nationalist space. In his embodied voice, which criticizes Jonathan's hypocrisy along with that of contemporary Bostonians, a measure of nationalist hope resides. Indeed, he appears as an outsider come to Boston to take in the parade: "I rose this morning early to get betimes in Boston town," he relates to the reader. "Here's a good place at the corner. . . . I must stand and see the show."[33] Later he will adopt a similar position to address the "Yankee phantoms," their descendants—the "smart grandsons [and] their wives [who] gaze at them from the windows"—and the "gentlemen of Boston."[34]

Whitman had not yet visited Boston when he published the poem in 1855.[35] Indeed, the narrator's perspective roughly corresponds to that of the New York newspaper reporters who allowed Whitman to witness the sad parade that carried Burns back to bondage in the summer of 1854, and, less directly, as that of Whitman himself as a New York news reader. The *Tribune* of June 3, 1854, suggests such an interpretation, for it contained a series of dispatches beginning early on the morning of June 2 and coverage that established many details that Whitman's poem relates; these included descriptions of the spectators lining Boston's streets and windows on the previous day, the federal forces, and even references to the Revolutionary-era controversies over quartered troops.[36] That day's news also demonstrated that the population around Boston had been moved by the radical Unitarian preacher Theodore Parker to protest as well as witness the state's deference to slave power by draping buildings in black and tolling bells in neighboring towns.[37]

All this indicates that, in rehearsing the local crisis in Boston as a news event shared via telegraph and cheap newsprint in New York, and in highlighting through his narrator a response that honored the Revolution's spirit, Whitman was evoking not merely the Burns rendition but the presentist memory circuit it sparked. This model of national memory clearly contrasted to the traditionalist version the poem abominates, and the true slave power represented by the corpse of King George. As a vision of empowered news reading and response, "A Boston Ballad" offers a more productive avenue by which a form of national power might intrude upon the local scene and organize identity around a much more recent past. The poem's satirical savaging of a traditionalist expression of American nationalism is, from this perspective, premised upon a more positive presentist model. Founded on news sharing, it was also linked to what Parker called, in a sermon two days after the extradition, "the spirit of our fathers—the spirit of justice and liberty in your heart, and in my heart, and in the hearts of us all."[38] The religious vitality and political potential Whitman saw in this sort of presentist alternative helps explain the poet's eagerness to appeal to Anglophobia rather than merely abolitionism and thus somewhat improbably to figure a sensationalized intersectional dispute as a conflict with a diabolically traditionalist foreign power.

That power could only be exerted through the sort of transatlantic memory circuit the poem imaginatively enacts. Exhuming King George, Whitman taps into the distrust antebellum northerners instinctively felt toward British meddling as well as their militant pride in the Revolutionary War, redirecting his readers' crusading belligerence away from the South and toward that "wonderful little island" that could not share American news. Indeed, in order to gain an audience with the dead King George, the traditionalists in Boston and in the national government would have to complete a far lengthier transatlantic circuit. They would have to "send a committee to England," as the narrator advises, there to "find a swift Yankee clipper—here is freight for you blackbellied clipper,/Up with your anchor! shake out your sails!—steer straight toward Boston bay."[39] In this transatlantic exchange, which is also a new British invasion, a dead past can only be shared as slowly circulating freight; yet the narrator's own position, and that of Whitman himself as a near instantaneous witness to "Boston town," indicates precisely the lively and liberated form of shared history upon which a true national poetry could be based.

"A Boston Ballad," as many readers have observed, is not a great poem. Yet it contains within it a compelling reflection on the sharing of both transatlantic and national history. Its inclusion within the first edition of *Leaves of Grass* may be justified by its indirect gesture to the domestic news as a mnemonic support for Whitman's free verse and by its corresponding repudiation of British memory as the ultimate source of slavery and thus American divisions. For a poet who would define himself as aesthetically and spiritually committed to the American union, the intersectional hostility stirred up by the Burns affair posed an obvious problem that "A Boston Ballad" attempted to ameliorate. The poem's strategic deployment of the news to vanquish an old transatlantic foe neatly avoided sectionalism and made American slavery, somewhat counterintuitively, a foreign-based threat to revolutionary presentist memory. This same transatlantic memory war would echo through the first three editions of *Leaves of Grass*. It would transmute sectional divisions into an Emersonian-style quarrel between the young democracy of Whitman's poetry and aristocratic Europe's debased politics and invidious literary influence.[40]

"Feel the Ground Swell": Recalling News and Nation

"A Boston Ballad" attacked sectionalism indirectly. Like its partner poem, "Resurgemus," it conflated slavery with transatlantic traditionalism while offering an alternative approach to national memory based in America's sharing of news. Yet the American news's content challenged Whitman's attempt to displace ongoing sectional animosities onto a foreign opponent. Signs that American news readers were dividing along hardening sectional lines could be found in the front pages of the same newspapers from which Whitman had drawn his poetic vision of Burns's expulsion from Boston.

The same June 3 edition of the *Tribune* that Whitman might have gotten up early to read, for example, displayed the growing sectional breach on an editorial page stocked with sectional fury. In addition to a scathing attack on those who had colluded in Burns's capture, Greeley's morning paper would have featured prominent reactions to Virginia's efforts to overcome the personal liberty laws of New York. Southerners hoping to bring their slaves north without fear, the *Tribune* complained, were seeking "to overthrow the local law of this State, and extend the local law of Virginia over us."[41]

Yet it was the Kansas-Nebraska Act's passage that earned the *Tribune*'s most violently sectional response:

> The Northern people are not a dueling or a bowie-knife people, and are slow to move to earnest strife. But when they are roused they are very apt to make their resistance tell.... We already feel the ground swell beneath our feet, and we see the distant clouds gathering in the sky which betoken the storm which is to wreck these fond expectations and overwhelm those faithless men who have betrayed the North, in a wild and stormy sea of political commotion.... If [the slave states] propose to secede in the event of the North's demanding and obtaining the exclusion of Slavery from Kansas and Nebraska, they had better lose no time in preparing to go.... We tell the Southern invaders that they have gone one step too far this time.[42]

If such prominent statements of national divisions were not enough to convince Whitman of the challenges a unionist poet would face, the *Tribune* also advertised at the top of the page "The North and the South: A Pamphlet of Forty Pages, Containing a series of articles reprinted from The New-York Tribune."[43] Just below this advertisement was another, however, pitched "to advertisers." It was for the *Weekly Tribune*, which with a circulation of 110,000, was "undoubtedly the best advertising medium in the United States." "Those who wish to make their business known to the country," the ad asserted, "would do well to try the *Weekly Tribune*."[44] If Greeley's paper seemed busy dividing the country by bolstering northern resolve, it was simultaneously tying it together, especially by connecting the eastern regions of New England and the mid-Atlantic to newer midwestern states through its weekly edition.

Considering the incendiary content of the *Tribune* pamphlet, these advertisements seem starkly contradictory. Yet both can be interpreted as hypernationalist expressions that articulate more robust national attachments to country through the geographical expansion of news.[45] Similarly, when the *Tribune* challenged hesitant northern readers to oppose southern slave power more firmly, it was merely repeating a dialed-down version of the charge it regularly leveled against doughface politicians—namely, that they were not bound closely enough to the area they represented to stand up for its free state status. The paper typically accused these northern accomplices in the southern agenda—those both Whitman and Greeley had previously branded as Judases in its pages—of caring for nothing but money and therefore having no country. Within the United States' representative system, their selling of votes amounted to auctioning off their attachment to home states and districts. In demanding deeper northern commitments, therefore, the *Tribune* was not exactly repudiating the standing union of states but rather demanding a deeper connection to the terra firma of one's country.[46]

Something similar was happening in the South. William Gilmore Simms, who had been one of Whitman's predecessors in calling for an independent American literature, shifted his allegiance and began to argue that southern letters needed to be liberated from northern publishing dominance.[47] That same year Simms would ask his fellow southerners, "Are we to draw our intellectual sustenance from the bosom of a distant and imperious relative, instead of from a mother?" This was precisely the sort of question Whitman (or an only slightly earlier version of Simms) would have asked concerning British influence, but the "imperious relative" Simms meant was not Britain but the North.[48] Simms had posed the question in the *Southern Quarterly Review* a few months after the Burns affair, and like Whitman's Burns poem, his concerns reflected the sectionalist upheavals spurred by the Kansas-Nebraska Act. Yet what he was calling for was not so different from what he had once hoped to achieve in declaring American literary independence from British dominance, or what Greeley and Whitman implicitly demanded from fellow northerners. The core critique of the status quo stemmed from an idealized nationality founded on proximity and immediacy in opposition to distance and abstraction. In transferring allegiance from the United States to the South, Simms appears a fickle nationalist, but this misses the point that Simms was always driving at: in all its forms his nationalism sought out a relatively familiar and localized public attachment for literature as well as politics.

Confusing in many ways, his stance becomes comprehensible as a hypernationalist response to a crisis in nationalism that absorbed the Anglo-American world. Rhetorically at least, he is most keen to support neither slavery nor even the South. Rather, the sustenance he seeks is the familial sustenance of national memory. Simms was certainly politically opposed to Whitman in 1856. Nevertheless, both writers sought a revitalized version of national literature by narrowing their vision of place and history; faced with evidence of anemic attachments and partisan rancor rife within larger cultural systems of federalism and Anglophone culture, each was rejecting them in favor of a more intimate relation to blood, land, and spirit.

Almost by definition, the broader Anglophone culture could not provide this sort of belonging. As the common basis for all literatures in English, it instead set the negative standard for Simms's positive accounts of literature as mother's milk. Resistance to the abstractions that Anglophone news presented throughout 1855 and 1856 inspired the northern press to vent hostility toward British claims on America as well as increasingly virulent anti-southern feelings. But inasmuch as national feeling arose from a sense of relative rather than absolute proximity, its attachments remained somewhat arbitrary and (as Simms proved) could be adjusted.[49]

Thus, considered as signs of potentially portable nationalist feeling, the divisive sectionalist disputes of the mid-1850s represented a resource as well as an obstacle for a would-be national bard. Whitman could not refute such hypernationalist passions in the name of cool compromise. Instead he sought to redeploy them as a firebreak against secession by redirecting them toward the old British foe. In this effort, Whitman would find a surprising ally in partisan news. For although the northern newspapers had muddled nationalist identifications with reports of sectionalized public responses to the Kansas crisis, they had also publicized Britain's meddling in the Western Hemisphere and reminded American audiences of a more dramatic transatlantic distinction in news sharing.

Drawing inspiration from the potential to share domestic news with relative immediacy, Whitman's 1855 and 1856 editions of *Leaves of Grass* recast the transatlantic information cycle as an argument for a unified national literature. As the Crimean recruitment scandal broke open, eventually leading to the expulsion of British diplomats in the summer of 1856, Whitman set about publishing the second edition of *Leaves of Grass*.

In this expanded edition, the poet would aggressively resist British influence as a greater national threat than sectionalism and would repudiate slavery as an international traditionalist conspiracy to undermine America's presentist ideals.

Thus his most explicit attack on slavery that summer focused on the international slave trade and Cuba; published in *Life Illustrated* in August, "The Slave Trade" would train its ire on northern contributions to a global slave economy, noting the departure of slave ships from New York and Salem, Massachusetts, to supply labor to horrific Cuban plantations that the old Spanish overlords had imposed on the island. The challenge to the American nation in the piece arrives not from sectionalist violence but an absent passion for the inherently presentist liberty of an imagined New World.[50]

The second edition of *Leaves of Grass* delivered on this presentist ideal of freedom through form and content. It framed the sharing of news on the domestic memory circuit as a practice that could keep national unity in creative tension with British historical and literary traditionalism. In the poet's visionary future, the United States could transcend its own divisions only by finalizing its poetic and political break with Britain, expanding inexorably into a real and figurative West, and eventually, like the prophetic vision of Israel, drawing all nations to itself. But to achieve this the entity that Whitman denominated "The States" would have to overcome the challenge exposed by expansion into Kansas and actually become "united." Whitman would later summarize the objectives of *Leaves of Grass* to Horace Traubel by insisting that "above everything else it stands for unity," but this unity required a new politics as well as a new poetics, and both forms of unity depended on highlighting transatlantic divisions.[51]

All the antebellum editions of *Leaves of Grass* to some degree sought to convert sectional divisions into a quarrel between the young nation of Whitman's new poetry and old England's abiding political and literary influence. The 1856 edition, which packed twenty new poems along with the twelve from the quarto-sized first edition into a barely pocket-sized format, worked in concert with the very recently published 1855 edition to pursue that end in a particularly powerful way. It included several new poems that focused on Anglo-American tensions, raised the specter of transatlantic traditionalism, and emphasized America's special connection to the recent past and future. It also repackaged those from the year before in ways that reinforced that forward thrust. It would, for example, reprint both the news poems of 1855, "Resurgemus" and "A Boston Ballad," which had appeared untitled but in sequence in the previous version of *Leaves of Grass*. In 1856, however, they receive dates as well as titles that mark them as celebrations of the lively spirit of 1776 that Whitman associated with antislavery's presentist crusade. Their dating places their international themes firmly within a recent American history organized according to its own nationalist calendar: "Poem of the Dead Young Men of Europe, the 72d and 73d Years of These States" and "Poem of Apparitions in Boston, the 78th Year of These States." Whitman's dating identifies the Declaration of Independence (rather than the Constitution) as the point of origin shared by all states, making the Revolution's refusal of traditionalist authority the characterizing mark of the North and South's shared spiritual history.

Whitman's new arrangement also places these similarly titled poetic reflections on the Revolutions of 1848 and Burns's extradition in the midst of poems that present the United States as the nationalizer of universal truth, the country that gives a divine spirit a particular place and time in which to operate. Whitman's arrangement surrounds these internationally themed news poems with poems emphasizing the relatively intimate scene around which American news revolves, contrasting universals to particulars and the past to the present. Thus the news poems appear in their 1856 context as confirmation that the founding of America represents the apotheosis of a new presentist orientation to memory, one which all people contain as a potential and which true American poetry must embody. Liberty, whether found in free people or free verse, begins for Whitman with liberty from the authoritative past of traditionalist memory. Although souls the world over yearn for such liberty, America had given it a place to practice its unique relation to history.[52] In their 1856 forms, "Poem of the Dead Young Men of Europe, the 72d and 73d Years of These States" and "Poem of Apparitions in Boston, the 78th Year of These States" mutually reinforce internal motifs involving spiritual apparitions and resurrection; taken together they suggest that the global spirit of liberty will receive its body in the perfection of an American nation that refuses to bow to tradition. Reconfiguring his calendar of historical events around America's revolutionary impulse rather than Jesus's birth, the second edition expands on an idea that "An English and an American Poet" had also proposed: namely, that poetry could "compete" with the "works of nature" and stand in such perfect relation to historical experience that it became its own divinely inspired form of American history.[53]

In part because the 1856 edition followed so closely on the heels of the first, Whitman would not only allude to American news but also symbolically reproduce its circulating effects. Indeed, despite the general tendency to privilege the first edition as Whitman's masterpiece, there is some reason to regard the two, separated by scarcely a year and appearing under the same title, as a single effort on the part of Whitman to introduce his mature poetry to the world. For only as a double iteration did *Leaves of Grass* allow Whitman to also introduce the world back into his poetry in the form of a special section of reprinted reviews and responses that appeared at the end of the 1856 edition. The second version of *Leaves of Grass* thus can present itself as a stage in a circuit of memory, one that records reciprocal loops of shared history in which it is fundamentally implicated. In this capacity, it functions less like a typical book and more like a nineteenth-century national newspaper: it structures its content around an assumed audience of present-day readers situated on the cusp of a future response, but it also records that response as part of its content. Thus it operates as a kind of living symbol of a presentist memory circuit.

The approach is consistent with Whitman's history as a newspaper writer and editor whose early poetry, as chapter 3 showed, also sought to engage this sort of temporality through form and content. Yet in the intervening years the sectionalist conflict had provided fresh urgency to the presentist project that sought to link national memory to the most recent past. Nowhere is Whitman's dominant presentist aesthetic more literally embodied than in the tight connection the poet built between the first two editions of his first book. It is no coincidence that he undertook this project at a time when nations seemed to be eroding more each day in the transatlantic news.

What *Leaves* Left Behind: Whitman's Embodied Memory Circuit

The first edition of *Leaves of Grass*, published with a run of 795 copies, was first advertised in the *Tribune* on July 6, 1855. The first poem, which would later be titled "Song of Myself," introduces itself as a song of the reader as well: "I celebrate myself, / And what I assume you shall assume / For every atom belonging to me as good belongs to you." Again and again through the lengthy poem and much that follows it, Whitman demands his readers share in his own intimate history of self; body, soul, and world, he builds a context for collective memory around his own poetic "I." But he also assumes that the book was merely the launching point of a memory circuit that would prompt thousands of readers to celebrate themselves as well. The book thus begins by calling on its reader to locate his or her own authenticity by sharing in the poet's recent history. Though it found few buyers, it soon garnered the responses that it demanded from a small number of advocates. The most important was Emerson, to whom Whitman had sent a complimentary copy of the first edition. Emerson had read it quickly and rapturously. But as he would write in his sparkling response on July 21, "I did not know until I, last night, saw the book advertised in a newspaper, that I could trust the name as real & available for a Post-office. I wish to see my benefactor, & have felt much like striking my tasks, & visiting New York to pay you my respects."[54]

Beyond the extraordinary good fortune of gaining a proof of admiration from one of America's most influential writers, Whitman must have been gratified by Emerson's air of urgent immediacy and his rehearsal of the circuit of increasingly intimate connections into which Whitman's book had woven him. As a reader, Emerson had shared in Whitman's poetic remembrance of his recent past, then had been convinced of Whitman's reality by a newspaper, which had led to an intimate letter and, even more important, the desire for an immediate face-to-face visit to Whitman's New York home.

Rather than savoring this sign of intimate attachment alone, Whitman cast the letter back into the news cycle, sending it to Horace Greeley, who had also publicly heralded Whitman's "rare poetic gifts."[55] It appeared in October, the same month as "An English and an American Poet," and it gave English as well as American reviewers further incentive to plumb the book for the greatness the Sage of Concord had apparently seen in a rough poet from Brooklyn.[56] As one British reviewer of *Leaves of Grass* (ruefully if not sarcastically) explained, "What Emerson has pronounced to be good must not be lightly treated."[57]

Armed with these reviews, his own self-congratulatory assessments, and Emerson's all-important imprimatur, Whitman made its first update impossible to overlook even by those who would leave it unread: brazenly drawing on what must have seemed to many an already overtaxed endorsement, Whitman emblazoned the volume's spine with Emerson's generous salutation: "I greet you at the beginning of a great career." Whitman had not secured Emerson's permission to share his private response, so the packaging of the second edition was, by most lights, an extreme breach of etiquette, a tawdry ploy gaudily paraded in gold letters.

Yet from another perspective, Emerson's blurb imprinted the body of Whitman's book with a symbol of its past and future as a medium of shared and sacred history. If Whitman's new collection of his poetry began with "I celebrate myself / And what I assume you shall assume," the book itself began with Emerson's delivery on that promise, his "I" greeting Whitman's "you" in kind. There on the spine where the reader would place her hand lay the trace of the shared history it had already brought into being. Moreover, because Whitman had chosen a line from the letter that pointed not to the past but to the future, that 1856 reader was enveloped in the same cycle of memory in which the poet and the Sage of Concord were already bound. Undoubtedly, Whitman was making the most of a means to notoriety. Nevertheless, the response-driven logic of *Leaves* suggests that Whitman was extending Emerson's celebratory salutation beyond himself and to the ordinary reader's own "career."

In doing so he was merely fulfilling Emerson's own expectations for American poets and American scholars. Moreover, though it departs from ordinary understandings of critical endorsements, such a generous reading of Whitman's unorthodox 1856 boast is consistent with the poet's brand of egotism, which (like Emerson's) is always consciously pushing beyond itself to grant equal or greater license to his readers. Whitman linked his self-presentation as an author who was keen to be surpassed by his readers with the larger American problem of traditionalist authority and the dangerous potential of his own words to become such an authority that would constrain the future liberty of others. As he put it in "Song of Myself," which he titled "Poem of Walt Whitman, an American" in the 1856 edition, "He most honors my style who learns under it to destroy the teacher."[58] Whitman's vision of national memory, like his breed of poetry, could not merely be a matter of the present showing deference to an honored past, even if that past included his own works. To do so was no safer than raising the corpse of King George.

Thus, in terms of its relation to the traditionalist authority, the second edition of *Leaves of Grass* actually held a more crucial position than the first, because it helped Whitman put the good news he preached into practice. By referring self-consciously to *Leaves of Grass* as a living entity that was still growing, Whitman was able to build a cycling memory circuit from his own words and those who responded to them, and out of that movement to demonstrate the model of presentist memory that he saw as America's unique heritage and destiny.

Partly to make this point, Whitman excised his original 1855 prose preface, replacing it with material that echoed the preface's prophecy that the United States required a new form of poetry and was itself a new kind of poem. He reiterated that sentiment, along with many key passages from the preface, in "Poem of Many In One," which begins "A nation announcing itself" and insists, "Mighty bards have done their work, and passed to other spheres, / One work forever remains, the work of surpassing all they have done."[59] In a telling revision of the first words of the first edition, "America does not repel the past," the poetic update offers a list of seeming qualifications that are in fact clarifications:

> America, curious toward foreign characters, stands sternly by its own,
> Stands removed, spacious, composite, sound,
> Sees itself promulger of men and women, initiates the true use of precedents,
> Does not repel them or the past or what they have produced under their forms, or amid other politics, or amid the idea of castes, or the old religions.[60]

Whitman's America, like his memory circuit, did not reject the past; it nevertheless entirely refused the notion of traditionalist authority in the name of a thriving present diversity. It perceived its identity in the true men and women of the future rather than any Old World heritage, and it initiated a new form of sacred memory through the "true use of precedents" by an authoritative contemporary moment. All that had preceded contemporary America became intimate and potent only by becoming subservient and useful to Whitman's modern compatriots, the nation's "own" who must remain merely curious about the "foreign characters" who had so often overawed these novice nationalists in part because they represented the traditionalist authority of the past. Thus the nationalism of the aptly named "Poem of the Many in One" conflates time with space to refuse an embodied relation to foreign characters still enslaved by their histories.[61]

Several other changes to the 1856 edition helped set *Leaves of Grass* firmly within this alternative American circuit of shared history and apart from such foreign characters bound by traditionalist attachments to the past. "Leaves-Droppings," appended at the end of the book, demonstrated the limited appeal Whitman's poetry exercised on British readers and the reprinted endorsement by an unquestionably American character in Emerson. Essentially a reprise of reviews, "Leaves-Droppings" allowed Whitman not only to trumpet Emerson's one-page letter but also to publish his own thirteen-page prose response to it, in which the poet estimated "the average annual call for my Poems [at] ten or twenty thousand copies— more, quite likely." This odd afterword, like the book's spine, seemed rudely to abuse Emerson's gracious act. It allowed a relatively unknown literary renegade to acknowledge the father of transcendentalism as "friend and master," peer and forbear—and to drag a literary eminence into an appallingly crass public relations campaign.[62]

Yet seen in the context of Whitman's challenge to traditionalism in all its forms, this immoderate act of self-aggrandizement also becomes a presentist intervention. All Whitman's efforts did not immediately drive Whitman's sales anywhere near the level he predicted. They did, however, make Whitman more difficult to ignore, and today they provide an important insight into the poet's vision of his relationship to his audience. If, as Ivan Marki suggests, the original 1855 preface had set up a test to determine whether the poems that followed constituted a new national poetry, the 1856 supplement sought to prove that Whitman had passed that exam by providing evidence of a circuit of sacred presentist memory.[63] In calling Emerson both his reader and his "master," and simultaneously hinting that Whitman would go beyond him, he was also projecting a circuit of shared history and a model of presentist remembering that he hoped his own readers would adopt by the thousands. Implicitly, Whitman presents both Emerson and himself as inspired readers of each other's work at the beginning of a brilliant career that was always just beginning; locked in a tight cycle of mutual influence, both proceeded together. Brothers and friends as well as master and disciple, they traveled the cutting edge of a sacred national history forged by modern news.[64]

Further indications that Whitman was not merely using Emerson for simple self-promotion can also be found in the body of reviews he reprinted in "Leaves-Droppings." These critiques did not contradict his egotism but rather supplied a further rationale for his boasting, though not because they were all glowing in their praise. In general Whitman did not shy away from negative or quizzical responses to his work so long as they were predicated on his distinctiveness. As one of his biographers notes, "He was undeterred by hostile critics, whose attacks he almost relished."[65]

Yet this does not go quite far enough, for the attacks were not merely privately relished but also intentionally publicized. Indeed, early criticism fueled a publicity campaign premised on nationalist divisions, and even in his self-reviews Whitman seemed happy to model both his poetry's formal unconventionality and its manifold rejections by conventional readers. Thus both the positive and negative reviews in "Leaves-Droppings" shared a common element that justified their inclusion. All of them recognize the obvious lack of orthodoxy in his verse, and with only one exception, Whitman's handpicked reviews explicitly characterized him as a national poet with a uniquely American and resolutely non-British modern voice. This conclusion is hardly surprising given that the bulk of these observations were offered either by the poet himself or by transatlantic readers. Of the nine reviews represented in "Leaves-Droppings" four are from British journals, and two, including "An English and an American Poet," are likely by an anonymous Whitman. In sum, Whitman's British critics, perhaps especially those who condemned him, ratified his self-advertised image as the prototypical American.[66]

In particular, the British reviews were able to confirm the distinction between Whitman's American originality and the more imitative American poets that had come before. Perhaps influenced by Emerson's support, one reviewer regarded this new "American prodigy" in the light of America's anxiety "that she has no national poet—that each one of her children of song has relied too much on European inspiration, and clung too fervently to the old conventionalities." While some British critics responded more positively than others, all recognized Whitman as a uniquely American voice. In the first line of the opinions section of "Leaves-Droppings," the *London Weekly Dispatch* declares *Leaves of Grass* "one of the most extraordinary specimens of Yankee intelligence and American eccentricity in authorship, it is possible to conceive."[67]

Other British journals echoed the assessment, with the more negative British reviews identifying the nationalistic peculiarities of *Leaves of Grass* in order to characterize them as indictments of American society at large, which produced not only the poet but also readers willing to adopt his vision of shared national history. The reviewers, in other words, could comment on the original *Leaves* not merely as a book but also as an alienated memory circuit.[68] George Eliot summarized the early responses on either side of the Atlantic, noting that Whitman had "been received by a section of his countrymen as a sort of prophet, and by Englishmen as a kind of fool."[69]

Alienated transatlantic observers who censured the response among this prophet's countrymen merely played into Whitman's plan to articulate a presentist mode of shared history. Similarly, by contrasting American and British public responses, they underscored his poems' lawless forms, moral indiscretions, and refusals of convention as profoundly American shortcomings, unwittingly providing arrows for the national bard's quiver. Foreign critics might use this strange new poetry to condemn an inherently vulgar American democracy's failure to honor established social as well as aesthetic systems. Yet in doing so they inevitably suggested the essential unity between Whitman's poetry and America's democratic distinctiveness. Thus Whitman's publication within the second edition of *Leaves of Grass* of several shocked and mildly condescending British appraisals helped make his case that America now possessed a "latter-day" poetry commensurate with its uniquely presentist commitments. Even if *Leaves of Grass* sounded to one obtuse American reviewer like the "soul of a sentimental donkey that had died of disappointed love," British ears confirmed that the beast brayed in an American idiom.[70]

The publicized assumption that Whitman spoke for a national culture defined by its divergence from British traditionalism helped enable Whitman's 1856 framing of *Leaves of Grass* as a new poetics grounded in America's common attachment to the recent past. Arriving under headings indicating their sources in foreign periodicals, the reviewers' damning testimony of the 1855 edition as a distinctively American memory circuit also highlighted the inevitable distinction in how the news could be shared. Moreover, the Whitmanian memory circuit provided evidence of national unity that might be difficult to discern elsewhere. In an era when Kansas or Cuba could make the nation's shared past look fleeting to British eyes, Whitman managed to give them an indisputable American, and an indisputably American response to the prophetic vision of history he presented. Their scorn, like Emerson's praise, offered proof that such a vision could function not just as poetry but also as a uniquely American mode of memory.

Framing Emerson's response as a bulwark against a transatlantic threat represented an important step in Whitman's attempt to craft the original American literature that Emerson had encouraged in his early essays.[71] In recognizing Whitman as the voice of the United States and commending "the solid sense of the book" as "the most extraordinary piece of wit and wisdom that America has yet contributed," Emerson fused the poetic prophet's self-reliance with his own enraptured American response.[72] By explicitly choosing the American transcendentalist over Tennyson as his "master," and by taking up the mission to free American poetry from what he called "that huge English flow" in his self-published reply to Emerson, Whitman presented his radically democratic chants as an alternative to the form of shared history perpetuated by English masters. The exacting Tennyson might write well enough for his own little island, but Emerson and Whitman agreed that it would take an extravagant, spacious, unfettered poet of the most recent past to write the national literature of the

United States. Expressing Anglophobic disdain for British literary dominance was one way to convince readers in the age of Emerson that *Leaves of Grass* represented an authentically American spirit. Yet the 1856 edition, as a material memory circuit that had no transatlantic peer or precedent, also demonstrated how such a spirit arose from the sacred ground of presentist memory.[73]

British scorn for American readers as well as poets helped justify the attempt in *Leaves of Grass* to rescue an authentically American literature from British masters, and transatlantic critical rejection also served to address Whitman's more immediate concerns about the ongoing sectional crisis of the 1850s. Like the later 1860 edition, the 1855–56 cycle encouraged American readers, North and South, to acknowledge their shared nationalism even as they accepted Whitman as their national poet. This appeal depended on subordinating fractious sectional divisions to a more fundamental quarrel, the struggle between the democratic nation his poetry represented and old England's continuing influence on its erstwhile colonies. Emerson's endorsement had moved from an inspiring poetic encounter with a first edition to an advertisement in a newspaper, then to a surprisingly intimate letter containing the promise of a face-to-face encounter, and finally to inclusion within a new edition of the same book. Thus its historical trajectory tacitly confirmed the recent past's potential to bind American spirits together in a tight domestic cycle of print and response.

By the same token, when Britain rejected a foreign voice and a distant shared history of the American scene, it implicitly alienated all American readers from Britain's shared history as well as Britain's literary precedents. Thus it reinforced the national foundation of the federal union with a uniquely American sense of history. When the poet confided in his letter to Emerson that "here are to be attained results never elsewhere thought possible," he stipulated—in what at first seems a non sequitur—that American literature should not only "withdraw from precedents, and be directed to men and women [but] also to The States in their federalness," that is, their sovereign commitment to unity. In the face of real political division, Whitman saw the desired break with Old World precedents as a means to achieve America's ideal spiritual union of distinct "states"; merging his own favorite bodily metaphors with the familiar language of the Apostle Paul, Whitman inserted the federal union into the church's traditional role as the mystical body of Christ, insisting to his American master that "the union of the parts of the body is not more necessary to their life than the union of These States is to their life."[74]

In 1850 Whitman had turned Christ out of heaven to find him in the plight of American slaves; in 1856 he found a divinely unified American spirit in the struggle against an alien memory circuit's traditionalist enslavements. Seizing on the conservative impulse behind Britain's "medieval dreams," he showed British readers the progress that they were sure to regard as "regression" and recorded the recoil of "English ears" from an American poetry grounded in American news.[75] Even British reformers were not immune from the reaction, and when Emerson finally determined to recommend *Leaves of Grass* to Carlyle, he did so somewhat cautiously for "the book throve so badly with the few to whom I showed it." Nevertheless, Emerson referred to the book as the "news" that prompted his letter after a yearlong interlude while he waited for "anything really good [to] happen here,—any stroke of good sense or virtue in our politics, or of great sense in a book." Now Emerson had finally determined to send "one book . . . a nondescript monster which yet had terrible eyes and buffalo strength, and was indisputably American," but he evinces little hope of a positive response. "It is called *Leaves of Grass*,—was written and printed by a journeyman printer in Brooklyn, New York, named Walter Whitman; and after you have looked into it, if you think, as you may, that it is only an auctioneer's inventory of a warehouse, you can light your pipe with it."[76] All indications are that Carlyle did just that.

"Come and See"

While Whitman's spiritual elevation of American nationalism can seem excessively jingoistic in retrospect, it occurred during a period when the Union's survival could not be taken for granted. Even as Whitman published his early paeans to an independent and unified American identity, transatlantic dependencies were becoming more vexing, and late antebellum sectional conflicts were dividing the American body politic in two. Thus Whitman was attempting to become the national poet for "The States" just when those states were least united. His evocations of mystical union arose from the threat of real disunion in August of 1856—the month when he claimed to have written his response to Emerson. Newspapers, and in particular the *Tribune,* had spent that summer fanning the flames of the antislavery crusade in Bleeding Kansas and tracking its spread from the western territory to the seat of government in Washington. The only way to maintain faith in the American nation under such circumstances was to relocate its sacred history within the very spirit that was threatening to tear the old political union apart.

When Emerson had written to Carlyle in 1854, he had described the growing Kansas crisis in a bid to convince his friend to "come and see the Jonathanization of John [Bull]." Merging national characters, Emerson indicated that both faced threats from internal divisions as well as external influences. Fresh from his western tour, Emerson insisted that "America is growing furiously, town and state." Yet he was unmistakably uneasy about a national destiny he found in the news: "New Kansas, new Nebraska looming up in these days." Far from manifest, the destiny of the western states, and the nation underwriting their sovereign status, remained far from certain. In fact, Emerson saw "vicious politicians seething a wretched destiny for them already at Washington." What hope there was to find lay in the sacred history of an antislavery crusade. "The politicians shall be sodden, the States escape, please God! The fight of slave and freeman drawing nearer, the question is sharply, whether slavery or whether freedom shall be abolished. Come and see."[77]

Carlyle did not come to see. Indeed, he had criticized abolitionism during Emerson's prior visit. He had published a racist tract on "the Nigger Question" the year after Emerson's tour and then expressed those thoughts in a pamphlet that Emerson had likely reread just before his plea to Carlyle.[78] Though Emerson had for a time also been attracted to racialist thought, his experience with the antislavery movement in the 1850s had sent him in a new direction.[79] Two years later his *English Traits* would recall his prior visit with Carlyle to Stonehenge, "the oldest religious monument in Britain," which, as Richard Bridgman has noted, left the American "unmoved, even disappointed" and became linked with his presentist critique of a spiritually compromised British nation.[80] Expressing his thoughts concerning "England, an old and exhausted island" in the shadow of Stonehenge, he had drawn a strong rebuke from Carlyle. Yet the intervening years had only reinforced his conviction that, if it existed at all, the nation's true spirit and sacred history must lie in a distinctively American struggle against slavery.[81] Shortly after his publication of *English Traits* in the same month Whitman dated his letter, he would be moved to endorse a more violent struggle to free the nation from its shackles.[82]

In the autumn after the publication of *English Traits* and the second edition of *Leaves of Grass,* warnings that a Republican victory in the fall election would doom the Union helped give Democrat James Buchanan the presidency. While some celebrated the election of 1856 as an averted disaster, it signaled to many a deeper need for a nationalism tied to something more lasting than political half measures and compromise positions, what

Emerson had called the "wretched destiny" of "vicious politicians."[83] The Republicans quickly regrouped, taking a stronger line against the expansion of slave power into national territory they located both at the edges of the federal system and in the localities enthralled by the Fugitive Slave Act.[84] Four years later, the very same week Whitman finished typesetting on the last prewar edition of *Leaves of Grass,* the new party nominated Abraham Lincoln for president. It was an act that would eventually precipitate the division of the states that Walt Whitman had worked so hard to suppress. Yet it was also an expression of nationalist conviction on the part of northerners and a response to the same desires for an authentically shared history of the recent past that Whitman had powerfully evoked in his poetic rejections of Old World traditionalism.

Conclusion

The Yankees are a damned lot and republican institutions all rot.
—Sir William Hardman, 1861

The great New York papers at once appear'd ... with leaders that rang out over the land, with the loudest, most reverberating ring of clearest, wildest bugles, full of encouragement, hope, inspiration, unfaltering defiance.
—Walt Whitman, *Memoranda during the War*, 1876

The American Civil War was, among many other things, a climactic battle in the larger memory war. The fractious antebellum years had channeled the cultural power of news, literature, and religion into a powerful presentist mode of memory. The conflict with the traditionalist alternative continued to rage as the southern states began to secede and form their own national government. Transatlantic news of the conflict, once it began to circulate, confirmed American audiences' location within a twice-divided nation, as both transatlantic and sectional tensions rendered nearly all nationalist assumptions open to question. As a result, news took shape through both Anglo-American and North-South conflicts during wartime, and it continued to offer an avenue for hypernationalist responses that often ran counter to the interests of any of the unsteady states involved.

Under the pressure of civil conflict, communal fallacies flourished in both traditionalist and presentist modes. Some northern unionists appealed to a relatively ancient heritage to which a violently divided populace could somehow belong. Others sought a communal spirit in the common national history of the recent past, though that history no longer seemed to include southern whites. Faced with daily news of the growing sectional split, the recently elected Lincoln summoned the music of traditionalist remembrance and predicted that "the mystic chords of memory, stretching from every battle-field, and patriot grave, to every living heart and hearthstone, all over this broad land, will yet swell the chorus of the Union."[1] Shortly thereafter, however, Julia Ward Howe, channeling the crusading zeal born of Bleeding Kansas, would "read a fiery gospel writ in burnished rows of steel" and would set it to the tune of the old revivalist song that had only recently become "John Brown's Body."[2] Though Lincoln and Howe were adopting different modes, both unionist writers were harmonizing with older strains of national memory and striving to keep the national idea alive in a shared and sacred past.

This book's examination of how the transatlantic memory war was fought in the decades that preceded the fall of Fort Sumter helps illuminate how the Civil War was in many ways a contest over the dueling modes of national memory that defined a twice-divided nation. The book's conclusion will demonstrate how the demands of national memory set the terms for the war even before the representations and commemorations that followed the Confederacy's surrender.

National Memory and Transatlantic Diplomacy

Especially considered from a transatlantic perspective, the conflict appears as a struggle over claims to national legitimacy centering on mass populations' relative capacities to share a common history. That struggle was never purely domestic. Domestic politics would be difficult to define in an era of civil strife at any rate, and dueling governments worked out whatever approximated their domestic concerns with one eye trained on Europe. This was true on the level of policy, where international influences shaped everything from cotton quotas to emancipation timelines to military strategies. But transatlantic pressures had an even more fundamental influence on popular understandings of nationality and national memory. In particular, the powerful presence of transatlantic news compelled millions of northerners and southerners to experience and eventually remember the war through the filter of transatlantic relations.

Julia Ward Howe had imagined the war as an emboldened presentist crusade, and many a northern news reader would experience it in similar terms as the war proceeded. Yet such visions of a sacred American history, rising amid the ashes of civil conflict, were not likely to inspire British journalists who saw it as their duty to puncture all Yankee puffery. Thus northern war news's "fiery gospel" could soon define itself against the blasphemous resistance from abroad that also inhabited wartime newspapers. Slow rolling waves of transatlantic war news threatened the margins of the American press's first draft of Civil War history, pressuring the edges of America's wartime memory circuits. Standing for the authority of traditionalist precedents, many British observers judged an American holy war harshly, and in doing so they helped to justify its necessity for outraged northern nationalists.

The social importance of this transatlantic news is one reason the historian Alan Nevins could plausibly assert that "no battle, not Gettysburg, not the Wilderness, was more important than the contest waged in the diplomatic arena and the forum of public opinion."[3] The wartime contest to which Nevins referred was always part of a larger memory war that stretched back decades, and the two arenas of diplomacy and public opinion were corners of one great battlefield of national histories shared within a transatlantic communication network. On this battlefield, mass-marketed newspapers influenced wartime diplomats as well as ordinary readers. They became, as the *Times* had during the Crimean conflict that immediately preceded the American war, important "protagonists" within the nationalist narratives of modern warfare.[4] Papers that might previously have operated as mere organs of state propaganda became venues for the popular sharing of war history. Yet, crucially, they played that role against the backdrop of their limited international circulation.

This larger context of both transatlantic news and the long-standing transatlantic conflict over national memory has been largely overlooked, even as Civil War scholars have increasingly attended to the importance of the international scene.[5] Periodizing tendencies still frame the Civil War primarily as a single decisive break between "two distinct and largely asymmetrical areas" of American history rather than as part of the continuous flow of nineteenth-century history or as a more complex "multilinear upheaval."[6] At the same time, disciplinary boundaries and nationalist assumptions constrain it as a discrete military and political struggle between Americans rather than a broader set of related cultural events that transcended, challenged, and reshaped national cultures. Recognizing the part the Civil War played in the larger memory war resists these constraints.

The intersectional dispute clearly shaped itself in relation to international affairs, but more broadly the war can be seen as a part of a great global struggle to define and legitimate modern nationality within a dominant Anglophone culture. Faced with this broader picture, considering the international Civil War as a matter of diplomatic history begins to feel restrictive. This concluding discussion of the war years therefore reconnects the diplomatic struggle to the enveloping transatlantic context of popular news and the vexing issues of national memory that influenced literary as well as political and military developments.

The case of the United States' chief wartime diplomat illustrates the broader context of shared history within which diplomacy and public opinion took shape. Lincoln's wartime secretary of state, William H. Seward, enjoyed a career as an international figure and nationalist advocate that transcended his diplomatic role. Seward, like his old partner Horace Greeley, was a creature of the modern news, and he adeptly combined Anglophobia and his manipulation of the domestic news cycle to convert popular newspapers into political weapons. Seward's habitual focus on the international horizon arose from his understanding of nationalist news audiences; the red meat of his Anglophobia fed his public's need for shared history by linking news to a broader understanding of a distinctively presentist American memory.[7] A master at rallying nationalist feeling around domestic news sharing, Seward emerged from the wreckage of the Whig Party as the presumptive Republican standard-bearer.

As governor, senator, and presidential candidate from Whitman's home state of New York, Seward sought to dampen sectional tensions by railing against European monarchies and even occasionally beating a drum for a transatlantic war. His transatlantic belligerence in the name of national unity presaged the poet's own determination to present the primary threats to the Union as fundamentally external, despite all the countervailing evidence supplied by sectional partisanship. In the run-up to the Civil War, Seward had publicly predicted Canada's eventual annexation, railed against political repression by the British establishment, and provoked British leaders and diplomats. When he traveled to Britain just prior to his 1860 run at the Republican nomination, Seward arrived with the reputation of a "great Anglophobe" and opponent of British power.[8]

Up until the last convention ballot was cast, Seward was the de facto leader of the Republican Party and favorite for the nomination. But at the 1860 Republican nominating convention in Chicago, Seward encountered a newsman with even greater reach than either he or Thurlow Weed, and his old collaborator Horace Greeley would prove his nemesis. Greeley arrived not as a New Yorker but as a replacement delegate for the western state of Oregon and once there would wreck the front-running Seward's candidacy through his influence with delegations outside New York. The apparent oddity of representing a new state in which he did not live, and swinging the votes of delegations that hailed from states far from the *Tribune*'s base of operations, neatly expressed the sort of political influence Greeley wielded as a central node in a great national memory circuit.[9] Yet by helping secure Lincoln's nomination, Greeley still managed to give Seward the chance to expand the manipulation of Anglophobic news onto the international scene as the head of Lincoln's state department.

As Lincoln's secretary of state, Seward's public statements and private letters during the first months of the secession crisis would present transatlantic conflict as a common cause that could unite the sections, and once the war began, he would foment transatlantic hostility to energize unionism at home. Though it was often intended to excite popular responses through the domestic news cycle, Seward's animosity toward Britain became legendary, prompting one observer to describe the secretary as "an ogre fully resolved to eat all Englishmen raw."[10]

Throughout the Civil War era, then, Seward drew from the transatlantic news to craft public statements that were nominally aimed at the British but were really designed to enflame his home audience's nationalist sentiments.[11] This tactic, which Whitman had also deployed in his poetry and the publicity surrounding it, encouraged American news readers to treat their own response to news as well as Seward's provocations as a part of the nationalist memory circuit; just as important, that history would be validated by its alienation from British news that appeared in the same papers but well beyond the range of such cycles of shared history. While that history also alienated antebellum readers in southern states, which sometimes banned papers to avoid the common bond of news, the transatlantic time lag and the raw reality of transatlantic distance underwrote a less arbitrary Anglo-American division. That dynamic motivated wartime northern nationalists, including Whitman, to focus on European opponents, and it also helps explain why Seward would champion the idea of transatlantic war as a means to bolster intersectional unity.

Seward would bring the idea to Lincoln as part of his now famous April Fool's Day memorandum at the end of the administration's first month in office and two weeks before the fall of Fort Sumter. While the document, titled "Some Thoughts for the President's Consideration," has become somewhat notorious as an example of questionable judgment and policy, Seward had as usual consulted allies in the press and may have assumed he was merely channeling the sort of transatlantic hostility that he had profited from in the past.[12] And although Lincoln ignored Seward's calls for ginning up transatlantic conflict in support of a "continental spirit," Seward would often return to the idea whenever Confederate sympathy in Britain's newspapers seemed likely to spill over into pro-southern policies.[13] When he did so he could depend on distinctive nationalist anxieties and arguments that marked the era before the successful deployment of the transatlantic cable. Those same nationalist undercurrents meant that the wartime contest over national recognition, combined with the distinctive way the Anglophonic news was shared and interpreted in the early 1860s, would open a new front in the long-running memory war.

Paper Nation: Neutrality and Recognition

The Civil War's effects on Anglo-American relations boil down to a question of recognition that involved many niceties of diplomatic protocol and international law. Yet on a more fundamental level it entailed judgments about the legitimacy of nationality and national memory. Generally, the fight for transatlantic "recognition" is understood as a battle over whether the Confederacy had a right to autonomous existence as a nation, recognized on the international scene. Britain, and to a lesser degree France, were the keys to this diplomatic struggle, which has been ably covered by historians such as Brian Jenkins, Howard Jones, and Amanda Foreman.[14]

Less well understood, however, were the wider cultural implications of this diplomatic contest, which played out in the popular press as well as in councils and parliaments. Seen more broadly, transatlantic recognition was not an exclusively southern concern; it was the aim of the North as well, which bristled at any suggestion that the world, and in particular Britain, did not respect its national status enough to support its suppression of an internal rebellion. At a more metaphorical level, recognition was not about the transatlantic other at all but rather an attempt to achieve an elusive self-recognition that nationalist anxiety and hypernationalist promises of the press demanded.[15]

In this way, the diplomatic questions of recognition and the larger questions of national self-recognition in time of civil war tended to bleed into other cultural areas, including literature. At the onset of secession, the same British readers who recognized something distinctly American in the strange voice of a wild Brooklyn poet five years before would revisit their assumption that anything distinctly American existed. In its short life, the Confederacy would not only refuse Whitman's encompassing embrace but would develop its own national poetry in intentional opposition to Yankee—rather than British—alternatives.[16]

As chapters 5 and 6 suggested, the modern news's capacity both to foment communal anxieties and to project itself as a venue for nascent national history had helped fuel the divisions that inspired these poetic developments even as it led to the war. Moreover, just as antebellum news had become a primary locus of internal divisions, presentist memory organized around war news would continue to generate schisms, as the 1850s political disputes transformed into arguments over wartime events and the meaning of shared American histories. During those same years, unionist defenses of a common American heritage would struggle to stay afloat against the tide of counterevidence generated by a bitter war fought on an almost unimaginable scale. Although observers have long noted the stronger national system that developed in the aftermath of the war, popular nationalism arose in both the North and the South against the background of potential national annihilation. Intersectional and transatlantic news in the antebellum era had challenged unionist beliefs in a common national tradition; by the same token, news in the war years staggered that communal imagination.

For northern readers, news that might otherwise have tied the country together often became merely another sign of its fracture. For all its technical grandeur, the modern news network ran aground of many of the same technical and political challenges that had occasionally plagued coverage of the Crimean War and Bleeding Kansas. The papers carried multiple versions of events, as official histories vied with alternative accounts produced both within and outside the nominal borders of the sections. Thus the presentist memory of the Union had to contend not merely with the transmitted facts of internecine conflict but with the dubiousness of the facts themselves. For a national imagination that was indelibly bound up in the modern news experience, war news whispered not only that the nation might be lost to the conflict but that it had never really existed.

British news readers were quick to acknowledge this constant subtext of American war coverage. Many realized that the war, even before it officially began in 1861, demolished many of the claims American nationalists had been making for years. Such observers were, furthermore, not always discreet in expressing their doubts concerning the legitimacy of American national memory; thus as accounts of the American war in British newspapers proliferated, they tended to confirm British notions that America had always been something of a paper nation. The diplomatic policy of neutrality and the concomitant cultural stance created one of the most powerful outlets for British suspicions about the United States' supposed foundation in a distinctive national past. In this sense, Britain's declaration of neutrality in the spring of 1861, as much as any other single event, dictated how the war would be imagined and fought.

While neutrality cast doubt on the notion of a single American nationality, American attempts to curry favor with a potential transatlantic ally further addled the national imagination. Before the war began in earnest, South Carolinians had voiced to the famous British war journalist William Howard Russell a desire to refute the Revolution by returning to monarchy—"to go back tomorrow if we could"—providing one of many signs that the transatlantic aspects of the Civil War were redrawing the borders of national memory. Northern newspapers that had covered Russell's reports also showed how transatlantic exchanges of war news could reveal Anglo-American affinities that distinguished the warring sections from each other; Russell avowed that Confederate monarchism had been "repeated over and over again" on his southern tour with such "wonderful strength and monotony" as to summon applause from the ghost of George III.[17]

While militant northern presentists might thrill at the chance to roust the South's vestigial Toryism from its aristocratic fiefdom, the suggestion of transatlantic affiliation by either section posed a double challenge to US nationalism. Any proclamation of Anglo-southern or Anglo-northern connection in the press tended to project the sectional divide onto a preexisting nationalist opposition. More importantly, however, it could threaten the revolutionary precept that had to some degree underwritten all previous forms of American nationalism: the insistence that America, by irrevocably breaking with European precedents, had initiated a new relation to national history and could not be reconciled to the Old World.

As the war progressed, this core nationalist principle often seemed to founder on the shoals of a transatlantic paradox. Both North and South underscored their respective compatibility with British audiences and interests as they sought British assistance in accomplishing their nationalist war aims. Southerners came to cherish British defenses of a culture associated with British heritage and bloodlines. Northerners came to recognize kindred spirits among British radicals who were closer to them politically and culturally than many southerners. This led to the paradox of wartime Anglophilia; as Britain publicly proclaimed the Confederacy a distinct political entity and then temporized endlessly about its potential role in the war, the dueling American quests for British support conspired to define both sections in relation to transatlantic audiences and in opposition to each other. Diplomacy demanded that Confederate and Union representatives convince British observers to honor their own long-standing transatlantic affinity for a relatively new nation of questionable legitimacy. Yet to do so invariably undercut the distinctiveness of American identity and the exclusivity of American memory. This process tended to make both sets of nationalist claims appear as paper-thin pretenses, as insubstantial as the transatlantic press's laughable image of a novel American monarchy.[18]

Courting British public opinion became a major war aim for both North and South in ways that transcended diplomacy. Indeed, popular audiences throughout the South always assumed that the Confederacy might not have to fight alone. The French, whose intervention in a previous American revolution had been decisive, might be enticed to intercede if their interests (in Mexico, for instance) aligned with the Confederacy's. But the British, sharing so much historically and culturally with the South, were even more promising. Britain's humming textile industry meant its politicians would have to take a keen interest in any war that threatened nearly 90 percent of the world's cotton supply. Thus Britain's declaration of neutrality in 1861 stoked southern hopes and northern anxieties about intervention that lasted throughout the war. It meant transatlantic attitudes would not only be closely monitored but would define the conflict for the soldiers, politicians, diplomats, and editors upon whom the American war's outcome depended.

This tenuous neutrality hung over virtually the entire conflict, lending credence to the South's "offensive-defensive" strategy, encouraging southern planners to believe that they could win a long war by pursuing a defensive struggle with flashes of offensive brilliance. Before the war, "it was assumed that simply withholding cotton would quickly force political recognition of the new Confederacy" and many southern leaders continued to hope that if they could hold out until the loss of cotton sufficiently threatened Britain's economy, the British government would be forced to intervene directly.[19] When Britain granted the South's belligerent status early in the war, many southerners wrongly supposed that each passing month would increase the likelihood of more aggressive foreign mediation on their behalf. This belief lent credence to following an overall strategy of defensive war and diminished the sting of the first Confederate defeats.

At the same time, the positive British response to the Confederacy's early successes bolstered the theory that a truly convincing southern victory could shock the states of Europe into quick recognition and helped encourage Robert E. Lee's two northern invasions of 1862 and 1863. Both incursions resulted in Confederate retreats, and the second ended in disaster at Gettysburg. Thus they had precisely the opposite effect on international opinion as their planners intended and weakened the southern cause, diplomatically as well as militarily. These, for the southern war effort, amounted to nearly the same thing, for the government was banking on external assistance from British supporters and northern "peace" parties that would operate in conjunction with the Confederacy's military successes.[20]

For the Union, Britain's neutrality (so long as it held) meant the North would have no "second front" and could devote its superior resources to squeezing the South into submission from all sides. With no need to contend with the British navy, the North could strengthen its initially porous blockade on southern ports and rest content so long as only a dwindling percentage of transatlantic shipments made it to and from European markets. Meanwhile the Union's larger, better-equipped armies and freshwater navy would force southern defenders to cede control over more and more territory. In most ways, then, British neutrality benefited the North. Yet to many in both North and South, the British government's designation of the Confederacy as a belligerent foretold the eventual international acceptance of southern nationhood and therefore of the antebellum Union's dissolution.

News emanating from the diplomatic sphere reinforced this impression. In one of history's great ironies, American national interests, in two distinctive and incompatible varieties, would come to serve at the pleasure of the queen and her ministers. In early May of 1861, the foreign minister, Lord Russell, had been visited by southern commissioners who claimed to represent a new nation-state defended by men of English blood and emphasizing common interests in trade and "constitutional government."[21] Russell would also soon receive northern counterparts. The new American president whose election had precipitated secession had drawn his own ambassador from a family whose "chief effort," according to the delegation's junior representative, Henry Adams, "had aimed at bringing the Government of England into intelligent cooperation with the objects and interests of America."[22] Though John Adams had helped launch the original American Revolution, Charles Francis Adams, Henry's father and Lincoln's new minister to the Court of St. James, had been tasked with securing British help in suppressing its sequel.

British officials faced a difficult task. They had to determine, based on their grasp of news from the war, which of two dueling delegations represented a legitimate nation and which represented a false one; their response, which they transmitted through mass-produced newspapers as well as diplomatic communiques, would ultimately be "both" and "neither." Britain would maintain official relations with Washington and would treat both the Confederacy and the United States as important trading partners and potentially dangerous powers on the world stage; yet it would refuse to grant either side the priceless aura of unquestionable national legitimacy.

Though neutrality may have been a practical necessity, it prevented Britain's straightforward acknowledgment of American national realities. Since the 1860s, observers have often implicitly criticized disappointed southerners and especially northerners for failing to understand the legal and economic rationale behind Britain's neutral stance. Certainly many Americans did not have the wherewithal to grasp such minutiae. Nevertheless, casting neutrality merely as a moderate diplomatic response to civil conflict ignores important cultural effects of which nineteenth-century news readers were keenly aware. In particular, Britain's neutral policy profoundly threatened the American masses' ability to believe in their own national legitimacy as a recognizable people grounded in a common past.

Considered as a broader cultural stance, British neutrality on questions of American nationality was nothing new. Determining who or what represented the American nation was increasingly important but never easy for British observers, and many were not shy about communicating their perplexity to their transatlantic peers. Indeed, as Sam W. Haynes shows, "By the early 1840s, an entire generation of Americans had been raised to maturity with the animadversions of foreign critics ringing in its ears."[23] American newspapers and politicians, though locked with their audiences in loops of shared history, still managed to project internal conflicts across the water in the 1850s. Thus in the decade before the war, the British press, even when acknowledging the American populace's national potential, had noted with consternation its institutional incapacity to channel its fractious energies.[24] British neutrality, by refusing to take for granted the nationalist claims of either side, expressed in legal terms Americans' historical inability to convince transatlantic audiences of their own national legitimacy.

Thus the coming of the war, and the near simultaneous arrival of diplomatic missions from dueling governments, confirmed a long-standing representational failure in no uncertain terms. Northern and southern nations became equally suspect in important ways through their diplomatic appeals, both because they contradicted each other and because they were forced to appeal to a common Anglo-American heritage. Despite the continuing presence of southern unionists, the Confederate delegation insisted it represented a nation of 20 million wholeheartedly secessionist people of mostly English blood.[25] The Union representatives asserted that the secessionists were attempting to carry out a rebellion led by a slave power that was inimical to inborn English as well as American liberty.

Early in the war the Confederacy stood some chance of achieving either full diplomatic recognition for a southern nation or British mediation that would ultimately force the North to accept the South's independence. News of Lord Russell's first interactions with the southern delegation and the apparently pro-southern slant of British public opinion deeply disturbed the Adams delegation. As Henry recalled in *The Education of Henry Adams*, "No one in England—literally no one—doubted that Jefferson Davis had made or would make a nation, and nearly all were glad of it."[26] Russell and other British representatives would insist that they favored neither side in the conflict. Yet the Adamses were neither wrong nor unique in seeing tacit encouragement of southern nationalism and a challenge to their own national union behind Britain's supposedly even-handed neutrality. By unabashedly dealing with their former colonies as a divided entity, the British government seemed to have closed the book on American nationalism as it had been previously imagined.

The Twice-Divided Nation, Nationalist Blasphemers, and Transatlantic War News

Or perhaps, because neutrality was seen as a temporary policy, it would be more accurate to say that the book of American nationalism remained uncomfortably open. American news readers, like Lincoln's ambassadors, understood that transatlantic perceptions of battlefield events could alter British beliefs about the legitimacy of the southern nation and even propel the British government toward the official Confederate recognition that might end the war and permanently divide America. Thus the fate of two American nations teetered unsteadily on how news was conveyed to the British one.

The British ruling class would continue to navigate, with limited success, the tangle of competing expectations and obligations that the American nation-state's unravelling had imposed on them. Yet it seems clear that the queen's ministers and the British press found cathartic satisfaction in this otherwise irritating engagement with America's national crisis.[27] After many years of concerns over whether America's political deficiencies would lead to Anglo-American war, that result now seemed to have been visited on the Americans themselves as their vaunted revolutionary republic devoured itself.[28]

Many prominent British leaders supposed that the United States had been a nation-state only in name; it had demonstrated the incapacity of republican institutions to hold the Americans' imagined nationality together. It had no real memory, and thus no real basis beyond the paper contract of its so-called Constitution. Britain's official neutrality emerged from months of complicated internal and external disputes over the Confederacy's status under international law. Nevertheless, the basic terms of the policy also reflected an instinctive suspicion of American nationality among the queen's ministers. Prime Minister Palmerston, one of the most confident proponents of British nationalism in the 1850s, proved far more dubious of America's national union. He informed the queen that a permanent breakup was inevitable at the beginning of 1861, when only one southern state had officially seceded.[29] Lord Russell, though more sympathetic than Ambassador Adams feared, had nevertheless agreed with Palmerston that the United States would separate. According to Russell, a divided America would become "one Republic to be constituted on the principle of freedom & personal liberty—the other on the principle of slavery & the mutual surrender of fugitives."[30]

Thus, though the letter of neutrality's law did not officially recognize the Confederacy as a nation-state, its spirit also tacitly revoked the recognition conferred by the Treaty of Paris on the United States in 1783. This helps explain why its transatlantic disclosure, and the combined official and unofficial British actions that immediately flowed from it, leveled a psychological blow against unionists far out of proportion to its actual results. On the whole, British neutrality benefited the northern war effort.[31] Yet it intensified the uncertainty hovering around American nationality by partially legitimating the sectional division and projecting it upon the international scene.

In most ways, British predictions of an inevitable regional division in 1861 simply reproduced the image of the sectionalist conflict that had bubbled up from transatlantic news in the 1850s.[32] Nevertheless, many northern journals proved particularly unmeasured in responding to what seemed a callous British refusal to support a holy war against an infernal rebellion of slaveholders. An editorial in *Harper's Weekly* caught the belligerent combination of stung pride, moralistic outrage, and territorial desire. Citing evidence of strong southern sympathy among British editors and politicians, the editorial attacked the queen's policy and promised that war with Britain would "insure the annexation of Canada." Partly because the international news network carried it back to southern cities, such support was as dangerous as any blow British arms might level against the North. "War with England," the journal declared, "would not injure us more than such British sympathy with the rebels as is foreshadowed in the Queen's proclamation, the declarations of the Ministry, and the tone of the London press."[33] Greeley's *Tribune* initially tried to minimize the damage that news of British sympathy was exacting on international relations. Yet it became increasingly clear as numerous Anglo-American conflicts played out in the press that British observers held veto power over the editor's own nationality as well as that of his erstwhile southern countrymen.

It was difficult to be told that one's nation had never actually existed, worse to be so informed by the power against which that nationality had always been principally defined. But the ultimate insult for the likes of Greeley lay in the British suggestion that America's sacred national history, including the crusade against the antislavery movement, had been built on a sham. The forms of internationalism and Anglophilia to which Greeley and his fellow Americans were most susceptible had always been based on the premise that American nationality was a given; Britain's refusal to acknowledge the American union's authenticity violated that premise and was understandably treated as a betrayal.[34]

Yet by the end of the war's first year, transatlantic reporting had supplied ample evidence for a loss of confidence in American national memory. An image of vexed nationalism gradually coalesced on the muddled canvas of transatlantic reporting, with all sides contending not just over the political legitimacy of governments based in Washington, Richmond, and London but also over the mnemonic basis for nationhood—or to use the more common parlance, what was required to "make" a nation and who had the right to decide when such a nation had been made. News of the war's progress continuously challenged and splintered the practical and symbolic foundations of nations, as everything from the value of currency to the appropriate number of stars to fly on a national flag became matters to be decided on the often inscrutable battlefield. Since the South had no plans to occupy the free states, most northerners were not exposed to the same level of threat as southerners. Nevertheless, readers in both sections took up their daily papers knowing that their most recent history might have already confirmed the old Union's demise or the Confederacy's end, and the shared transatlantic news network intensified these anxieties.

Britain's imperfectly implemented neutrality suggested that, far from being a self-evident fact of nature or sacred writ, an American nation was a slippery thing whose legitimacy was difficult to discern but ultimately subject to British judgments. At the same time, the transatlantic communication network stoked long-standing nationalist resentments by conveying

British news of the American war and with it the scornful attitude of the mainstream British press toward the fraudulent American nations such news seemed to expose. As British observers adjudicated between competing American claims of national legitimacy, they created a new context for rehearsing the same traditionalist British criticisms that American presentists had been disputing for decades. Moreover, Anglophones could no longer regard such transatlantic animus as merely a good-natured debate among Anglophone cousins. During wartime, British judgments about national legitimacy always had the potential to become self-fulfilling prophecies; if British public opinion or the public's representatives in Parliament were to reject unionist assertions, for example, British recognition of the Confederacy or mediation in the conflict might permanently disband that very Union. Thus the war and the tenuousness of British neutrality raised the stakes of British judgments about American nationalism, making such transatlantic dismissiveness dangerous as well as insulting to northerners.

Northern media reacted to this ambiguous situation with suspicion, which, given the benefits the British policy actually conveyed to the Union, sometimes bordered on delusion. Northern Anglophobia arose less from real transatlantic threats than from the worry that the war had given the British a deciding vote on whether their nation, as well as the Confederacy, had any claim on its sacred memory. However agonizing this new transatlantic dependency became for northerners, Britain's power demanded that its vote be secured, and, like it or not, northern representatives would have to compete for it. British neutrality, in other words, went far beyond the question of southern recognition. The policy presented significant challenges to northerners' self-recognition as a national public, and the access to transatlantic as well as intersectional war news tended to accentuate the psychological challenge of living in a twice-divided nation.

"They Came in Good Time for They Were Needed": Recalling the Memory Circuit of Bull Run

Even the highest representatives of the American nation-state proved vulnerable to the transatlantic news's dismantling of nationalist beliefs. The greatest blow to the confidence of the Adams delegation combined a Union defeat with an attack on the veracity of the northern press. In early August of 1861, London editors had received independent accounts of the Battle of Bull Run from its correspondents along with the New York papers' much more positive versions at the beginning of August. These had caused a great stir, especially the *Times* of London's battlefield dispatches filed by William Howard Russell, which described the Union troops' flight toward Washington and then blasted the northern press for covering up a humiliating rout. Dismissing the credibility of the northern papers along with the northern army, Russell struck a profoundly powerful blow against the American national crusade. In addition to cataloging the retreat, his dispatches salted an old nationalist wound by supporting Britain's traditionalist criticisms of Brother Jonathan and his dependence on unscrupulous editors. The enterprising New York papers, which had celebrated prematurely in correspondence written from the field before the tide had turned against the Union, were recast as false prophets peddling a phony history. The South's early victory would convince many British readers that the northern effort to restore the Union was hopeless, and their impressions hardened before any northern response was possible. Many British leaders would express this opinion as well, in private if not in public. It was the Great Exhibition all over again but with no Greeley on the scene to counter the momentum of British reportage. Reading Russell's accounts, a despairing Henry Adams later wrote that he "had hugged himself in his solitude when the story of the battle of Bull Run appeared in the *Times*" on August 6.[35]

Two weeks later, the same reporting that leveled Adams in London completed the transatlantic circuit to arrive once again in New York. Beginning on August 20 northern readers from Boston to Chicago read Russell's eyewitness accounts and frank criticism of the North's official history of the battle. Worse still, they were compelled to endure the widespread British scorn provoked by the *Times*'s celebrated correspondent.[36] Russell's own paper mercilessly ridiculed both the Union army and northern war reporting as shams. Scoffing at Anglophobic belligerence of the sort Seward had perfected as empty boasting, the world's most important paper characterized the symbols of a proud northern nationalism as absurd fabrications and ridiculed the credulity of northern readers. Calling Bull Run no more than a tempest in a teapot, the editors mocked the American war as a childish farce. "The fact is, that we do not like to laugh, and the sense of the ridiculous comes too strong over us when we would be serious," the paper sneered. "[Bull Run] is a great battle without the dignity of danger, or the painful interest of great carnage. There are all the ridiculous incidents of stark fear and rabid terror, without much real peril, and with very little actual suffering." As avid readers of American war news, the editorialist concluded, "we begin to feel that we have been cheated out of our sympathies."[37]

Nations typically seem to solidify in times of war, but the United States after Bull Run seemed to be rapidly dissolving before a global audience. Northern newspapers had now been implicated in this distressing development, and they swiftly made the *Times*'s special correspondent their scapegoat, savaging the reporter they now called "Bull Run Russell." To impugn his credibility, the *Chicago Tribune* even attacked Russell's most famous Crimean War report, protesting that although Russell with "Tennyson has sung the deeds of those heroes" of the Light Brigade, authoritative histories of the Crimean War counted few dead among the now legendary "six hundred." Northern readers, their Anglophobia aroused, followed their papers' lead. Russell was encouraged to seek sanctuary in the British embassy lest he be physically as well as verbally attacked.[38]

But the genie was out of the bottle. That Russell aroused such hostility only underscored the devastating authority of reportage from Manassas, filed by the world's most celebrated war correspondent and published in the world's most respected newspaper. The violence of a southern slaveocracy had repelled Russell, and he was privately pro-Union. Yet his story of the routed army's flight from hostile Virginia's soil seriously eroded the public confidence the northern papers had for weeks tried hard to bolster—confidence in the national press, in the national army, the national cause, and, by extension in time of civil war, the national union. Northern editors who had followed Russell's progress and reprinted his reports turned either cold or apoplectic when he exposed the entire northern press apparatus. Arriving almost a month after the fighting ceased, his reporting certified the Confederate cause's viability as a demonstrated fact of international history and forced Greeley to renounce his early hopes concerning British attitudes. The *Tribune* printed portions of Russell's account of the Union debacle under the waspish disclaimer that "the following are extracts from the letter of W. H. Russell to the *London Times*, describing the rout of Bull Run. It is to be noted that he was not present at the fight, having come upon the ground just before the retreat commenced."[39] Thereupon the *Tribune* severed its association with Bull Run Russell.[40]

Years later when Walt Whitman published his Civil War notes in 1876's *Memoranda during the War*, he would remember his former publisher's service as a presentist warrior, even as he implicitly recorded the challenge posed by the powerful British press. By then he had already published several war poems that elevated nationalist war news as a medium for prophetic action and several more that cast the Civil War as a struggle against Old World pressures.[41] His later prosaic recollections, however, offer a clearer picture of the lasting impact of domestic and transatlantic news on both the nation's memory of the war and his own.

Whitman's account of the northern response to the debacle at Bull Run celebrated the emboldening power of sharing news along a tight daily or even twice daily memory circuit. After the Union army's retreat, Whitman recalled that "the great New York papers at once appear'd, (commencing that very evening, and following it up the next morning, and incessantly through many days afterwards,) with leaders that rang out over the land, with the loudest, most reverberating ring of clearest, wildest bugles, full of encouragement, hope, inspiration, unfaltering defiance. Those magnificent editorials! They never flagg'd for a fortnight."[42] Viewing the experience in retrospect, Whitman knew that such reporting had taken more than mere editorial license with the facts from the battle. He also knew but did not say that these editorials would "flag" when it became apparent that northern fraudulence had already been exposed to ridicule within a transatlantic news cycle. For just as the newspaper campaign to bolster northern morale was wrapping up, the northern public received the unwelcome reminder that the definitive history of the battle was not in the hands of their own partisan press.

It had arrived, of course, by transatlantic mail steamer in the form of British newspapers. Russell's revelations leveled a severe blow to the North's nationalist war memory that had steadily reconstructed itself around several weeks of the heartening editorials to which Whitman referred.[43] Even after Russell's access to the front was restricted, northerners had reason to worry that southern sympathizers in the press and Parliament might spur the British government to more active participation in the American war. Northern papers during the war's first two years would report on the depressingly widespread British conviction that a divided United States represented the new status quo in North America. The timing of Russell's damaging Bull Run reports may partially explain why Whitman's *Memoranda* recorded an entry addressing foreign hostility toward the United States just following his tribute to the heroic New York papers of 1861. "The happening to our America, abroad as well as at home, these years, is indeed most strange," Whitman had written. "The Democratic Republic has paid her to-day the terrible and resplendent compliment of the united wish of all the nations of the world that her Union should be broken, her future cut off, and that she should be compell'd to descend to the level of kingdoms and empires ordinarily great."[44]

The controversy over Bull Run's transatlantic news coverage amounted to a second national embarrassment one step removed from the first coverage of the actual military retreat. The transatlantic time lag had effectively exposed northern readers' nationalist beliefs to justifiable scorn from abroad and had done so at a time when British opinions about American nationality carried real military consequences. This was one reason why Whitman's war poetry made room for the "doubtful news" of the war, news he clearly associated with what he called in one war poem the "Quicksand years that whirl me I know not whither." Conflating metaphors of time and space, the poetic narrator of 1865's *Drum-Taps* would address the nationalist culture built around news. "Your schemes, politics, fail—lines give way—substances mock and elude me," the poet complained. "Out of politics, triumphs, battles, death—what at last finally remains? / When shows break up, what but One's-Self is sure?" Whitman might have been speaking for many thousands of northern news readers for whom the national ground had become uncertain even as their faith in their common history had been shaken by sectional and transatlantic challenges to the northern press.[45]

Yet for many years after, Whitman would cast in glowing terms the New York papers' capacity to shape the historical understanding of Bull Run around a stable Union. The editorials "came in good time for they were needed," Whitman insisted fifteen years after the battle, "for in the humiliation of Bull Run, the popular feeling North, from its extreme of superciliousness, recoil'd to the depth of gloom and apprehension."[46] Russell's reporting had of course exercised a veto over the northern press's emboldening official history, and so Whitman's carefully limited recollection suggests a chauvinist doubling down on the unionist suppression of earlier battlefield losses. Nevertheless, in another way, Whitman's memory accurately reflects a capacity the northern news network would eventually demonstrate. The unwelcome intervention of British news had exposed the northern accounts as false after scarcely a fortnight. It had undercut all "those magnificent editorials" along with the northern faith in the Union and its presentist capacity to share in the sacred history of the recent past. Nevertheless, returning to those clippings in 1876, on the centenary of the Declaration of Independence, Whitman had several reasons to proclaim that such faith had been vindicated.

First, despite the many failures of the domestic wartime press of both sections, the war produced and circulated an unprecedented amount of news that was explicitly tied to national existence. Moreover, they did so with unprecedented speed. This meant that a mass audience of American readers found the most significant indications of their shared national history and future destiny in accounts of the most recent past, enhancing their sense of themselves as a nation with a unique reliance on presentist memory.

Second, in repudiating the implicitly traditionalist criticisms they found in British war news, northern readers could become more adamantly nationalistic and presentist. British criticisms tended to insist that the innovative system of democratic governance was partly to blame for the breakup of the Union. Some even argued that the incapacity of republican forms to contain great geographical spans was a timeless principle demonstrated in the ancient world long before southern secessionists confirmed it.[47] This argument suggested not merely that the American nation was suspect but also that it was irredeemable, and it left very little room for northern unionists to maintain their own nationality without completely disproving traditionalist understandings of national identity and memory. In essence, unionists would have to demonstrate that their idea of a "new nation" was not inherently contradictory. Thus Britain's traditionalist critique of republican governance encouraged northerners to support their defense of republican nationality through positive news from the front, the recovery of southern territory, and a spirit of voluntary service to the Union cause exhibited by soldier and civilian alike. Union victories supported not just a cause but the American idea that stable democratic nations could be based in the recent past, even as they comprised a large and expanding geographical territory, and thus quelled northern anxieties even as they countered transatlantic criticisms.[48]

Third, the first transatlantic cable's failure left a significant time lag between British and American war news; this meant that despite all its shortcomings, the domestic news narrative by the end of the war was demonstrably more reliable and coherent than the British version that appeared in adjacent columns of newsprint. Supercilious British accounts of the conflict often hit the American papers nearly a month after the original precipitating battlefield events had occurred. The late arrival of British reports produced the distinctive anxiety felt in the North after Bull Run's fraudulent history was revealed. Yet Bull Run Russell turned out to be an outlier. Far more often late-breaking British responses merely appeared to be behind the times in their grasp of the war as well as their notions of what made a nation. British correspondents would often get the story wrong, in ways that made their increasing anti-northern prejudice obvious. But more important, even when they got the story right, subsequent battlefield events made British judgments obsolete far sooner than news could travel the monthly transatlantic circuit.

All of this gave northern unionists the sense that the history they were making through news reading was theirs alone, worked out in explicit opposition to their old British nemesis. By the end of the war, northern papers had proven the merits of their own narrative; the Union's victory had demonstrated the validity of the northern press's partisan outlook in the face of its supposedly impartial international refutation. Moreover, it was the British press, especially the *Times*, that would be exposed to American readerships as fraudulent.[49] By the time Americans read the transatlantic version of the American war, it was often strikingly clear that the British were out of touch with the realities that appeared, with relative firmness, in adjacent columns of a national newspaper like the *Tribune*. This meant that the sacred national history of the recent past, developed in the antebellum period, could have its authenticity partially verified through constant comparison with an outdated British vision of the conflict. Though it troubled nationalist certainties, the traditionalist position British observers often adopted—as a venerable Old World nation fit to judge the paper pretender it saw across the water—helped cement northern attachments to presentist national memory.

"The Hot Lesson of General Hatred"

Thus in the summer of 1864, when an article in the *Atlantic* surveyed two large volumes containing "the diplomatic correspondence between the State Department and our ministers to foreign powers during the present contest," its author could regard them from a position of relative security. By that point, G. M. Towle could plausibly claim that the British view of the war arose from anachronistic news, traditionalist prejudices, and outmoded political ideas. Towle prefaced his article by insisting that the United States had always been seen by the European powers primarily as a political innovation, a potentially dangerous democratic experiment in nationality to be proven on the ground of the present. He singled out the federal system's capacity to incorporate new states within a single national republic; this idea had proved particularly problematic for the traditionalist nation-states of the Old World and "the representatives and supporters of medieval systems of state-craft." The United States, "starting on a totally new system . . . running counter to every prejudice and every conclusion of the Old-World statesmen . . . were forced to prove their institutions by experience, before they could assume the dignity of a first-class power." In the wake of the successes that had followed the American Revolution, "the politicians of Europe had been amazed to find that their unanimous prediction of the frailty of our political system had totally failed."[50]

Yet despite the treaties by which the "British ministry recognized the nationality of the United States," it remained "difficult for [English statesmen] to conceive that an entirely novel frame of government, deriving its genius from an idea, and regardless of precedent, could live to shame a system which had received the sanction of centuries of success." By the late antebellum years, "one ray of hope remained to the enemies of republican government" appearing in the transatlantic news of a growing sectional conflict. These British opponents "watched Slavery with an anxious eye. . . . In that they saw the apple of discord which might destroy our Union. They observed with exultation the increasing influence of those who warred upon slavery in the North, and the increasing insolence of those who would nationalize it in the South."[51]

Now that the war against slavery was under way, neutral Britain refused to regard it "as the rightful exercise of a complete nationality to suppress insurrection"; despite its antislavery convictions, Britain gave hope to a diabolical system of human bondage even as it continued to deny the United States' most basic claim of national legitimacy, "to be treated as a friendly sovereign state." In short, Britain had revoked the Treaty of Paris, in spirit if not in fact. Summarizing the situation, Towle quoted Secretary of State Seward, whose long-standing Anglophobic suspicions had hardened into settled law during a civil war marked by fractious transatlantic diplomacy and battles over public opinion. "Mr. Seward has well expressed our attitude toward England in a few words," Towle observed. "'The United States claim, and they must continually claim, that in this war they are a whole sovereign nation, and entitled to the same respect, as such, that they accord to Great Britain. Great Britain does not treat them as such a sovereign.'"[52]

The *Atlantic* was hardly unique in taking umbrage at Britain's continuing neutrality, southern sympathy, and occasional hostility toward the Union cause. Yet if the title of Towle's article, "Our Recent Foreign Relations," suggested a certain irony in a transatlantic refusal to acknowledge American nationality, that refusal also provided an additional incentive for northern nationalists to break their habitual deference to British precedents. Indeed, Whitman himself would celebrate British doubters as a spur to greater national independence in literature. His antebellum poetic efforts had embodied and enshrined a presentist national memory circuit to counter British traditionalism, and he put pen to paper during the war to ensure that the American news's transatlantic alienation would never be forgotten. By celebrating New York editors like Greeley as bulwarks of the Civil War years' shaky nationalism, Whitman was also celebrating a victory over

British influence that he hoped to extend to his own career as a national poet operating within a domestic memory circuit. In making public confession of his own nationalist doubts after Bull Run, he was also pointing the way toward the ultimate victory of a mode of memory he had been prophetically summoning since the 1850s. That victory lay in ceaseless resistance, not against the South, but rather against the British traditionalism that had refused to recognize the Union and its liberating holy war.

Whitman and other northerners sensed the real presence of the American nation during the Civil War as a matter of feeling and of faith. Frances Clarke has noted a clear relationship between northerners' experience of British hostility to their cause and the religious enthusiasm other historians observed operating in the ranks and on the home front, "the sheer intensity and virtual unanimity of Northern conviction that the Union armies were hastening the day of the Lord."[53] Yet only the war's outcome would allow that nation finally to manifest itself as a fact that the whole world would be compelled to acknowledge. Phillip Schaff, who periodically interpreted American religion to European audiences, would echo the conservative theologian John Williamson Nevin's judgments in an address on July 4, 1865—that the "war, reaching out to the world-astounding issue in which it has now come to its close, stands revealed to our faith emphatically as God's work. . . . Our national deliverance has been wrought for us, as a world-historical act, by God himself. . . . God has done great things for us, whereof we are glad; and this, itself, is our best reason for believing that he will do for us, still greater things hereafter. He will not forsake the work of his own hands."[54] For countless northerners, that work was America. As Towle wrapped up his reflections in the *Atlantic*, he looked forward to that same future using political terms, merging the struggle to validate a new "republican system" with a crusade reverberating through a "Christian world" tied to news of the American war. "If we should fail," Towle declared, "the thrones of despots are fixed for centuries; if we triumph, in due time they will vanish and crumble into the dust. . . . To such an end we fight, and suffer, and wait; the greater the stake, the more fearful the ordeal; but Providence smiles upon those whose aim is freedom, and through danger guides to consummation."[55]

For Whitman in particular, as a presentist poet dedicated to an embattled Union and the development of national literature, America was a spirit to be followed out from the shadows of transatlantic traditionalism through the common practices of remembering the nation together in the news. British wartime hostility only increased his dedication to a uniquely

American identity taking shape in the transatlantic news as well as his own poetry. Indeed, at the height of internecine war with the South, the poet was still scanning the eastern horizon as it appeared in his home papers for signs of foreign hostility. When he, along with Towle and countless other northern nationalists, surmised that it was Europe's "ardent prayer that the United States may be effectually split, crippled, and dismember'd by [the war]," he welcomed such animosity in much the same spirit in which he had embraced his first negative British reviews of *Leaves of Grass*. In his wartime notes that reappeared in his *Memoranda* a century after the Revolution, the poet had clearly sensed an opportunity: "We are all too prone to wander from ourselves, to affect Europe, and watch her frowns and smiles. We need the hot lesson of general hatred, and henceforth must never forget it. Never again will we trust the moral sense nor abstract friendliness of a single government of the old world."[56]

Thus the would-be national bard stood at the centenary of American independence, summoning the resentments born of transatlantic news. In so doing he reiterated the central concerns of his poetic quest for American originality and redirected sectional aggression abroad. Slowly emerging from the destruction wrought by the hypernationalist zeal of the previous decade, Whitman recalled his wartime hopes that British hostility would launch an era of more confident presentist nationalism. Looking forward into the nation's second century of political independence, he would assume that the twin claims of American union and American literature would be validated through a history shared by millions, written on the sacred ground of the most recent past.

NOTES

Preface

1. Benedict Anderson emphasizes the war dead's importance to national identity, while Gary Wills and Drew Gilpin Faust both describe the Gettysburg Address as a means of marshaling the dead to defend the political viability of a dubious national union. See Anderson, *Imagined Communities: Reflections on the Origin and Spread of Nationalism* (London: Verso, 1991), 7; Gary Wills, *Lincoln at Gettysburg: The Words That Remade America* (New York: Simon and Schuster, 1992), 133–34; Drew Gilpin Faust, *The Republic of Suffering: Death and the American Civil War* (New York: Alfred A. Knopf, 2008), 100–101.

2. For data and analysis of this grammatical shift, see Bryan Santin, Daniel Murphy, and Mathew Wilkens, "Is or Are: The 'United States' in Nineteenth-Century Print Culture," *American Quarterly* 68, no.1 (March 2016): 101–3.

3. George P. Fletcher argues that the Gettysburg Address provided the vital foundation for a second constitution. See Fletcher, *Our Secret Constitution: How Lincoln Redefined American Democracy* (Oxford: Oxford University Press, 2001), 27–28.

4. Eric Hobsbawm, introduction to *The Invention of Tradition*, ed. Eric Hobsbawm and Terrence Ranger (Cambridge: Cambridge University Press, 1983), 1–14.

5. John R. Gillis, "Memory and Identity: The History of a Relationship," in *Commemorations: The Politics of National Identity*, ed. John R. Gillis (Princeton, NJ: Princeton University Press, 1994), 7.

6. See Anderson, *Imagined Communities*, 6; Anthony D. Smith, *Chosen Peoples: Sacred Sources of National Identity* (New York: Oxford University Press, 2003), 22; Jacqueline Rose, *States of Fantasy* (Oxford: Clarendon Press, 1996), 4.

7. Thomas C. Leonard, *The Power of the Press: The Birth of American Political Reporting* (New York: Oxford University Press, 1986), 79–95; Howard Holzer, *Lincoln and the Power of the Press: The War for Public Opinion* (New York: Simon and Schuster, 2014), 146.

Introduction

1. Hereafter the weekly edition of the *New-York Tribune*, which was distributed throughout the country, is referred to and cited as *"Weekly Tribune,"* while the daily edition will be referred to and cited as *"New-York Tribune."*

2. The *Tribune* advertised this special edition printed "on the departure of each Mail Steamer for Liverpool" for four dollars a year. *Weekly Tribune*, 12 January 1850.

3. Greeley testified before the committee on two occasions, on May 30 and June 3, 1851. See "Report from the Select Committee on Newspaper Stamps; Together with the Proceedings of the Committee, Minutes of Evidence, Appendix, and Index," Sessional Papers (4 February–8 August 1851), 17:393–95, 438–41. Decades later, Frederic Hudson accurately reproduced substantial excerpts from Greeley's testimony; see his *Journalism in the United States, from 1690 to 1872* (1873; New York: Harper and Row, 1969), 540–48.

4. In 1850 the *Tribune* reached circulation figures of 18,600 and 41,400 for the daily and weekly editions, respectively; by 1851 Greeley would have been printing well over 150,000 papers a week, many of which would have been read by more than one person. See Adam Tuchinsky, *Horace Greeley's "New-York Tribune": Civil War–Era Socialism and the Crisis of Free Labor* (Ithaca, NY: Cornell University Press, 2009), 145.

5. Plans for the Westminster competition were submitted on December 1, 1835; the winning bid was announced at the end of February 1836 and the cornerstone laid in 1840. See Roland Quinault, "Westminster and the Victorian Constitution," *Transactions of the Royal Historical Society*, 6th ser., 2 (1992): 94; Caroline Shenton, *Mr. Barry's War: Rebuilding the Houses of Parliament after the Great Fire of 1834* (Oxford: Oxford University Press, 2016), 42–46.

6. From the 1840s, this "'American-style' emphasis on speed" formed "a critical element of American culture" and target for British prejudice in an otherwise collaborative Anglo-American relationship. See Joel H. Wiener, "'Get the News! Get the News!'–Speed in Transatlantic Journalism, 1830–1914," in *Anglo-American Media Interactions, 1850–2000*, ed. Joel H. Wiener and Mark Hampton (New York: Palgrave Macmillan, 2007), 55, 50.

7. Though he uses different terminology, Michael Kammen notes a similar shift in *Mystic Chords of Memory: The Transformation of Tradition in American Culture* (New York: Alfred A. Knopf, 1991), 41–100. My own view assumes that collective memory supported progressive as well as conservative stances in the United States, in part because memory's presentist mode relied on democratically oriented news. For other studies that closely link news to memory, see Richard Terdiman, *Present Past: Modernity and the Memory Crisis* (Ithaca, NY: Cornell University Press, 1994), 37–38; Carol Reardon, *Pickett's Charge in History and Memory* (Chapel Hill: University of North Carolina Press, 1997), 39–61.

8. Although lead architect Charles Barry's professionalism obscured the religious zeal of his chief collaborator, A. W. N. Pugin, the Westminster site bore obvious associations with the "politics, religion and class-ridden traditions of the past"; moreover, religious

arguments against "pagan" architecture motivated the decision to rebuild in a Gothic style. See Shenton, *Mr. Barry's War*, 40, 12.

9. Charles Taylor, partly because of his interest in careful definitions of secularism, has a different view of this sort of immanent history, and here I do not mean to echo his notion of an "immanent frame," which he explicitly contrasts with transcendence; although presentist national memory arose from what Taylor might call "secular" time, this is not the only way to define the experience of "horizontal" historical attachment, and Taylor recognizes that such "secularism" allowed for significant religious involvements. Nevertheless, Taylor's descriptions of immanence do not seem to me to fully capture American understandings of sacred history in the Civil War era, in part because, as others have noted, "vertical" associations and figural interpretations continued to inform modern American notions of sacred history, and in part because those notions also associated horizontal time with Christian scripture and history. See Charles Taylor, *A Secular Age* (Cambridge, MA: Harvard University Press, 2007), 552, 208–9; see also Taylor, *Modern Social Imaginaries* (Durham, NC: Duke University Press, 2004), 157–59; on "vertical time" as an American literary strategy, see Robert Weisbuch, *Atlantic Double-Cross: American Literature and British Influence in the Age of Emerson* (Chicago: University of Chicago Press, 1986), 154, 176–78.

10. This book deploys the term "transatlantic" in its broadest and admittedly imprecise sense. David Armitage introduced an alternative terminology to help organize the field of Atlantic or transatlantic history, one which proposes "Circum-Atlantic" as a way to designate work that focused on Atlantic exchanges, "Cis-Atlantic" to identify studies of particular Atlantic locales, while reserving "Trans-Atlantic" for comparative works; as Laura Stevens points out, literary or cultural works tend to utilize some aspects of all three methodologies. This study implicitly treats the three as linked, partly because the real and conceptual distinctions between exchanges, locales, and comparisons were rarely hard and fast for nineteenth-century Anglo-Americans, for whom the Atlantic was simultaneously a bridge, a shared border, and a barrier. Thus deploying a categorical distinction for the sake of analytical clarity might kill off what remained a live question for the cultures under analysis. For similar reasons, "transatlantic" stands neither for a diametrically opposed alternative to nationalism in this book nor as merely a neutral frame within which nationalism developed. See David Armitage, "Three Concepts of Atlantic History," in *The British Atlantic World, 1500–1800*, ed. David Armitage and Michael J. Braddick (London: Palgrave, 2002), 11–30; Laura M. Stevens, "Transatlanticism Now," *American Literary History* 16, no. 1 (Spring 2004): 93–102; see also Amanda Claybaugh, "New Fields, Conventional Habits, and the Legacy of *Atlantic Double-Cross*," *American Literary History* 20, no. 3 (Fall 2008): 439–48.

11. As Paul Giles has suggested, only the Union's victory allowed the geographical basis for a unified US identity to harden into an unquestioned creed. See Giles, *The Global Remapping of American Literature* (Princeton, NJ: Princeton University Press, 2010), 9–10.

12. Weisbuch, *Atlantic Double-Cross*; Elisa Tamarkin, *Anglophilia: Deference, Devotion, and Antebellum America* (Chicago: University of Chicago Press, 2008); Christopher

Hanlon, *America's England: Antebellum Literature and Atlantic Sectionalism* (Oxford: Oxford University Press, 2013); Sam W. Haynes, *Unfinished Revolution: The Early American Republic in a British World* (Charlottesville: University of Virginia Press, 2011).

13. The recent diversification of transatlantic studies has superseded approaches associated with Robert Weisbuch that highlighted anxieties related to Old World influence; the current trend leans toward nuanced descriptions of complex reciprocal loops and cultural entanglements. The shift is not surprising, for Weisbuch had announced his own "misgivings" about the "new prejudice" his analysis of transatlantic "enmity" might engender, while simultaneously acknowledging his debt to a previous generation of scholars, in particular Walter Jackson Bate and Harold Bloom. All of this suggests an inevitably cyclical debate over emphasis within the field. This book's own position within that debate tends to subvert generic and nationalist boundaries while reinforcing some aspects of anxiously nationalist divisions that are difficult to avoid in the study of memory—an inevitably anxious category that implies a level of existential uncertainty. Moreover, nineteenth-century Anglophones could not avoid realities of British power and legacies of revolutionary nationalism that influenced even their more cosmopolitan exchanges. Thus while the book confirms that nationalist anxiety and hostility were not the only transatlantic moods, it often finds them lurking just under the surface, like a repressed itch. Weisbuch, *Atlantic Double-Cross,* xviii. For a review of newer work and the response to Weisbuch, see Claybaugh, "New Fields."

14. "Yet America is a poem in our eyes; its ample geography dazzles the imagination, and it will not wait long for metres." Emerson, "The Poet," 304. Unless otherwise noted, all works by Emerson are cited by title and page reference in Ralph Waldo Emerson, *The Essential Writings of Ralph Waldo Emerson,* ed. Mary Oliver (New York: Modern Library, 2000). "The United States themselves are essentially the greatest poem." Walt Whitman, *Leaves of Grass* (1855), iii. For all cited editions of Walt Whitman's *Leaves of Grass, Drum-Taps, Sequel to Drum-Taps,* and *Memoranda during the War,* see *The Walt Whitman Archive,* ed. Ed Folsom and Kenneth M. Price, http://www.whitmanarchive.org. Hereafter cited as *Leaves* (1855, 1856, 1860, 1867), *Drum-Taps* (1865), *Sequel to Drum-Taps* (1865), and *Memoranda* (1876).

15. See Pierre Nora, "Between Memory and History," general introduction to *Realms of Memory: The Construction of the French Past,* ed. Pierre Nora, trans. Arthur Goldhammer (New York: Columbia University Press, 1996), 1–20; see also Nora, "Between Memory and History: Les Lieux de Memoire," *Representations* 26 (Spring 1989): 7–24. Nora's essay helped launch contemporary scholarship on collective memory, though nationalism's critics have long noted the past's role in the "illusory communal life" of the state. Karl Marx, "The German Ideology," in *Karl Marx, Frederick Engels: Collected Works,* 50 vols. (New York: International Publishers, 1975), 5:46.

16. Gillis, "Memory and Identity," 8.

17. Often these nationalist constructions include an element of imagined kinship crucial to their mass acceptance; see Azar Gat, *Nations: The Long History and Deep Roots of Political Ethnicity and Nationalism* (New York: Cambridge University Press, 2012), 1–43, esp. 38–39.

18. Jan Assmann, *Religion and Cultural Memory: Ten Studies*, trans. Rodney Livingstone (Stanford, CA: Stanford University Press, 2006), 95.

19. "Memory is fluid and works in ways in which we are scarcely aware. The categories in which we discuss memory should thus be indefinite enough to avoid any sense of rigid boundaries separating one 'type' of memory from another." James J. Fentress and Chris Wickham, *Social Memory: New Perspectives on the Past* (1992; Oxford: Blackwell, 2009), 25.

20. The modern founder of memory studies, Maurice Halbwachs, emphasized the social origins of much remembrance and the imperfections of individual memory. See Halbwachs, *On Collective Memory*, ed. and trans. Lewis A. Coser (Chicago: University of Chicago Press, 1992), 47–51. See also Terdiman, *Present Past*, 7.

21. Terdiman, *Present Past*, 9; Paul Connerton, *How Societies Remember* (New York: Cambridge University Press, 1989), 6.

22. Daniel Schacter, *The Seven Sins of Memory: How the Mind Forgets and Remembers* (Boston: Houghton Mifflin, 2001), 4.

23. The remembered past, and an individual's identity as a person with a history, inevitably contains troubling lacuna; yet more fundamentally, recalling the distant past divides the present subject. Nietzsche traced this uniquely human burden of self-dividing memory to consciousness of "an uninterrupted having-been, a thing which lives by denying itself, consuming itself, and contradicting itself," in a process that death only confirms. Friedrich Nietzsche, *On the Advantage and Disadvantage of History for Life*, trans. Peter Preuss (Indianapolis: Hackett, 1980), 9.

24. For an overview of this debate, see Anthony D. Smith, *The Nation in History: Historiographical Debates about Ethnicity and Nationalism* (Hanover, NH: University Press of New England, 2000), 27–51.

25. The "modernist" scholar Eric Hobsbawm, though he argued that "nations do not make states and nationalisms but the other way around," assumed that the idea of an ancient nation formed an important element in modern nationalism's invention of tradition; similarly, even harsh critics of the modernist thesis who assert some level of continuity between ancient and modern nations also admit to modernists' "generally correct and significant precept" that modern developments opened the way for unprecedented mass involvement upon which modern nation-states depend. See Hobsbawm, *Nations and Nationalism since 1780: Programme, Myth, Reality* (Cambridge: Cambridge University Press, 1992), 10; and Hobsbawm, introduction to *Invention of Tradition*, 1–14; Gat, *Nations*, 9. For a perceptive analysis of points of agreement within this debate, see Annika Hvithamar, "Nationalism and Civil Religion," in *Holy Nations and Global Identities: Civil Religion, Nationalism, and Globalisation*, ed. Annika Hvithamar, Margit Warburg, and Brian Arly Jacobsen (Leiden: Brill, 2009), 101–8.

26. Terdiman, *Present Past*, 3–4.

27. Assmann, *Religion and Cultural Memory*, 81–100.

28. Anderson, *Imagined Communities*, 36.

29. Kammen, *Mystic Chords of Memory*, 130.

30. Assmann, *Religion and Cultural Memory*, 6, 95, 94.

31. Smith, *Nation in History*, 55.

32. Elisa Tamarkin has argued that an idealized British union remained relevant throughout the secessionist crisis; her rich insights help demonstrate how the experience of fracturing nationalism could produce both a proliferation of nationalist options and the desire for an imagined British past, one associated with a deeper experience of consanguinity and filial loyalty than either the actual domestic or international political spheres could provide. See Tamarkin, *Anglophilia*, 61–76.

33. This phrase was one of the most clichéd responses to modern technology in the nineteenth century. See Wolfgang Schivelbusch, *The Railway Journey: The Industrialization of Time and Space in the Nineteenth Century* (Berkeley: University of California Press, 1977), especially chapter 3, "Railroad Space and Railroad Time," 33–45.

34. As Hobsbawm tartly observes, modern nationalists' rejection of their own nations' novelty forms "a curious, but understandable, paradox": curious, because such nations are entirely dependent on the engines of modernity to function, understandable because their invented provenance enhances their political legitimacy. Hobsbawm, introduction to *The Invention of Tradition*, 14.

35. Pugin's "doctrine was equivocal. On the one hand, he insists that Gothic is the right style for modern times—indeed for every time. On the other, he turns with a shudder from modernity." Richard Jenkyns, *Westminster Abbey* (Cambridge, MA: Harvard University Press, 2005), 106.

36. David Paul Nord, *Communities of Journalism: A History of American Newspapers and Their Readers* (Urbana: University of Illinois Press, 2001), 89.

37. "The big events, the famous names and places, were brought closer to home by their appearance alongside local news, thus redirecting the . . . community spirit outward to the larger world." Ronald J. Zboray, *A Fictive People: Antebellum Economic Development and the American Reading Public* (New York: Oxford University Press, 1993), 127.

38. Mk 3:28–30; Mt 12:31–32; Lk 12:10. This scripturally inspired pejorative might seem to denote a presentist outlook, but it could also issue from arch traditionalists who tied spiritual authenticity to ancient standards. See Rosemary Hill, *God's Architect: Pugin and the Building of Romantic Britain* (2007; New York: Penguin, 2008), 241.

39. Smith, Gat, and Hvithamar all point to this modernist tendency to overlook religion's ongoing influence. See Smith, *Chosen Peoples*, 10; Hvithamar, "Nationalism and Civil Religion," 104; Gat, *Nations*, 11–14.

40. Anderson, *Imagined Communities*, 23–24.

41. Anderson, *Imagined Communities*, 24. Auerbach's original statement did not propose that prior Christian communities had no sense of history that was temporally or causally linked; rather he argued that a vertical linkage arose through a providential and "figural" interpretation of scripture and thus history. This figural understanding—inaugurated in the Christian tradition by the Apostle Paul, developed through the early church fathers and championed by Augustine—triumphed as the dominant view during the Middle Ages. Yet Auerbach also saw Augustine as exemplifying the Christian

capacity to accommodate a horizontal view of sacred history as "a continuous connection of events," through his explanations of church history as "the progress of the City of God on earth." Moreover, the more recent "temporal turn" in literary and cultural scholarship has raised many questions about stark medieval/modern division of temporality that Anderson and others have assumed. Most significant for this book's examination of nationally distinct Christian temporalities, Kathleen Davis has argued that the Venerable Bede's descriptions of English history challenged Augustine's notions of earthly temporality and that "the political struggles by Bede and others over conceptions of history and temporality *pluralize* 'the Middle Ages' and undermine the very categories that made medieval/modern periodization possible." See Erich Auerbach, *Mimesis: The Representation of Reality in Western Literature* (New York: Doubleday, 1953), 11, 65; Kathleen Davis, *Periodization and Sovereignty: How Ideas of Feudalism and Secularization Govern the Politics of Time* (Philadelphia: University of Pennsylvania Press, 2012), 104.

42. Smith, *Chosen Peoples*, 10.

43. Hvithamar, "Nationalism and Civil Religion," 106. My colleague Slavica Jakelic makes a similar claim from a different perspective, by pointing out the tendency of modernist scholars, including Anderson and more surprisingly Smith, to regard religion as both epiphenomenal to modern national identifications and also diminished by that association. See her *Collectivistic Religions: Religion, Choice, and Identity in Late Modernity* (Burlington: Ashgate, 2010), 15–27.

44. Anderson does not seem to acknowledge that the Reformation shift in collective imagination was potentially consistent with previous notions of Christian history. Thus he seems to brand two varieties of "simultaneity," both of which were potentially fundamental to Christian piety, as essentially incompatible. This clean historical and conceptual break seems rather too neat. Thus when Anderson goes so far as to suggest that "the word 'meanwhile' cannot be of real significance" until the advent of modern newspapers, he is pushing a valid distinction into a hyperbolic register. There is no reason, after all, why the so-called messianic simultaneity of past and future in a providential and prophetic present should preclude a belief in the importance of simultaneous temporal coincidence nor a progressive account of church history. Anderson, *Imagined Communities*, 24.

45. As Anderson put it succinctly, "the dawn of the age of nationalism" was "the dusk of religious modes of thought"; similarly, he holds that Luther's Reformation launched the expansion of print and vernacular languages that made secular nationalism possible, yet he deemphasizes that movement's religious content. Anderson, *Imagined Communities*, 11, 39–40.

46. Quoted in Weisbuch, *Atlantic Double-Cross*, 71.

47. Smith, *Chosen Peoples*, 263 n2; see also Gat, *Nations*, 389 n18. To some extent, the debate between modernists and their critics hinges on semantics, since what counts as religious or secular seems central to the controversy. For Anderson, nationalism clearly responds to something like a spiritual need for "continuity" and "meaning" that under some definitions might suggest religious content. Yet Smith's basic objection is good as far as it

goes: Anderson and many fellow modernists deemphasize religion's continued influence on nationalism up to the present day. See Anderson, *Imagined Communities*, 24.

48. Protestant presentists tended to resist traditionalist authority by identifying with the biblical church, and the most extreme sought its restoration with primitivist zeal; see Theodore Dwight Bozeman, *To Live Ancient Lives: The Primitivist Dimension in Puritanism* (Chapel Hill: University of North Carolina Press, 1988), 11. Nineteenth-century British traditionalists usually shaped their ideals of religious and political unity around visions of the medieval church and were sometimes nearly as critical of contemporary Roman Catholicism as they were of Protestantism. See Owen Chadwick, *The Mind of the Oxford Movement* (Stanford, CA: Stanford University Press, 1960), 39; see also Hill, *God's Architect*, 222.

49. See Taylor, *Secular Age*, 544.

50. Gat, *Nations*, 11.

51. *Illustrated London News*, Exhibition Supplement, 23 August 1851, 250.

52. Weisbuch stressed the opposition and generative tension between a dominant and influential Britain and an anxiously uncultured American rival, but his model of "ontological anxiety" does not focus on how transatlantic news provided a material basis to both generate and defray American anxieties over the sharing of history. See Weisbuch, *Atlantic Double-Cross*, 249–57.

53. The shared English language inspired nationalists, including Whitman, to champion a distinctively American dialect. See Benjamin T. Spencer, *Quest for Nationality: An American Literary Campaign* (Syracuse, NY: Syracuse University Press, 1957), 130–34.

54. Thus Pugin insisted that, despite its largely Protestant population and state church, England was the Catholic nation par excellence. "Catholicism is so interwoven with every thing sacred, honourable, or glorious in England, that three centuries of puritanism, indifference, and infidelity, have not been able effectually to separate it. It clings to this land. And develops itself from time to time, as the better feelings of a naturally honourable man who had been betrayed into sin." A. W. N. Pugin, *An Apology for the Revival of Christian Architecture in England* (1843; Edinburgh: John Grant, 1895), 50.

55. Young England arose among Tories as an alternative model of British conservatism at a time when Whigs controlled Parliament, though its members "never acted as a disciplined Parliamentary group." See Richard Faber, *Young England* (London: Faber and Faber, 1987), 115.

56. Mitchell Snay, *Horace Greeley and the Politics of Reform in Nineteenth-Century America* (Lanham, MD: Rowman and Littlefield, 2011), 87.

57. In fact, Ryan K. Smith demonstrates how anti-Catholic voices at midcentury were already contemplating strategic cooption of Gothic forms of art and architecture to stave off the threat of Catholic conversions. See Smith, *Gothic Arches, Latin Crosses: Anti-Catholicism and American Church Designs in the Nineteenth Century* (Chapel Hill: University of North Carolina Press, 2006), 17–18, 46–50.

58. Greeley's role as an agitator in the Civil War arose partly from the revolutionary potential he discerned in antebellum news of sectional conflict; meanwhile simultaneous

currents of traditionalism ultimately inspired the sympathies of Confederate supporters such as A. J. B. Beresford Hope, who promoted the Confederacy in Britain as a recovered aristocracy of pure English bloodlines and conservative religion rather than a revolutionary cause or a popular rebellion. See A. J. B. Beresford Hope, *A Popular View of the American Civil War* (London: James Ridgeway, 1861); and Hope, *The Social and Political Bearings of the American Disruption* (London: William Ridgway, 1863).

59. Big Ben was begun in 1848 and was operational in 1859, although the bell soon had to be replaced; the overhanging design and the clock's numerals were based on Pugin's ideas. See Quinault, "Westminster," 95.

Part I. Revival and Revolution

1. Jenkyns, *Westminster Abbey*, 10–11.
2. Jenkyns, *Westminster Abbey*, 26–28.
3. Susanne Hoeber Rudolph, "Religious Transnationalism," in *Religion in Global Civil Society*, ed. Mark Juergensmeyer (New York: Oxford University Press, 2005), 190.
4. The resulting system "is the unique province of neither church nor state [nor] always or usually clearly differentiated either from the church or state." John Coleman, quoted in Annika Hvithamar and Margit Warburg, "Introducing Civil Religion, Nationalism and Globalisation," in Hvithamar, Warburg, and Jacobsen, *Holy Nations and Global Identities*, 4.
5. As Anthony Smith observes, "We need to avoid the temptations of seeing nationalism as a straightforward, albeit modified, continuation of traditional religions, or simply as a secularized version of traditional religions." Smith, *Chosen Peoples*, 17. See also Gat, *Nations*, 14.
6. Andrea Fredericksen, "Parliament's Genus Loci: The Politics of Place after the 1834 Fire," in *The Houses of Parliament: History, Art, Architecture*, ed. Christine Riding and Jacqueline Riding (London: Merrill Publishers, 2000), 111. Under public pressure, Prime Minster Peel had given a select parliamentary committee the responsibility for determining plans for Parliament's accommodation; see Shenton, *Mr. Barry's War*, 12.
7. Liah Greenfeld, *Nationalism: Five Roads to Modernity* (Cambridge, MA: Harvard University Press, 1992), 3–4, 7.
8. Dan McKanan, *Prophetic Encounters: Religion and the American Radical Tradition* (Boston: Beacon, 2011), 74.
9. Shenton, *Mr. Barry's War*, 40.

1. Memory for the Masses

1. Greeley's relative radicalism is a central theme of two recent biographies. See Tuchinsky, *Greeley's "Tribune"*; Robert C. Williams, *Horace Greeley: Champion of American Freedom* (New York: New York University Press, 2006).

2. These phrases appeared as part of the full title of *Contrasts,* beginning with the first edition in 1836. In later editions, Pugin sought to "maintain the principle of contrasting Catholic excellence with modern degeneracy," but especially in his mature view he presented Protestantism as the outcome rather than a cause of European Christianity's inconsistency, which had left the true faith riddled with "internal decay." Thus in contemporary architecture, Pugin avowed that "wherever that [modern] degeneracy is observable, be it in Protestant or Catholic countries, it will be found to proceed from the decay of true Catholic principles and practice." A. W. N. Pugin, *Contrasts* (London: Charles Dolman, 1841), iii–v.

3. S. Lang, "The Principles of the Gothic Revival in England," *Journal of the Society of Architectural Historians* 25, no.4 (December 1966): 261. Lang emphasizes Pugin's Catholic belief in the one true church as the source for his architectural convictions.

4. The Westminster fire and the debate over the rebuilding project launched Pugin's public architectural career. Prior to his involvement with Barry, he brought out his 1835 *Letter to Hakewill,* in which he both publicly declared himself an architect and strongly disagreed with the addressee's advocacy for renovating Westminster in the classical style. The first edition of *Contrasts* was published the following year. See Rosemary Hill, "Reformation to Millennium: Pugin's *Contrasts* in the History of English Thought," *Journal of the Society of Architectural Historians* 58, no.1 (March 1999): 29. See also, Hill, *God's Architect,* 147–49.

5. See Pugin, *Apology,* 7. The centrality of this impulse led Hobsbawm to point to revivalist architecture as one of the chief embodiments of "the longing for the unity of man in nature" that motivated "the romantic critique of the [bourgeois] world." Eric Hobsbawm, *The Age of Revolution, 1789–1848* (1962; New York: Vintage, 1996), 263–64. Amanda Foreman also notes that the Westminster planners' refusal of neoclassical options projected an aggressive national pride, in "a bold, even arrogant London that dared other cities to emulate its style," though too much emulation would certainly run counter to Pugin's stated goal of developing a particularly national style. See Foreman, *World on Fire: Britain's Crucial Role in the American Civil War* (New York: Random House, 2010), 40.

6. Pugin, *Apology,* 9–10, 6. Pugin's decisive turn to a nationalized mode of Gothic architecture came in 1840 and corresponded with his idealization of the late thirteenth century. See Hill, *God's Architect,* 226–27.

7. Pugin, *The True Principles of Pointed or Christian Architecture* (1853; Oxford: St. Barnabas, 1969), 47–48.

8. See Pugin, *Apology,* 51. See also Faber, *Young England,* 110.

9. Michael Alexander, *Medievalism: The Middle Ages in Modern England* (New Haven, CT: Yale University Press, 2017), xviii. See also Hill, "Reformation to Millennium," 32–40.

10. Chadwick, *Mind,* 39.

11. See Tuchinsky, *Greeley's "Tribune,"* 145.

12. Greeley and McElrath began with a few thousand dollars of capital and within a year could boast a circulation of nearly ten thousand. Tuchinsky, *Greeley's "Tribune,"* 9.

13. The *Tribune* began advertising these rates for its weekly, semiweekly, daily, and European editions early in 1850. *Weekly Tribune*, 12 January 1850.

14. Many other witnesses were called during the weeks Greeley testified, including editors of major London papers. See "Report from the Select Committee," 17:393–441.

15. Tuchinsky, *Greeley's "Tribune,"* 146.

16. The Chartists' working-class periodical campaigns for a more representative, democratic, and equitable political system emerged in the wake of the Reform Act of 1832. Historians have long tended to date Chartism's last great surge and its gradual demise to this midcentury moment, the passing of which also corresponded with a move to target the last remaining taxes on knowledge. See Joel H. Wiener, *The War of the Unstamped: The Movement to Repeal the British Newspaper Tax, 1830–1836* (Ithaca, NY: Cornell University Press, 1969), xi–xii; Neville Kirk, *The Growth of Working Class Reformism in Mid-Victorian England* (Urbana: University of Illinois Press, 1985), 2–26.

17. See Kevin Gilmartin, *Print Politics: The Press and Radical Opposition in Early Nineteenth-Century England* (Cambridge: Cambridge University Press, 1996), 74.

18. See Wiener, *War of the Unstamped*, 52–82; Bob Clarke, *From Grub Street to Fleet Street: An Illustrated History of English Newspapers to 1899* (Aldershot: Ashgate, 2004), 233–39.

19. Linda Colley, *Britons: Forging the Nation, 1707–1837* (New Haven, CT: Yale University Press, 1992), 369.

20. See "Report from the Select Committee," 17:393–95, 438–41. Richard Cobden was present for both Greeley's appearances on May 30 and June 3 and initiated the line of questioning referring to working-class reading habits discussed below. The committee ultimately declined to recommend a specific taxation policy but did propose that the news itself was an inappropriate target of government taxation. Under the British tax code in 1850 Greeley could not have made a profit selling his paper to a working-class audience, which was very much the taxes' intent; reduced stamp duties after 1836 still left the mainstream British papers the province of the upper and upper middle classes, and the political implications of this policy led radical politicians to agitate for repeal after 1849. Had the reduced 1850 duty been applied to Greeley's paper, it would have more than doubled the *Tribune*'s price. See Wiener, *War of the Unstamped*, xi–xii; Clarke, *From Grub Street*, 237.

21. Hudson, *Journalism*, 542, 544.

22. Hudson, *Journalism*, 542

23. Hudson, *Journalism*, 541–42, 545.

24. Hudson, *Journalism*, 545.

25. Hudson, *Journalism*, 545.

26. Hudson, *Journalism*, 546–47.

27. Hudson, *Journalism*, 548.

28. McKanan, *Prophetic Encounters*, 74.

29. "He had begun to think and talk about the possibility of another kind of journalism in New York. One could not look at the weekly shiploads landing at the Battery without

wondering what effect these might have on America.... They knew so little of their new home.... They would want [a newspaper] now." William Harlon Hale, *Horace Greeley: Voice of the People* (New York: Harper and Row, 1950), 24.

30. Michael F. Holt, *The Rise and Fall of the American Whig Party: Jacksonian Politics and the Onset of the Civil War* (New York: Oxford University Press, 1999), 105–6.

31. Snay, *Horace Greeley*, 46.

32. Williams, *Horace Greeley*, 51–55.

33. Quoted in Snay, *Horace Greeley*, 92.

34. Williams, *Horace Greeley*, 52–53.

35. In 1847, in the heat of the *Tribune*'s rivalry with the *Herald*, Greeley had commissioned an independent assessment of the two papers' circulation. Although he lost his bet, he publicized the data to prove how far he had come; tabulating the average daily, weekly, and semiweekly figures, the *Tribune* weighed in at 28,195 copies, the *Herald* at 28,946. See Hudson, *Journalism*, 529.

36. Although Greeley shipped a west coast edition by boat, issues of the *Tribune*, like other shipments, were restricted both by the lack of continuous rail service to the Pacific and the lack of significant settlements; nevertheless, some of his greatest gains in the 1840s and 1850s came in midwestern frontier states.

37. Menahem Blondheim, *News over the Wires: The Telegraph and the Flow of Public Information in America, 1844–1897* (Cambridge, MA: Harvard University Press, 1994), 32–33.

38. Greeley "had been advising distressed mechanics to head west since 1837" and that year's attendant panic, and advocates for homestead legislation sought his support throughout the 1840s, since "the *Weekly Tribune* had the potential to propagandize land reform ... in the agricultural Midwest where homestead proposals resonated with farmers in the Great Lakes Region." Tuchinsky, *Greeley's "Tribune,"* 135.

39. *New-York Tribune*, 27 March 1850; *Weekly Tribune*, 30 March 1850.

40. See Horace Greeley, *Recollections of a Busy Life* (New York: J. B. Ford, 1868), 137. Greeley maintained this posture publicly long after the paper's founding; see *Weekly Tribune*, 12 January 1856, 8.

41. For the role of modern news in this major political realignment, see Leonard, *Power of the Press*, 79–95.

42. For Greeley's reputation as iconoclastic social reformer, see Frank Luther Mott, *American Journalism: A History, 1690–1960*, 3rd ed. (New York: Macmillan, 1962), 276–77.

43. Quoted in Williams, *Horace Greeley*, 66.

44. Mott, *American Journalism*, 277.

45. "History, as yet, has left in the United States but so thin and impalpable a deposit that we very soon touch the hard substratum of nature; and nature herself, in the western world, has the peculiarity of seeming rather crude and immature." Henry James, *Hawthorne* (New York: Harper and Brothers, 1899), 12. See Weisbuch, *Atlantic Double-Cross*, xi–xii.

46. For the relevance of the geographical peculiarities of the colonial situation see Anderson, *Imagined Communities*, 188.

47. The real "fatality of transatlantic birth" also provided bodily legitimation for the hemispheric distinction. Anderson, *Imagined Communities*, 57–58.

48. Whitman, *Leaves* (1855), iii.

49. Drawing on Mercea Eliade, Weisbuch makes a "subtle" connection between an essentially Christian temporality and a myth of the West that was interpreted by the Puritans and other American Protestants to represent the New World; Christianity's broader "redemption of Time and History" to which Eliade referred, however, did not depend on the myth of the West and thus could support other American cultural elements that reciprocally reinforced its forward thrust. See Weisbuch, *Atlantic Double-Cross*, 70–71.

50. Weisbuch adjusts Sacvan Bercovitch's theory of Puritan influence on American romanticism, which located Puritan notions of national election at the origins of a more or less continuous American tradition, in order to account for their rediscovery and revitalization in the age of Emerson. See Sacvan Bercovitch, *The Puritan Origins of the American Self* (New Haven, CT: Yale University Press, 1975), 165; Weisbuch, *Atlantic Double-Cross*, 77–79.

51. Chapter 2 examines this paradox and its relationship both to modern news and to primitivist identifications with the apostolic church.

52. Indeed, even today American evangelicalism "is rooted in an expectation of strong emotional and physical manifestations of people's religious experiences." Meredith B. McGuire, *Lived Religion: Faith and Practice in Everyday Life* (New York: Oxford University Press, 2008), 74.

53. Nathan O. Hatch, *The Democratization of American Christianity* (New Haven, CT: Yale University Press, 1989), 22.

54. McGuire, *Lived Religion*, 73.

55. The Presbyterian experience in the American West helps underscore this tendency of imposed orthodoxy to inspire schism. See Sydney E. Ahlstrom, *A Religious History of the American People* (New Haven, CT: Yale University Press, 1975), 444–45.

56. Though defined in various ways, "lived religion" centers on religious practice as a zone of redefinition and resistance, in which the sacred mixes with mundane experiences and materials. See David D. Hall, ed., *Lived Religion in America: Toward a History of Practice* (Princeton, NJ: Princeton University Press, 1997), xi, 6–7.

57. James Davison Hunter, *American Evangelicalism: Conservative Religion and the Quandary of Modernity* (New Brunswick, NJ: Rutgers University Press, 1982), 65, quoted in Harold K. Bush Jr., *American Declarations: Rebellion and Repentance in American Cultural History* (Urbana: University of Illinois Press, 1999), 189 n14.

58. Quoted in Sydney Mead, *The Lively Experiment: The Shaping of Christianity in America* (New York: Harper and Row: 1963), x.

59. In explaining Pugin's early interactions with "the new enthusiasm" for the British past, Hill notes that, although literature originally inspired architecture, in the early 1800s "each fed the other." Hill, *God's Architect*, 51.

60. Catharine L. Albanese, *A Republic of Mind and Spirit: A Cultural History of American Metaphysical Religion* (New Haven, CT: Yale University Press, 2007), 123.

61. Albanese, *A Republic of Mind and Spirit*, 5.

62. "What is called collective memory is not a remembering but a stipulating: that *this is important*." Susan Sontag, *Regarding the Pain of Others* (New York: Picador, 2003), 86. For a detailed and nuanced description of such selection, see Barry Schwartz, *Abraham Lincoln and the Forge of National Memory* (Chicago: University of Chicago Press, 2003), 10–23.

63. Karl Marx and Frederick Engels, *Collected Works*, 6: 487–89. Marx worked on the document, sometimes in cooperation with Engels and sometimes on his own, from December of 1847 through January of 1848, beginning in London and completing the work in Brussels. Mark and Engels, *Collected Works*, 6: 697–98n257.

64. Indeed, one critic credits the *Manifesto* as "the best available description" of an era dominated by a sense of accelerating change. Walter Russell Mead, *God and Gold: Britain, America, and the Making of the Modern World* (New York: Alfred A. Knopf, 2007), 286.

65. Hill, *God's Architect*, 215.

66. The congress met at the Red Lion Hotel in Soho, on the corner of Great Windmill an Archer streets. Marxists Internet Archive, "The Communist League," https://www.marxists.org/archive/marx/works/1847/communist-league/index.htm.

67. See Hale, *Horace Greeley*, 1–18.

68. Pugin, *Apology*, 211.

69. McKanan, *Prophetic Encounters*, 74.

70. As Gat and others have argued, many of these prior experiences of unity were recognizably national in their own right. See Gat, *Nations*, 67–131.

2. Enslaved to the Past

1. See Robert Daniel Koch, *Ralph Waldo Emerson in Europe: Class, Race, and Revolution in the Making of an American Thinker* (London: I. B. Tauris, 2012), 48–79.

2. Emerson, *English Traits*, 598. Richard Bridgman points to this section of *English Traits* as indicative of Emerson's struggle to imagine and justify the American inheritance of a British bloodline given its lack of vigor abroad and at home. As Ian Finseth points out, Emerson's slippery treatment of race in *English Traits* also emerges as a complex outgrowth of an even more complicated background, one that included multiple racial taxonomies and genealogies; Christopher Hanlon interprets the book's rhetoric of Anglo-American racial bloodlines as an attempt to address problems of American sectionalism through creative engagements with Britain's history of ethnic conflict, which ultimately suggested the nation's dependence on a process of racial melioration rather than racial determinism. See Bridgman, "From Greenough to 'Nowhere': Emerson's *English Traits*," *New England Quarterly Review* 59, no.4 (December 1986): 469–85; Finseth, "Evolution, Cosmopolitanism, and Emerson's Antislavery Politics," *American Literature* 77, no.4 (December 2005): 728–60; Hanlon, *America's England*, 21–40.

3. Emerson, *English Traits*, 573, 574.

4. Emerson, *English Traits*, 572.

5. Emerson, *English Traits*, 592.

6. Emerson, *English Traits*, 592, 593, 596, 597. Emerson also saw a link between the *Times*'s circulation and the revolutionary fervor of 1848, which prompted Carlyle to subscribe. See Ralph Waldo Emerson, *The Journals and Miscellaneous Notebooks of Ralph Waldo Emerson*, 16 vols., ed. Merton M. Sealts Jr. (Cambridge, MA: Belknap Press of Harvard University Press, 1960–82), 10:196, 228–29, 231, 297.

7. Emerson, *English Traits*, 592.

8. Emerson, *English Traits*, 572.

9. Emerson, *English Traits*, 575.

10. *The Letters of Ralph Waldo Emerson*, 10 vols., ed. Ralph L. Rusk and Eleanor M. Tilton (New York: Columbia University Press, 1939–95), 7:141–42, quoted in Barbara Packer, "Signing Off: Religious Indifference in America," in *There Before Us: Religion, Literature, and Culture from Emerson to Wendell Berry*, ed. Roger Lundin (Grand Rapids, MI: William B. Eerdmans, 2007), 5.

11. "The power of the newspaper is familiar in America and in accordance with our political system. In England, it stands in antagonism with the feudal institutions." Emerson, *English Traits*, 592.

12. Emerson, *English Traits*, 593–97.

13. Explaining Emerson's leaving his pastorate, Robert D. Richardson observes that "if anything, Emerson believed too much, not too little." Later, Emerson would suggest that "Transcendentalism is the Saturnalia or excess of Faith." Richardson, *Emerson: The Mind on Fire* (Berkeley: University of California Press, 1995), 125; Emerson, "The Transcendentalist," 85.

14. As he put it in June of that year, "In order to be a good minister it was necessary to leave the ministry." Quoted in Richardson, *Emerson*, 126. Emerson continued to preach on a more limited basis after leaving Second Church, though as Gay Wilson Allen observes, his "delight in being an itinerant preacher was another indication that Emerson was beginning to find a second vocation" as a popular speaker on the lecture circuit. See Allen, *Waldo Emerson: A Biography* (New York: Viking, 1981), 226.

15. Emerson, "The Lord's Supper," 107.

16. Emerson, "The Lord's Supper," 101.

17. Emerson, "The Lord's Supper," 101–2.

18. Emerson, "The Lord's Supper," 106–7.

19. Emerson, "The Lord's Supper," 107.

20. Emerson, *English Traits*, 573.

21. Emerson, "The Lord's Supper," 102–103.

22. Emerson, "The Lord's Supper," 108.

23. Bush, *American Declarations*, 112.

24. Philip F. Gura, *American Transcendentalism: A History* (New York: Hill and Wang, 2007), 13.

25. Packer, "Signing Off," 22. Richardson also traces the genesis of American transcendentalism to Emerson's recognition that "the 'reason' of Milton, Coleridge, and the Germans was another name for what the Quakers recognized as the inner light. The same phenomenon was explained philosophically and logically by one group; it was made practically available and psychologically real by the other." Richardson, *Emerson*, 167.

26. Richardson notes that Emerson's understanding of communion drew on the Quaker idea that Christ instituted not merely a "modernized Passover" but also a rejection of ceremonialism in favor of spirit; bread and wine became "metaphors for the spiritual state of being one with Christ." Richardson, *Emerson*, 126.

27. Indeed, Emerson viewed "Romanism" as the unwelcome outcome of the English Church's adherence to tradition in the wake of German higher criticism. See Emerson, *English Traits*, 577.

28. Many later conceptualizations of horizontal time seem to elide the abiding centrality of the antitraditionalist impulse within Christian theology, practice, history, and especially scripture; nevertheless, Erich Auerbach's seminal articulation locates a similar impulse behind figural interpretations of history as well as the gospel accounts of Christ's life. See Auerbach, *Mimesis*, 42, 63–64.

29. This basis in the New Testament helps explain why adherents to later Christian traditions could still dismiss traditionalism as "the dead faith of the living," to borrow Jaroslav Pelikan's famous formulation. As Pelikan noted, Emerson leveled this precise criticism at all of tradition in his advocacy for a "new born bard of the Holy Ghost." See Jaroslav Pelikan, *The Vindication of Tradition* (New Haven, CT: Yale University Press, 1984), 65–66.

30. Quoted in Richardson, *Emerson*, 158.

31. Gail E. Husch, *Something Coming: Apocalyptic Expectation and Mid-Nineteenth-Century American Painting* (Hanover, NH: University Press of New England, 2000), 3. The American impulse to identify news with the end times appears in other eras. See Ruth H. Bloch, *Visionary Republic: Millennial Themes in American Thought, 1756–1800* (New York: Cambridge University Press, 1985); Paul Boyer, *When Time Shall Be No More: Prophecy Belief in Modern American Culture* (New York: Belknap, 1994).

32. Emerson, *Journals*, 10:329.

33. Michael Rogin, *Subversive Genealogy: The Politics and Art of Herman Melville* (New York: Alfred A. Knopf, 1983), 34.

34. Eduardo Cadava, *Emerson and the Climates of History* (Stanford, CA: Stanford University Press, 1997), 107.

35. The picture sketched here differs somewhat from an image of the Revolution as a triumph of what Charles Taylor refers to as "secular" time, but which in Taylor's view may still leave ample space for its own varieties of religious involvement. On my reading, neither Taylor's vision of revolutions generally as "anti-structure to end all anti-structure" nor his association of the American Revolution with what Eliade calls a "time of origins" fully captures the spiritual potency of Emerson's radical refusal of retrospection; on the other hand, Taylor's notion of Emerson as attempting "a new positive form

of religion" suggests the possibility for a more radical merger of secular and higher time. Emerson and other presentists seem to believe that actions undertaken in horizontal or ordinary time can carry ultimate spiritual authority without abandoning an essential connection to an eternal God or participation in a divine order as "ontic necessities." See Taylor, *Secular Age*, 53, 208–9; see also Taylor, *Modern Social Imaginaries*, 156–57, 186–88.

36. Quoted in Allen, *Waldo Emerson*, 187.

37. See Emerson, *Nature*, 3.

38. Pugin had also characterized his opponents as "blasphemer[s] against the holy Ghost." See Hill, *God's Architect*, 241.

39. Emerson, "The Lord's Supper," 108.

40. Indeed, Garrison's projection of personal ego allowed him to adopt "the revivalist idiom of testimony in a way that appealed to both revivalists and liberals who admired revivalist zeal." McKanan, *Prophetic Encounters*, 42. Nord stresses the "participatory character" of the *Liberator* and Garrison's determination to make the paper speak not merely for himself but for others. Nord, *Communities of Journalism*, 99–100.

41. Nord, *Communities of Journalism*, 98.

42. McKanan, *Prophetic Encounters*, 40.

43. McKanan, *Prophetic Encounters*, 42.

44. Alfred F. Young, *The Shoemaker and the Tea Party: Memory and the American Revolution* (New York: Beacon, 2000), 153. Young notes that abolitionists and advocates of the working class often advanced radical appropriations of Bunker Hill in the antebellum era.

45. Ford Risley, *Abolition and the Press: The Moral Struggle against Slavery* (Evanston, IL: Northwestern University Press, 2008), x.

46. This reading of the abolitionist project is only roughly compatible with other interpretations that identify the abolitionists' many rhetorical appeals to eighteenth-century revolution as a kind of determined anachronism. For an outstanding example of such a perspective, see Robert Fanuzzi, *Abolition's Public Sphere* (Minneapolis: University of Minnesota Press, 2003). While Fanuzzi offers a compelling description of abolitionism's anachronistic relationship to history, I argue that abolitionist references to a revolutionary past are typically prophetic rather than merely anachronistic. This is to say that late abolitionism's apparent anachronism corresponded to a presentist mode of memory that, partly through their efforts, was becoming dominant in the antebellum era.

47. The *Liberator*'s first issue insisted slavery was an emergency demanding immediate action. "Tell a man whose house ins on fire, to give a moderate alarm; tell him to moderately rescue his wife from the hands of the ravisher; tell the mother to gradually extricate her babe from the fire into which it has fallen;—but urge me not to use moderation in a cause like the present." Garrison, *Liberator* 1, no. 1 (1 January 1831).

48. Although they were not entirely compatible, proslavery forces could eventually choose between authoritative visions of the past provided by the Bible or the sort of supposedly scientific analysis prominently displayed in Josiah C. Nott and George R. Gliddon's *Types of Mankind: or, Ethnological Researches: Based upon the Ancient Monuments,*

Paintings, Sculptures, and Crania of Races, and upon Their Natural Geographical, Philological and Biblical History (Philadelphia: J. B. Lippincot, 1854).

49. Mark A. Noll, *America's God: From Jonathan Edwards to Abraham Lincoln* (New York: Oxford University Press, 2005), 391, 395.

50. Michael Schudson, *The Power of News* (Cambridge, MA: Harvard University Press, 1995), 25.

51. See Risley, *Abolition and the Press*, 25; Leonard L. Richards, *The Slave Power: The Free North and Southern Domination, 1780–1860* (Baton Rouge: Louisiana State University Press, 2000), 128.

52. This success was not without costs to abolitionist publishers, since cheap papers could also threaten the bottom lines of long-standing antislavery publications like the *National Era*. See Risley, *Abolition and the Press*, 148.

53. As Haynes points out, however, for Garrison "the ideals enshrined in the Declaration were universal and divinely inspired" and thus did not constrain him from seeking out British allies. Haynes, *Unfinished Revolution*, 189. See also Fanuzzi, *Abolition's Public Sphere*, 1–82.

54. Risley, *Abolition and the Press*, 6.

55. Haynes, *Unfinished Revolution*, 194–95.

56. Hill, *God's Architect*, 165; Bush, *American Declarations*, 112.

57. Greeley, *Recollections*, 86.

58. Emerson, *English Traits*, 575; Emerson to Carlyle, 11 March 1854, in *The Correspondence of Thomas Carlyle and Ralph Waldo Emerson*, 2 vols. (Boston: Ticknor, 1888), 2:266.

59. Packer, "Signing Off," 10.

60. Quoted in Packer, "Signing Off," 21.

61. Packer, "Signing Off," 22.

3. The News and Walt Whitman

1. Whitman published his account in the 7 March 1842 issue of the *New York Aurora*. See Martin Klammer, *Whitman, Slavery, and the Emergence of "Leaves of Grass"* (University Park: Pennsylvania State University Press, 1995), 46.

2. Emerson, "The Poet," 305.

3. Greeley defended Whitman's poetic gifts publicly in 1850, and the *Tribune*'s enthusiastic review of *Leaves of Grass* earned him the ridicule of American critics who disallowed Whitman's genius and even his status as a poet. See Jerome Loving, *Walt Whitman: The Song of Himself* (Berkeley: University of California Press, 2000), 153, 187–88.

4. On Whitman's antitraditionalism, especially in relation to British precedents, see Kenneth M. Price, *Whitman and Tradition: The Poet in His Century* (New Haven, CT: Yale University Press, 1990), 8–34.

5. Whitman, "Letter to Ralph Waldo Emerson," in *Leaves* (1856), 346.

6. Betsy Erkkilä, "'To Paris with My Love': Whitman among the French Revisited," *Revue Française D'Études Américaines* 108 (May 2006): 9.

7. See Klammer, *Whitman*, 27-60.

8. Whitman's New Orleans interlude has long been a source of speculation about Whitman's personal and poetic development; Klammer has noted how his work clipping news from other papers corresponded to an expanded view of African Americans. See Loving, *Walt Whitman*, 114; Klammer, *Whitman*, 56-60.

9. Klammer points out that "despite the conventional tone and diction" the 1850 poems as a group have "at least worked the slavery issue into the shape of poetry" in a way that foreshadows the racial perspective of the original *Leaves of Grass*. Klammer, *Whitman*, 83.

10. American news also influenced the style of Whitman's poetry. See Shelley Fisher Fishkin, *From Fact to Fiction: Journalism and Imaginative Writing in America* (Baltimore: Johns Hopkins University Press, 1985), 13-51.

11. See Cadava, *Emerson*, 107. Later Emerson would respond publicly to Webster's speech with several of his own, including one on the Fugitive Slave Law delivered March 7, 1854; see Ronald A Bosco and Joel Myerson, eds. *The Later Lectures of Ralph Waldo Emerson, 1843-1871*, 2 vols. (Athens: University of Georgia Press, 2001), 1:333-47.

12. Precise accounts of congressional speeches are difficult to establish in this period; newspapers depended on correspondents' shorthand notes for some versions of speeches and allowed the speaker to amend the text before the publication of others. As Charles M. Wiltse points out, Webster published a "revised and corrected" version of the speech in the *Boston Atlas* on March 11; this became the basis for several pamphlet editions from a variety of presses in New York and elsewhere. It therefore seems likely that Whitman would have had ready access to this amended version by the time he wrote his poetic response in June, though he doubtless also had read summary reports and perhaps even transcripts of the original. In this paragraph and hereafter the account corresponds to the amended version, though I note the discrepancies with the original printed transcription; the reference to the "golden chain," for example, does not appear in the *National Intelligencer* version published on March 8. Daniel Webster, "The Constitution and the Union," in *The Papers of Daniel Webster: Speeches and Formal Writings*, ed. Charles M. Wiltse (Hanover, NH: University Press of New England, 1988), 2:515, 550.

13. *New-York Tribune*, 11 March 1850, 2.

14. *New-York Tribune*, 9 March 1850, 1.

15. Walt Whitman, "Song for a Certain Congressman," *New York Evening Post*, 2 March 1850, 2, http://www.whitmanarchive.org/published/periodical/poems/per.00004.

16. Mark A. Noll, *God and Race in American Politics: A Short History* (Princeton, NJ: Princeton University Press, 2008), 34.

17. Webster, "The Constitution and the Union," 519-22.

18. See Walt Whitman, "Blood-Money," *New-York Tribune*, supplement, 22 March 1850, 1, https://whitmanarchive.org/published/periodical/poems/per.00089.

19. Even readers who have recognized Whitman's reliance on biblical imagery, language, and themes often regard the connection as relatively superficial. See, for example, Jimmie M. Killingsworth, *Whitman's Poetry of the Body: Sexuality, Politics, and Text* (Chapel Hill: University of North Carolina Press, 1989), 127-30.

20. McKanan, *Prophetic Encounters*, 74.

21. The great twentieth-century New Testament interpreter William Barclay articulates this attitude toward the gospel succinctly: "In the early days . . . Christianity was not argument about a dead person, however great; it was encounter with a living presence." Barclay, *The Mind of St. Paul* (New York: Harper and Row, 1958), 114–15.

22. In the synoptic gospels Christ establishes the supper as a commemoration of the death that Judas, identified as Christ's betrayer, brings about in each of the narratives. See Mt 26:14–29; Mk 14:10–25; Lk 22:3–23.

23. Jesus makes this connection especially visceral in the Gospel of John by dipping bread into wine and passing it to Judas to identify him as the betrayer. See Jn 13:26.

24. Jonathan Edwards, quoted in George M. Marsden, *Jonathan Edwards: A Life* (New Haven, CT: Yale University Press, 2003), 354.

25. Jerome Loving, for example, devotes considerable attention to the poem but refers to it as a response to Webster that "was essentially a modern rendering of Judas's betrayal of Christ." See Loving, *Walt Whitman*, 153.

26. 1 Cor 11:17, 22.

27. 1 Cor 11:23–27. The words do not appear in the Gospel of John, in which Jesus pauses during supper to wash his disciples' feet. The synoptic gospels follow a more standardized account, although the words of institution differ somewhat. See Mt 26:14–29; Mk 14:10–25; Lk 22:3–23.

28. Emerson, "The Lord's Supper," 99.

29. Emerson credits the Quakers for having "good reasons" to abandon the communion ritual; as several scholars have noted, Emerson relied on Thomas Clarkson's 1806 work *A Portraiture of Quakerism* as a source for his own argument. See Marie C. Turpie, "A Quaker Source for Emerson's Sermon on the Lord's Supper," *New England Quarterly* 17 (1944): 95–101. See also Packer, "Signing Off," 7n16. Whitman was also influenced by Quakerism and would have been familiar with such arguments. Indeed, Whitman's original intention to portray schism in favorable terms may also have had a Quaker association for him, for he would later recall the "two opposed meeting houses in one enclave" that he had witnessed on Long Island and told Horace Traubel in 1890: "I don't know if any sect has such a democratic feeling—one fence elsewhere rarely includes two bands of worshipers!" See Horace Traubel, *With Walt Whitman in Camden*, vol. 6, ed. Gertrude Traubel and William White (Carbondale: Southern Illinois University Press, 1982), 259. The sense of sectarian division that adheres to the poem may also have explained why it did not appear in the 1855 *Leaves of Grass*. In 1889 Whitman more or less confirmed Traubel's suspicion that late editions of *Leaves of Grass* had excluded it "on sectional grounds," explaining, "There is a partisanship in the poem which makes it to some extent nonexact—nonrepresentative." See Horace Traubel, *With Walt Whitman in Camden*, vol. 5, ed. Gertrude Traubel (Carbondale: Southern Illinois University Press, 1964), 207.

30. Jn 1:36.

31. Paul also refers to Christ as the paschal lamb in 1 Corinthians, the same epistle that contains references to this tradition and the words of institution (1 Cor 5:7 and 11:23–26).

Raymond Brown notes that some of the earliest first-century Christians seem to have passed on to Paul the communal and commemorative breaking of the bread and that the notion of divine presence in the act may have developed from even earlier Jewish practices. See Brown, *An Introduction to the New Testament* (New York: Doubleday, 1997), 288–89.

32. Ernst van den Hemel, "Things That Matter: The *Extra Calvinisticum,* the Eucharist, and John Calvin's Unstable Materiality," in *Things: Religion and the Question of Materiality,* ed. Dick Houtman and Brigit Meyer (New York: Fordham University Press, 2012), 63. Van den Hemel shows how Calvin's theological adjustment of doctrines of the Eucharist was not merely a compromise between the Lutheran and Zwinglian views but rather a position deeply rooted in Calvin's theology and his belief in the potential for divine immanence in the material everyday experience of the present.

33. These correspondences do not necessarily contradict David Kuebrich's claim that Whitman intended to advance a post-Christian religion. See Kuebrich, *Minor Prophecy: Walt Whitman's New American Religion* (Bloomington: Indiana University Press, 1989); Kuebrich, "Religion and the Poet-Prophet," in *A Companion to Walt Whitman,* ed. Donald Kummings (2007; Oxford: Wiley-Blackwell, 2009), 197–215.

34. Whitman's use of "finish" in apparent reference to Jesus's upcoming passion echoes Jesus's final word from the cross in the gospel of John. See Jn 19:30.

35. The Greek word used by Jesus in the synoptic gospels was translated by nineteenth-century Bibles as "covenant" or "testament."

36. "The Reclamation in Free States of Fugitive Slaves," *New-York Tribune,* 20 March 1850, 2.

37. The report, "Webster's Speech," is actually from March 11 but was published in the March 16 edition. *New-York Tribune,* 16 March 1850, 1.

38. *New-York Tribune,* 20 March 1850, 1.

39. *New-York Tribune,* 20 March 1850, 1.

40. Frances M. Clarke, *War Stories: Suffering and Sacrifice in the Civil War North* (Chicago: University of Chicago Press, 2011), 16–17.

41. These lines were added to amended versions of the speech. Webster, "The Constitution and the Union," 551.

42. *New-York Tribune,* 14 June 1850, 3.

43. In the same edition of the *Tribune* that responded to Webster's speech, the paper's Paris correspondent defended himself against the charge of radicalism by attacking the European caste system and unrepresentative governments as the equivalent of plantation slavery. *New-York Tribune,* 14 June 1850, 3.

44. These *Tribune* writers celebrated European revolution as a sign of the coming of "Universal Emancipation," and European revolutionaries such as Giuseppe Mazzini saw the United States as a model for nationalism's triumph over entrenched monarchical traditions. See Williams, *Horace Greeley,* 129, 137.

45. See Tuchinsky, *Greeley's "Tribune,"* 84–85.

46. Andrew Delbanco, *Melville: His World and Work* (New York: Alfred A. Knopf, 2005), 103.

47. McKanan, *Prophetic Encounters*, 73

48. Walt Whitman, "Resurgemus," *New-York Tribune*, 21 June 1850, 3, https://whitmanarchive.org/published/periodical/poems/per.00088.

49. Mt 25:42–45.

50. Whitman, "Song for a Certain Congressman." The *Tribune* was regularly reporting on European slaves, American serfs, and especially the hypocrisy inherent in the example of Britain's impoverished and unrepresented masses during this period. *New-York Tribune*, 14 June 1850, 3.

51. See Mk 13:35 and Lk 13:25.

52. This form of Christian-infused spirituality also contained a literally "spiritualist" element, for the rage for spiritualism had recently become a mainstream phenomenon, partly through Greeley's popularization of such contemporary miracles that same year. *New-York Tribune*, 18 January 1850, 1. See Williams, *Horace Greeley*, 121–23; McKanan, *Prophetic Encounters*, 87.

53. Webster, "The Constitution and the Union," 548.

54. Whitman, "Song for a Certain Congressman."

55. Webster, "The Constitution and the Union," 548.

Part II. War Stories and Memory Circuits

1. In *The Communist Manifesto*, Marx had observed that the union of workers was "helped on by the improved means of communication that are created by modern industry and that place the workers of different localities in contact with one another." The *Manifesto* responds directly to the charge that communists were antinationalists by displacing the criticism: first onto exploitive ruling classes who ensure that "working men have no country" but finally onto history itself, which with the unification of the proletariat "will cause [national differences and antagonisms] to vanish still faster." Marx and Engels, *Collected Works* 6: 493, 502–3.

2. The paradox of violent nationalisms that arose despite the growth of international communication and commitments formed a catalyst for explorations of nationalism by several twentieth-century Marxist scholars, including Benedict Anderson. Anderson's specific quandary lay in explaining how nationalism not only remained pervasive within modern Marxist states but had led to war between those states. See Anderson, *Imagined Communities*, 1–4.

3. Susan-Mary Grant, "From Union to Nation? The Civil War and the Development of American Nationalism," in *Themes of the American Civil War*, 2nd ed., ed. Susan-Mary Grant (New York: Routledge, 2010), 300–301.

4. Timothy Sweet, *Traces of War: Poetry, Photography, and the Crisis of the Union* (Baltimore: Johns Hopkins University Press, 1990), 13.

5. Martha Schoolman, *Abolitionist Geographies* (Minneapolis: University of Minnesota Press, 2007), 7.

4. Palaces of Memory

1. Anderson recognizes a more complex picture in the Americas, where administrative units combined with common languages to create multiple nationalisms within a larger imperial cultural system; Trish Loughran's analysis of communication networks' incapacity to overcome geographical and cultural barriers throughout the early national period—which she aptly describes as simultaneity's "ragged emergence across time in this or that form"—suggests a more complex process by which identity and temporalities were nationalized much more unevenly. See Anderson, *Imagined Communities*, 57; Loughran, *The Republic in Print: Print Culture in the Age of U.S. Nation Building, 1770–1870* (New York: Columbia University Press, 2007), 346.

2. As Michael Alexander notes, such contradictions were suppressed at the popular level under the patriotic zeal of the post-Napoleonic period; they tended to complicate the task of traditionalist theorists, however, as Pugin's difficulties in selecting a national style from among various Gothic alternatives illustrated. Alexander, *Medievalism*, 64–65; see Hill, *God's Architect*, 226–27. See also Jenkyns, *Westminster Abbey*, 18–22.

3. The reinstitution of the Catholic hierarchy in 1850 sparked widespread anti-Catholic protests, and by the time Greeley visited, Newman was offering popular lectures denouncing anti-Catholicism. Crucially, however, Newman and other converts had first sought to reform an essentially English form of Protestant church and state through "a scholarly defense of and a historical reverence for Church tradition and authority" and the return to "highly ritualistic worship" in the Church of England. C. Brad Faught, *The Oxford Movement: A Thematic History of the Tractarians and Their Times* (University Park: Pennsylvania State University Press, 2003), 30.

4. This universal horizon is compatible with some theories of nationalism, and Greenfeld even suggests that "a nation coextensive with humanity is in no way a contradiction in terms." Greenfeld, *Nationalism*, 7. Below I show how this universalist potential within nineteenth-century Anglo-American nationalisms could motivate the exclusionary limitations that defined those nationalisms in practice, because that abstract potential could trigger social and psychological desires for exclusively shared histories that legitimated national belonging as more than an abstract affiliation.

5. This discussion draws on Jeffrey Auerbach's excellent analysis of the exhibition in its national context, *The Great Exhibition of 1851: A Nation on Display* (New Haven, CT: Yale University Press, 1999). See also Hermione Hobhouse, *The Crystal Palace and the Great Exhibition: Art, Science and Productive Industry; A History of the Royal Commission for the Exhibition of 1851* (London: Athlon, 2002).

6. Leonard, *Power of the Press*, 79–95.

7. This hypernationalist impulse, which arises from a weakening faith in national legitimacy under the specific threat of relatively abstract universalist identifications, differs somewhat from the related psychological states described by Greenfeld and Rose. See Greenfeld, *Nationalism*, 15–17, 488; Rose, *States of Fantasy*, 4.

8. Geoffrey Cantor, *Religion and the Great Exhibition of 1851* (New York: Oxford University Press, 2011), 28.

9. The *Economist* reported that daily attendance on May 30, 1851, when Greeley first testified, was fifty-five thousand, twice the number that had attended the palace's grand opening at the beginning of the month. Even for elites, being in a crowd formed part of the experience of the Great Exhibition, which averaged more than a million visitors a month; especially toward the end of the summer, after the price of admission dropped, Britons of all classes flocked to the exhibit; by the end of the summer, the *Times* found that the sidewalks around Hyde Park were "swarming with dense black columns of pedestrians, all wending their way to the Crystal Palace." See Auerbach, *Great Exhibition*, 147–48, 251n122, 252n152.

10. "Pugin loathed the Crystal Palace," but his anachronistic exhibition of a medieval court drew praise in the press as well as ridicule from those who saw it "as backward and outdated, antithetical to progress" and thus contrary to the spirit of the exhibition. See Hill, *God's Architect*, 453; Auerbach, *Great Exhibition*, 116.

11. Auerbach, *Great Exhibition*, 45.

12. There would always be local distinctions in newspapers. Nevertheless, the dawn of the Associated Press and more broadly the midcentury development of a standardized system of gathering and disseminating news was undertaken, according to the New York Associated Press's general agent, Daniel Craig, to achieve and enforce "a uniformity and concert of action" even between competing presses with the goal of "transmitting, from one end of the Union to the other, all important news." Craig quoted in Blondheim, *News over the Wires*, 98.

13. In 1851 the wet-plate process made possible the mass distribution of two new photographic formats: the stereograph and the carte de visite. In England alone from 1861 to 1867, between 2 and 3 billion cartes de visite may have been sold. William C. Darrah, *Cartes de Visite in Nineteenth Century Photography* (Gettysburg, PA: Darrah, 1981), 6.

14. As Charles Taylor and others have observed, the absence of mediation characterized the modern shift to secular or horizontal time. See Taylor, *Secular Age*, 209–10; see also Taylor, *Modern Social Imaginaries*, 158.

15. "This principle lies at the basis of all nationalisms and justifies viewing them as expressions of the same general phenomenon." Greenfeld, *Nationalism*, 7.

16. The first channel cable was laid in 1850, although reliable telegraphic communication between London and Paris was only established in the fall of 1851. Even before his first telegraphic landline was established in 1844, Morse (who had originally conceived his vision of electric telegraph while on a transatlantic voyage) had informed the US government of the feasibility of a transatlantic cable in 1843. See John Steele Gordon, *A Thread across the Ocean: The Heroic Story of the Transatlantic Cable* (New York: Walker, 2002), 35; Blondheim, *News over the Wires*, 30.

17. *Times* of London, 6 August 1858. The editorial was at least as enthusiastic about the cable's capacity to overcome insecurities within Britain's global empire and to tighten political connections to Canada. As Hanlon observes, the widespread enthusiasm for

the transatlantic cable occasionally ascended to lyric heights in the press but was sometimes tinged with notes of anxiety and doubt. See Hanlon, *America's England*, 132–38.

18. The New York papers did all they could to lay the groundwork for the cable by extending telegraphic communication to the easternmost point at which they could intercept transatlantic ships carrying news from the Old World; see Blondheim, *News over the Wires*, 107–10.

19. By the time the exhibition opened, British historians had begun to read the revolutionary breach of the previous century as the result of British misunderstanding of a distant colonial situation. See William Smyth, *Lectures on Modern History from the Irruption of the Northern Nations to the Close of the American Revolution* (Cambridge: John Owen, 1841), 423–26.

20. Lawrence Fenton, *Palmerston and the Times: Foreign Policy, the Press and Public Opinion in Mid-Victorian Britain* (London: I. B. Taurus, 2013), 4.

21. Quoted in Auerbach, *Great Exhibition*, 163.

22. Cantor, *Religion and the Great Exhibition of 1851*, 185–86.

23. Paul Gilmore, *Aesthetic Materialism: Electricity and American Romanticism* (Stanford, CA: Stanford University Press, 2009), 21.

24. See Hudson, *Journalism*, 529; see also Wiener, "'Get the News!,'" 48–66; Blondheim, *News over the Wires*, 24.

25. "[Newspapers] and their discursive patterns have become essential to our modern construction of the world. Indeed, at times the 'world' and the 'news' might almost seem to have merged for us." Richard Terdiman, *Discourse/Counter-Discourse: the Theory and Practice of Symbolic Resistance in Nineteenth-Century France* (Ithaca, NY: Cornell University Press, 1985), 118.

26. Tamarkin's interest is obviously in Anglophilia, but one of her chief insights is that American acts and imagined acts of deference can be read as expressions of the desire for, or even the achievement of, an independent and secure national identity, a way to live "'Americanness' . . . in other languages of national expression." Tamarkin, *Anglophilia*, xxiv.

27. Thomas Peyser, *Utopia and Cosmopolis: Globalization in the Era of American Literary Realism* (Durham, NC: Duke University Press, 1998), 17. Auerbach argues that nationalism and internationalism "were present from the outset" as "the two columns upon which the exhibition was built." Auerbach, *Great Exhibition*, 159. The London builder Thomas Cubitt suggested to Prince Albert that an international exhibition would make the prince "a leading light among the nations," and, according to the minutes of the first meeting between Albert and representatives from the Society of Arts on June 30, 1849, the determination to internationalize the exhibition proceeded under the belief that "particular advantage to British industry might be derived from placing it in fair competition with that of other nations." See Hobhouse, *Crystal Palace*, 8–9.

28. Peyser, *Utopia and Cosmopolis*, 7.

29. Partly this climate was due to the period's many nationalist revolutions on which both sides in the Civil War later drew and which also helped inspire the Franco-Prussian

War of 1870. See Andre M. Fleche, *The Revolution of 1861: The American Civil War in the Age of Nationalist Conflict* (Chapel Hill: University of North Carolina Press, 2012), 11–37.

30. The American Civil War was only the most obvious indication of the decade's latent violence. In the wake of the Crimean War, "forty years of peace were now followed by four wars (fought from 1859 to 1871) that revolutionized the continent." Norman Rich, *Why the Crimean War? A Cautionary Tale* (New York: McGraw-Hill, 1991), 198.

31. Auerbach, *Great Exhibition*, 159. This was true even when the nationalist designation was somewhat tenuous, as was the case for what the *Illustrated London News* described as "the vast extent of territory embraced in the general name of Germany." *Illustrated London News*, 17 May 1851, 436.

32. Indeed, Greeley's Anglophobia nearly kept him from making the trip. See Williams, *Horace Greeley*, 156.

33. *Illustrated London News*, 17 May 1851, 432.

34. Such "taunts" were reprinted in American newspapers. See *New-York Times*, "The Great Exhibition—The American Department," 31 October 1851, 4.

35. Brother Jonathan appeared frequently in British and American newspapers from the period, where he helped readers distinguish the United States from its transatlantic counterparts.

36. Though somewhat restrained, the *Times* article of 18 April 1851 fairly represents the patronizing attitudes against which Greeley reacted: "Some misgivings are entertained as to the effectiveness of the American show, founded on a variety of causes. In the first place, the want of general supervision and control before their contributions were sent over made it impossible to secure a high class and select character for the whole collection. Then again the Americans are not so much a manufacturing as an agricultural community; and, lastly, their greatness lies in their expansive energies, and in the scale upon which they do everything." *Times* of London, 18 April 1851, 5.

37. *Illustrated London News*, Exhibition Supplement, 23 August 1851, 250.

38. *New-York Tribune*, 31 May 1851, 6; see also Horace Greeley, *Glances at Europe in a Series of Letters from Great Britain, France, Italy, Switzerland, &c. during the Summer of 1851, Including Notices of the Great Exhibition, or World's Fair* (New York: Dewitt and Davenport, 1851), 31.

39. *New-York Tribune*, 11 June 1851, 4; see also "Political Economy as Studied at the World's Exhibition," in Greeley, *Glances at Europe*, 92.

40. Years later Greeley would still bitterly recall that early in the exhibition "the great London journals were jeering at the poverty and shabbiness of our department." Greeley, *Recollections*, 273.

41. In the preface to the published volume of the letters, Greeley admits that "the letters in this volume which refer to the great Exhibition of Industry were mainly written when the persistent and unsparing disparagement of the British Press had created a general impression that the American Exposition was a mortifying failure, and when even some of the Americans in Europe, taking their cue from that Press, were declaring themselves

'ashamed of their country' because of such failure. Of course, these letters were written to correct the then prevalent errors. More recently, the tide has completely turned. . . . The truth lies midway between the extremes already indicated." Greeley, *Glances at Europe*, vi.

42. The circulation of the *Times* of London did not rise to seventy thousand until the mid-1850s. See Mott, *American Journalism*, 303.

43. See Williams, *Horace Greeley*, 125–51.

44. Weisbuch neatly summarizes the effect of this anxiety on antebellum literature: prompted by British criticism "American writers . . . would become aware of absences not only external in America but within, in the environment of the imagination." Weisbuch's focus on literary culture may lead him to deemphasize the balance provided by other forms of print culture, especially the distinctly American newspapers. See Weisbuch, *Atlantic Double-Cross*, xiii.

45. James H. Moorhead, *American Apocalypse: Yankee Protestants and the Civil War, 1860–1869* (New Haven, CT: Yale University Press, 1978), x, quoted in Clarke, "'Let All Nations See': Civil War Nationalism and the Memorialization of Wartime Volunteerism," *Civil War History* 52, no. 1 (2006): 90.

46. Auerbach, *Great Exhibition*, 183.

47. See Auerbach, *Great Exhibition*, 45, 114, 183.

48. *New-York Tribune*, 11 June 1851, 4; see also Greeley, *Glances*, 88.

49. Joseph Paxton, who had published a letter recommending free admission in the *Times* and been savaged for it by the same publication, recognized the commission's pricing structure as a "tax on knowledge." See Auerbach, *Great Exhibition*, 144.

50. Greeley, *Glances*, 88–89.

51. Tom Morley, "'The Arcana of That Great Machine': Politicians and *The Times* in the Late 1840s," *History* 73, no. 237 (February 1988): 38, quoted in Fenton, *Palmerston*, 10n2.

52. Greeley, *Glances*, 90.

53. Greeley, *Glances*, 90.

54. Auerbach, *Great Exhibition*, 189.

55. See Meredith McGill, *American Literature and the Culture of Reprinting, 1834–1853* (Philadelphia: University of Pennsylvania Press, 2003), 76–107.

56. Leslie Fiedler, quoted in Weisbuch, *Atlantic Double-Cross*, 81; see also Paul Giles, *Virtual Americas: Transnational Fictions and the Transatlantic Imaginary* (Durham, NC: Duke University Press, 2002), 16.

57. According to Pierre Nora's account of modern memory, it is precisely the recognition of this communal loss that sparks the development of nationalism's *lieux de mémoire*. "There are *lieux de mémoire*, sites of memory, because there are no longer *milieux de mémoire*, real environments of memory." Nora, "Between Memory and History," 7.

58. This notion of a limitation on the universal is central to many theories of nationalism; see Anderson, *Imagined Communities*, 7; Weisbuch, *Atlantic Double-Cross*, 58–60.

5. Wars and Rumors of Wars

1. The *Times* of London, quoted in Phillip Knightley, *The First Casualty: The War Correspondent as Hero and Myth-Maker from the Crimea to Iraq* (Baltimore: Johns Hopkins University Press, 2004), 9.

2. Broader transatlantic anxieties related to this embattled nationalism help explain what Martha Schoolman has described as a major thrust of late antebellum "abolitionist geographies," whereby "abolitionist paramilitarism" in places like Kansas contributed to the reframing of the South "as a zone to be invaded and subdued rather than fended off from the outside through efforts at Northern ideological self-purification." Schoolman, *Abolitionist Geographies*, 7.

3. Hanlon explains "Atlantic sectionalism," or "how sectionalism both shaped American apprehensions of England and configured itself in relation to these apprehensions." Hanlon, *America's England*, x.

4. See *New-York Times*, 27 November 1854.

5. *Speeches of John C. Calhoun*, ed. Richard K. Crallé (New York: D. Appleton, 1883), 550–51, 548, 552.

6. Greenfeld, *Nationalism*, 475, 479.

7. Calhoun, *Speeches*, 552.

8. As Linda Colley argues, "It was the coincidence of [Britain's] pan-Protestantism and its successive wars with a Catholic state [i.e., France] that did most to give it what Eugene Weber calls 'a true political personality.'" Colley, *Britons*, 369–70.

9. Palmerston's hopes were expressed to the cabinet and also to Lord Clarendon. Rich, *Why the Crimean War?*, 108–9.

10. The tsar had sought to gain the support of Christian Europe and neutralize British opposition to Russia by forwarding such a proposal in 1853. Yet in the zeal for war, Britons demonstrated a remarkable capacity to overcome qualms about aiding an Islamic empire. See Rich, *Why the Crimean War?*, 93–95; Orlando Figes, *The Crimean War: A History* (2011; New York: Picador, 2012), 150–51.

11. Indeed, the British army "had not fought in a major battle since Waterloo, and in many ways remained half a century behind the times." Russell's first letters from the front bore witness to the high command's poor organization, for while the French army had "learned how to supply an army on the march efficiently" this was "an area of expertise where their superiority over the British became apparent from the moment the two armies landed." Figes, *Crimean War*, 179. Noting the command's reliance on aristocratic bloodlines, Russell would write to his editor that "the management is infamous, and the contrast offered by our proceedings to the conduct of the French most painful." Quoted in Knightley, *First Casualty*, 5–6.

12. Quoted in Rich, *Why the Crimean War?*, 182.

13. Palmerston's reputation had been cemented while serving as foreign secretary during a controversy over his deployment of British naval power to seize compensation from Greece for British claimants living abroad; Palmerston's patriotic oration had ended the

flap over this "Pacifico Affair" by arguing that "a British subject, in whatever land he may be, shall feel confident that the watchful eye and the strong arm of England, will protect him against injustice and wrong." See Fenton, *Palmerston*, 113.

14. Clarendon to Lord Granville, 12 March 1856, quoted in Rich, *Why the Crimean War?*, 184.

15. Rich, *Why the Crimean War?*, 183.

16. "Napoleon's Policy—A Retrospect," *New-York Times*, 27 January 1855, 4; *New-York Tribune*, 6 May 1854, 5; "The Future of Turkey," *New-York Times*, 9 May 1854, 4.

17. "Napoleon's Policy–A Retrospect."

18. See Laurence Fenton, "Charles Rowcroft, Irish-Americans, and the 'Recruitment Affair,' 1855–1856," *Historical Journal* 53, no.4 (December 2010): 963–82.

19. Quoted in Bruce Chadwick, *1858: Abraham Lincoln, Jefferson Davis, Robert E. Lee, Ulysses S. Grant and the War They Failed to See* (Naperville, IL: Sourcebooks, 2008), 246–47.

20. *Illustrated London News*, 3 November 1855, 513.

21. *Illustrated London News*, 3 November 1855, 513–14.

22. Nicole Etcheson, *Bleeding Kansas: Contested Liberty in the Civil War Era* (Lawrence: University Press of Kansas, 2004), 46.

23. Parker quoted in Gura, *American Transcendentalism*, 255; Tuchinsky, *Greeley's "Tribune,"* 158. Greeley himself reputedly sent a six-inch cannon. See Henry Luther Stoddard, *Horace Greeley, Printer, Editor, Crusader* (New York: G. P. Putnam's Sons, 1946), 180.

24. "The federalist project thus amounts to the successful, if unlikely, conquest of both space and time by a theory, a consolidation, on a mass scale, of both territory and history—the very matrix of what it means to be a nation." Loughran, *Republic in Print*, 226.

25. Etcheson, *Bleeding Kansas*, 29,

26. Quoted in Adam I. P. Smith, *The Stormy Present: Conservatism and the Problem of Slavery in Northern Politics, 1846–1865* (Chapel Hill: University of North Carolina Press, 2017), 103.

27. Etcheson, *Bleeding Kansas*, 46, 48.

28. Taylor, *Modern Social Imaginaries*, 181, 180. See also Taylor, *Secular Age*, 197.

29. Etcheson, *Bleeding Kansas*, 46.

30. Etcheson, *Bleeding Kansas*, 29.

31. Republicans not only made the Ostend Manifesto a major campaign issue but branded Buchanan a piratical threat to the social order; see Smith, *Stormy Present*, 96–98.

32. Taylor, *Modern Social Imaginaries*, 185–94.

33. Mark A. Noll, *The Civil War as a Theological Crisis* (Chapel Hill: University of North Carolina Press, 2006), 4, 2. See also Noll, *America's God*, 386–401.

34. Greeley, *Recollections*, 294.

35. Holzer, *Lincoln*, 150.

36. Quoted in Holt, *Rise and Fall*, 844.

37. Violence that spiked in 1856 began much earlier, and the press promoted major

incidents involving militia groups, including the "Wakarusa War" of 1855, to demonstrate northern mettle as well as the political legitimacy of free-state groups. The *Weekly Tribune*'s usual practice of carrying a summary of news from various geographical areas on its front page in ordinary typeface was altered at several points during the Kansas controversy by outsized front-page stories of the violent struggle printed in blaring type. See Etcheson, *Bleeding Kansas*, 87; Williams, *Horace Greeley*, 189.

38. Early reports of the Whigs' demise as an intersectional party, though vehement and widespread after Kansas-Nebraska's initial passage, proved premature; the intersectional break over slavery's expansion became fatal when combined with the proliferation of political alternatives northern voters encountered during the subsequent congressional elections, which prevented Whig organizations from effectively channeling anti-Democratic sentiments; no free state featured a two-party race between Whigs and Democrats in 1854. See Holt, *Rise and Fall*, 822–57.

39. Smith, *Stormy Present*, 100.

40. *New-York Tribune*, 5 January 1854, quoted in Holzer, *Lincoln*, 153; see also Williams, *Horace Greeley*, 171.

41. Holzer, *Lincoln*, 146.

42. Leonard, *Power of the Press*, 90–91.

43. "The Presidency," *New-York Tribune*, 28 April 1856, 4.

44. Although this violent response to violent upheavals seems counterintuitive, Smith argues convincingly that "in the political imagination of Northerners, violence was both terrifying and emancipatory. It . . . increased their anxiety about the stability of their society . . . and gave them, at the same time, an imagined resolution . . . using violence as the only alternative to national destruction." Smith, *Stormy Present*, 99.

45. *Weekly Tribune*, 26 January 1856, 4.

46. David M. Potter, *The Impending Crisis, 1848–1861*, ed. Don E. Fehrenbacher (New York: Harper and Row, 1976), 219.

47. Sweet, *Traces of War*, especially 165–205; Sontag, *Regarding the Pain of Others*, 51–55.

48. Though Loughran's larger project focused on earlier periods, this particular description is of a *Tribune* map printed at the height of Bleeding Kansas. See Loughran, *Republic in Print*, 366.

49. "The Nebraska Infamy," *New-York Tribune*, 9 May 1854, 4.

50. *Weekly Tribune*, 26 January 1856, 4.

51. Popular sovereignty as well as southern responses to Kansas "completed [the] radicalization" of the *Tribune*, which became "for the first time, openly and aggressively sectional." See Tuchinsky, *Greeley's "Tribune,"* 157.

52. "Power of the Press," *Weekly Tribune*, 1 November 1856, 4.

53. *Weekly Tribune*, 1 November 1856, 4. The only *Tribune* club of more than forty members from Virginia in March 1850 was in Wheeling (now West Virginia). *Weekly Tribune*, 30 March 1850, 5.

54. *Weekly Tribune*, 1 November 1856, 4.

55. *New-York Tribune*, 9 May 1854, 4. The memorial petition, presented by Edward Everett, was signed by three thousand clergy. See Etcheson, *Bleeding Kansas*, 17–18.

56. Kansas news, as a medium for nationalist desires that simultaneously produced acute nationalist anxiety, suggests the sort of political fantasy that, in its idealization, "can be grounds for license or pleasure" but "can just as easily surface as fierce blockading protectiveness." Rose, *States of Fantasy*, 4.

57. The *Tribune* offered the dubious proposition that its tallies showed an increase "comparatively even greater in the Slave States" than in free states "having advanced in some at the rate of one hundred per cent." While it was true that South Carolina subscriptions increased from 17 to 38, this increase of 21 subscriptions is hardly impressive when compared, as it was in this column, with northern states like Indiana that increased by more than 5,000 subscriptions and 85 percent over the same months. *Weekly Tribune*, 1 November 1856, 4.

58. The *Tribune* was widely banned in the South, and Virginia had brought criminal charges for insurrection against Greeley in 1856. Suzanne Schultze, *Horace Greeley: A Bio-Bibliography*, Bibliographies and Indexes in American History 22 (New York: Greenwood, 1992), 30. The *Tribune* responded to this lawsuit enthusiastically. See *Weekly Tribune*, 1 November 1856, 4.

59. *New-York Tribune*, 18 May 1856, quoted in Williams, *Horace Greeley*, 173.

60. *New-York Tribune* 12 April 1855, quoted in Eric Foner, *Free Soil, Free Labor, Free Men: The Ideology of the Republican Party before the Civil War* (New York: Oxford University Press, 1970), 310.

61. This strategy of regional firmness included calling the secessionist "bluff" of southern leaders during the Kansas crisis, and Greeley would similarly advise both his readers and Lincoln to "let the erring sisters go in peace," though he would in virtually the same breath encourage the president to violently recover national ground from slavery's forces in Maryland and Virginia. All of this suggests Greeley's intense desire for the sense of geographically grounded national integrity that the territorial disputes so profoundly unsettled. See *Weekly Tribune*, 10 November 1860.

62. Quoted in Stoddard, *Greeley*, 181, 180.

63. Susan-Mary Grant, *North over South: Northern Nationalism and American Identity in the Antebellum Era* (Lawrence: University Press of Kansas, 2008), 8. Elsewhere Grant argues that the positive moral overtones of the northern victory concealed the true nature of antebellum northern nationalism and thus postbellum American nationalism as well. Grant, *North over South*, 4.

64. *Weekly Tribune*, 12 January 1856, 8.

65. Indeed, Greeley had largely abandoned reporting on Whig politics in the name of a "general fusion of all parties" in 1853 and later helped foster the growth of the Republican coalition through his influence on midwestern editors as well as readers. See Holt, *Rise and Fall*, 771, 859.

66. William Adelbert Dill, *Growth of Newspapers in the United States* (Lawrence: University of Kansas, 1928), 11–12.

67. *Weekly Tribune,* 12 January 1856, 8.

68. *Weekly Tribune,* 12 January 1856, 8.

69. See Etcheson, *Bleeding Kansas,* 169.

70. *Weekly Tribune,* 2 February 1856, 5.

71. *Weekly Tribune,* 2 February 1856, 5.

72. The encounter demonstrates how in these years the northern press ensured not only that, as Smith notes, "the imagery of violence—as both a threat and a response to the threat—suffused political language," but also that active participation in the news's violent history offered a means to political actualization; according to Greeley's account, the famous editor's ignorance of Rust's identity fueled the congressman's rage, and his repeated attacks ensured hundreds of thousands would recognize him as one of slavery's defenders. *Weekly Tribune,* 2 February 1856, 5.

73. James McPherson, *Battle Cry of Freedom: The Civil War Era* (New York: Ballantine Books, 1988), 150–53.

74. Quoted in McPherson, *Battle Cry of Freedom,* 151.

75. McPherson quotes this reformed Southern apologist in *Battle Cry of Freedom,* 151. David Donald's estimate of the speech's circulation is quoted in Potter, *Impending Crisis,* 219n40. The Sumner portrait was printed in the *Weekly Tribune,* 7 June 1856, 3.

76. *New-York Times,* 27 January 1855, 4; *New-York Times,* 9 May 1854, 4.

77. "War with England," *New-York Times,* 23 February 1856, 4.

78. *New-York Tribune,* 1 March 1856, 4.

79. For Phillips's concern with the transatlantic context and his account of the surprising centrality of religion to American civil strife in the 1850s and 1860s, see Phillips, *The Cousins' Wars: Religion, Politics, and the Triumph of Anglo-America* (New York: Basic Books, 2000), xii–xiii, 390–406.

80. In 1855, David Christy published *Cotton Is King* anonymously; Christy would respond explicitly to the *Tribune* review, published on July 19, in the preface to the second edition. See Christy, *Cotton Is King: Or the Culture of Cotton, and Its Relation to Agriculture, Manufactures and Commerce; to the Free Colored People, and to Those Who Believe That Slavery Is in Itself Sinful* (Cincinnati: Moore, Wilstack, Keys, 1855); see also "Cotton and Slavery," *New-York Tribune,* 19 July 1855, 3; Christy, "Preface to the Second Edition," in *Cotton Is King* (New York: Derby and Jackson, 1856), vii.

6. "Transatlantic Latter-Day Poetry"

1. Emerson, *English Traits,* 583, 584.

2. Emerson, *English Traits,* 580.

3. [George Eliot], "Transatlantic Latter-Day Poetry," *Leader* 7 (7 June 1856): 547–548. For Eliot's review and all subsequent cited criticism of the first edition in

periodicals, see *Walt Whitman Archive,* http://whitmanarchive.org/criticism/reviews/lg1855/index.html.

4. "Leaves of Grass," unsigned review of *Leaves of Grass,* by Walt Whitman, *Saturday Review* 1 (15 March 1856): 393–94.

5. [Eliot], "Transatlantic Latter-Day Poetry."

6. The relevant 1856 lines repurpose a crucial section of the 1855 preface, which insisted that "the direct trial of him who would be the greatest poet is today," to prove Whitman had passed "the final test of poems or any character" to become the national bard; they adopt the gerund form to convert 1855's present tense into established and ongoing facts. Whitman, *Leaves* (1855), iv, xi; Whitman, *Leaves* (1856), 184.

7. [Walt Whitman], "An English and an American Poet," *American Phrenological Journal* 22 (October 1855): 90–91.

8. See Haynes, *Unfinished Revolution,* 51–76.

9. Indeed, Whitman's terms correspond quite closely with scholars' typical emphasis on geographical contiguity, inherited ethnicity, cultural traditions, and religion—along with shared language and political sovereignty—as pillars of national belonging. See Gat, *Nations,* 23–26.

10. This working-class identity was not solely the mark of an outsider but also a central element in Whitman's understanding of himself as a national poet. See Edward Keyes Whitley, *American Bards: Walt Whitman and Other Unlikely Candidates for National Poet* (Chapel Hill: University of North Carolina Press, 2011), 157.

11. [Eliot], "Transatlantic Latter-Day Poetry."

12. [Whitman], "An English and an American Poet."

13. [Whitman], "An English and an American Poet."

14. These efforts bore little fruit in the United States, partly because of American outrage at the schemes' unveiling; ultimately Britain recruited just over ten thousand mercenaries, most of whom were German or Swiss. See Figes, *Crimean War,* 334.

15. Whitman, *Leaves* (1855), iv.

16. Whitman, *Leaves* (1855), iii.

17. Whitman, *Leaves* (1855), iii.

18. See Price, *Whitman and Tradition,* 15.

19. Whitman, *Leaves* (1855), iv.

20. Gura, *American Transcendentalism,* 245–48, 250–52.

21. Whitman, "Song for a Certain Congressman."

22. Klammer, *Whitman,* 103–6.

23. Whitman was hardly alone in considering slavery an aristocratic institution, and a good deal of the North's free labor rhetoric operated by contrast to both European social hierarchies based on inherited wealth and to an American South that was often accused of reproducing this same sort of feudal system.

24. Loving, *Walt Whitman,* 174.

25. [Whitman], "An English and an American Poet."

26. Whitman's 1855 audience was familiar with Jonathan from newspapers that cast him

as the American contrast to John Bull though he became increasingly associated with the northern war effort and was sometimes depicted in opposition to secessionist counterparts. See Charles Adams, *Slavery, Secession, and the Civil War: Views from the United Kingdom and Europe, 1856–1865* (Lanham, MD: Scarecrow, 2007), 316. *Brother Jonathan* was also the title of a New York literary journal where Whitman had occasionally published and that became a virulent advocate for national literature under the editorship of John Neal, though it also specialized in reprinting the work of British writers for an American audience. See Spencer, *Quest for Nationality*, 76, 114.

27. Whitman, *Leaves* (1855), 89.

28. Whitman, *Leaves* (1855), 89.

29. Webster famously described Bunker Hill as a landscape pregnant with political meaning where the postrevolutionary generation stood "among the sepulchres of our fathers . . . on ground distinguished by their valor, their constancy, and the shedding of their blood . . . not to fix an uncertain date in our annals, nor to draw into notice an obscure and unknown spot. If our humble purpose had never been conceived, if we ourselves had never been born, the 17th of June, 1775, would have been a day on which all subsequent history would have poured its light, and the eminence where we stand a point of attraction to the eyes of successive generations." Daniel Webster, *An Address Delivered at the Laying of the Corner Stone of the Bunker Hill Monument* (Boston: Cummings, Hilliard, 1825), 3–4. For an analysis of Emerson's radical objections to Webster's genuflection, see Cadava, *Emerson*, 91–148.

30. Whitman, *Leaves* (1855), 89–90. Whitman signaled pauses within poetic lines with four printed dots that resemble ellipsis points in the original 1855 version of the poem; to avoid confusion I've replaced them with dashes here and below.

31. Whitman, *Leaves* (1855), 90.

32. Whitman, *Leaves* (1855), 89.

33. Whitman, *Leaves* (1855), 89.

34. Whitman, *Leaves* (1855), 90.

35. Phillip Round notes that while Whitman's later descriptions of Boston emerged from visits to the city that began in 1860, this early vision is symbolic; as in previous news poems, Whitman's poetic rendering of New York newspaper reports from the city highlights the real capacity of news to connect the distinct American locales. See Round, "Boston, Massachusetts," in *The Walt Whitman Encyclopedia, Walt Whitman Archive*, http://www.whitmanarchive.org/criticism/current/encyclopedia/entry_76.html.

36. A *Tribune* editorial described Burns's extradition as a "show," and the dispatches from throughout the day called attention to the "dragoons" and the well-ordered Boston police and noted that "thousands of women filled the balconies and retained possession of the windows in Court and State-sts., up to the time of his [Burns's] departure." All of these details are mentioned in Whitman's poem. See *New-York Tribune*, 3 June 1854, 4–5. See also *New-York Times*, 3 June 1854, 1.

37. Gura, *American Transcendentalism*, 253.

38. Quoted in Gura, *American Transcendentalism*, 253.

39. Whitman, *Leaves* (1855), 90.

40. For example, the "Protoleaf" that opens the 1860 edition seems to subtly annex Canada as well as Cuba, both of which were recent flash points of Anglo-American controversy. See Whitman, *Leaves* (1860), 7, 19.

41. *New-York Tribune*, 3 June 1854, 4.

42. *New-York Tribune*, 3 June 1854, 4.

43. *New-York Tribune*, 3 June 1854, 4.

44. *New-York Tribune*, 3 June 1854, 4.

45. Geographical scope as well as numerical scale was one of the primary goals of the Associated Press's consolidation in the early 1850s. See Blondheim, *News over the Wires*, 99.

46. Weisbuch borrows Stephen Spender's notion of *patria* to develop this distinction between the true nation and its actuality, but the patriotic focus on the "country" also seems to have been basic to the way the *Tribune* projected an image of national authenticity even as it threatened to topple standing national institutions. See Weisbuch, *Atlantic Double-Cross*, 80–81.

47. Indeed, Simms had associated himself in the 1830s with the "Young America" circle of Evert A. Duyckinck, which was centered in New York City. See Haynes, *Unfinished Revolution*, 71.

48. Although similar arguments had been previously pursued on the grounds of regional identity, a full-blown literary nationalism emerged amid the general climate of intensifying sectionalist conflict in the mid-1850s; Simms was responding directly to an editorial on the Kansas-Nebraska controversy in *Harper's Monthly*. William Gilmore Simms, "Northern Periodicals Versus the South," *Southern Quarterly Review* 10, no.20 (October 1854): 510. See also Coleman Hutchison, *Apples and Ashes: Literature, Nationalism, and the Confederate States of America* (Athens: University of Georgia Press, 2012), 19, 54–55.

49. For an extended analysis of the vicissitudes of antebellum southerners' nationalist attachments, see Hutchison, *Apples and Ashes*, 18–31.

50. Walt Whitman, "New York Dissected," *Life Illustrated*, 2 August 1856, ed. Jason Stacy, *Walt Whitman Archive*, http://www.whitmanarchive.org/published/periodical/journalism/tei/per.00271.html.

51. Horace Traubel, *With Walt Whitman in Camden*, vol. 1 (Boston: Small, Maynard, 1906), 282.

52. The series of poems that surround "Resurgemus" focus on American history and its bard as exceeder of previous excellences while highlighting the international relevance of America's founding ideal of liberty. See Whitman, *Leaves* (1856), 249–78.

53. [Whitman], "An English and an American Poet."

54. The original of the letter may have been owned by Horace Traubel's widow; see Emerson, *Letters*, 4:520–21.

55. Quoted in Loving, *Walt Whitman*, 153.

56. *New-York Tribune*, 10 October 1855, 7.

57. Quoted in Whitman, *Leaves* (1856), 359. Emerson's public endorsement caused significant dismay among many of his literary friends. See Emerson, *Letters*, 4:520–21.

58. Whitman, *Leaves* (1856), 93.

59. Whitman, *Leaves* (1856), 182.

60. Whitman, *Leaves* (1856), 182–83.

61. Whitman, *Leaves* (1856), 182.

62. Whitman, *Leaves* (1856), 346.

63. Ivan Marki, "*Leaves of Grass,* 1855 Edition," *Walt Whitman Archive*, https://whitmanarchive.org/criticism/current/encyclopedia/entry_21.html.

64. Whitman's effort to present his relationship with Emerson as one of mutually reinforcing literary originators helps explain "the internal tensions within the complete letter," as well as Whitman's increasingly critical view, which Kenneth M. Price has argued became more virulent once Emerson was more firmly ensconced in the literary firmament. See Price, "Whitman on Emerson: New Light on the 1856 Open Letter," *American Literature* 56, no.4 (December 1984): 83–87.

65. Loving, *Walt Whitman*, 209.

66. Of the reviews reprinted from American periodicals, only those from the *Christian Spiritualist, Putnam's Monthly,* and the *Boston Intelligencer* were originally written by someone other than Whitman; they comprise fewer than six of the twenty-five printed pages of the "Opinions" section and do not detract from the general sense that, as Charles Eliot Norton wrote in his mostly negative review in *Putnam's,* "Aside from America, there is no quarter of the universe where such a production [as *Leaves of Grass*] could have had a genesis." Quoted in Whitman, *Leaves* (1856), 369. Whitman had begun self-publishing criticism of his work in 1855 when he bound reviews from the *North American Review, Putnam's,* and *London Eclectic Review*—along with three anonymous self-reviews—at the end of the first edition for its small second printing. See Loving, *Walt Whitman*, 507n12. As previously indicated, Whitman also seems to have occasionally pasted reviews clipped from newspapers to volumes he was sending to critics. As Leslie Elizabeth Eckel observes, "skeptical responses of [Whitman's] British reviewers," appended to the 1856 edition of *Leaves of Grass*, had allowed the poet to more convincingly frame his work as an incipient national literature. See Eckel, *Atlantic Citizens: Nineteenth-Century American Writers at Work in the World* (Edinburgh: Edinburgh University Press, 2013), 160.

67. Quoted in Whitman, *Leaves* (1856), 359, 374, 359.

68. George Eliot's review, discussed above, appeared under the title of the *London Leader*, where it had first appeared. The appalled reviewer in London's the *Critic* began, "We had ceased, we imagined to be surprised at anything that America could produce," and went on to argue that though "the words 'an American' [which appeared adjacent to the first reference to "Walt Whitman" in "Song of Myself"] are a surplusage." The United States, however, should not mistake *Leaves of Grass* for "the dawn of a thoroughly original literature, now there has arisen a man who scorns the Hellenic deities, who has no belief in, perhaps because he has no knowledge of, Homer and Shakespeare." The *Examiner* sarcastically dismissed as

signs of American vulgarity both "the new American prodigy" and American critics who dared compare him to Tennyson. Quoted in Whitman, *Leaves* (1856), 381–83, 374–75, 378.

69. Quoted in Whitman, *Leaves* (1856), 381.

70. Quoted in Whitman, *Leaves* (1856), 384.

71. These included "The American Scholar," "Self-Reliance," "Nature," and "The Poet," although Whitman later claimed Emerson had only a limited influence on *Leaves of Grass*. For an interpretation of this problem that sets Whitman's relationship to Emerson within the broader question of poetic originality and literary influence, see Price, *Whitman and Tradition*, 35–52.

72. Quoted in Whitman, *Leaves* (1856), 345.

73. Whitman, *Leaves* (1856), 348.

74. Whitman, *Leaves* (1856), 350. The use of a rhetoric of the body to inspire political unity in the early Christian Church informs many of the New Testament epistles but is most dramatically preserved in the twelfth chapter of Paul's first letter to the Corinthians, which, like *Leaves of Grass*, describes spiritual unity amid the diversity of individual characteristics through an extended metaphor of the physical form of a human being. See 1 Cor 12:4–6, 12–20; significantly, these are also some of the key biblical passages in which the slavery of the ancient world is mentioned and which were commonly cited in debates over American slavery in the 1850s; Paul here denies that the slave's status can bar inclusion within the Christian community at Corinth. For other examples of these central Pauline motifs, see Rom 12:4–5; Eph 1:22–23, 4:15–16, 5:30; Col 1:18–24, 2:19, 3:15. The wartime experience intensified the conviction, already evident in Whitman's early appropriation of biblical language, that the American nation's ability to maintain its cohesiveness despite its diverse makeup constituted a kind of spiritual force, "a moral and political unity in variety" that was only made fully manifest in the midst of civil war. See Whitman, *Memoranda* (1876), 65.

75. [Eliot], "Transatlantic Latter-Day Poetry."

76. Emerson to Carlyle, 6 May 1856, in *Correspondence*, 282–83. Some readers have seen this letter as an indication of Emerson's diminishing regard for Whitman. See Loving, *Walt Whitman*, 221; David S. Reynolds, *Walt Whitman's America: A Cultural Biography* (New York: Alfred A. Knopf, 1995), 343–44. The instability of Emerson and Carlyle's transatlantic friendship makes it difficult to take the discussion of Whitman at face value, however, given that the two critics now disagreed about a great deal, including the state of national literature. Despite his colorful description and his intuition of Carlyle's negative reaction, Emerson clearly frames Whitman's book as worthy, above all American books of its time, of Carlyle's consideration, and does so in the first letter he had sent to Carlyle in the year since *Leaves of Grass*'s publication.

77. Emerson to Carlyle, 11 March 1854, in *Correspondence*, 267.

78. Carlyle also responded dubiously to Emerson's characterization of Kansas as the ultimate battle between slavery and freedom. Carlyle to Emerson, 8 April 1854, in *Correspondence*, 272.

79. Koch, *Ralph Waldo Emerson in Europe*, 172.

80. Emerson, *English Traits*, 598; Bridgman, "From Greenough," 480.
81. Emerson to Carlyle, 11 March 1854, in *Correspondence*, 266.
82. Koch, *Ralph Waldo Emerson in Europe*, 194.
83. Emerson to Carlyle, 11 March 1854, in *Correspondence*, 266.
84. As James Oakes argues, Republicans shifted by the late 1850s to a belief that "the Constitution made freedom *national,* and that antislavery was therefore the only truly national politics." Oakes, *Freedom National: The Destruction of Slavery in the United States, 1861–1865* (New York: W. W. Norton, 2013), 43. See also McPherson, *Battle Cry of Freedom*, 158–61.

Conclusion

1. Abraham Lincoln, *The Collected Works of Abraham Lincoln*, 9 vols., ed. Roy P. Bassler (New Brunswick: Rutgers University Press, 1959), 4: 271. Ironically, Seward had helped craft Lincoln's argument that the militarization of what he had called an "irrepressible conflict" should now be considered unthinkable; Seward provided the impulse and many of the images behind the speech's justly renowned conclusion, though in a nod the usefulness of foreign foils he had added "aliens" to "enemies" as a contrast to "countrymen." See Lincoln, *Collected Works*, 4: 261–62n99. See also Joyce Kearns Goodwin, *Team of Rivals: The Political Genius of Abraham Lincoln* (New York: Simon and Schuster, 2005), 326.

2. Julia Ward Howe, "Battle Hymn of the Republic," *Atlantic* 9, no. 52 (February, 1862): 10. As Franny Nudelman notes, both songs "exemplified the tendency of nationalist culture to abstract the effects of violence" and to link military service and suffering "to a transcendent purpose." Perhaps more crucially, the former had transformed Brown from an enemy of the state into a paragon of unionist virtue and national spirit and had even initiated "the very process of transformation through which corpses . . . are reinterpreted as group spirit." Nudelman, *John Brown's Body: Slavery, Violence, and the Culture of War* (Chapel Hill, NC: University of North Carolina Press, 2004), 2, 15.

3. Quoted in Robert E. May, introduction to *The Union, the Confederacy, and the Atlantic Rim*, ed. Robert E. May (West Lafayette, IN: Purdue University Press, 1995), 23.

4. Knightley, *First Casualty*, 9

5. Studies of the war's transatlantic field often focus on diplomacy and/or British public opinion. See, for example, R. J. M. Blackett, *Divided Hearts: Britain and the American Civil War* (Baton Rouge: Louisiana State University Press, 2001); Foreman, *World on Fire*; Brian Jenkins, *Britain & The War for the Union*, 2 vols. (Montreal: McGill-Queen's University Press, 1974–80); Howard Jones, *Union in Peril: The Crisis over British Intervention in the Civil War* (Chapel Hill: University of North Carolina Press, 1992); Jones, *Blue and Gray Diplomacy: A History of Union and Confederate Foreign Relations* (Chapel Hill: University of North Carolina Press, 2010); Dean B. Mahin, *One War at a Time: The International Dimensions of the American Civil War* (Washington, DC: Brassey's, 1999); May,

Union; Don H. Doyle, *The Cause of All Nations: An International History of the American Civil War* (New York: Basic Books, 2015).

6. See Cody Marrs, *Nineteenth-Century American Literature and the Long Civil War* (New York: Cambridge University Press, 2015), 1, 3.

7. Seward's public positions on many topics, from westward expansion to Canadian annexation to the possibility for transatlantic war, roughly mirrored several of Whitman's poetic pronouncements, though from early in his career he was anxious to channel popular Anglophobic excitement and often held more nuanced personal views of transatlantic relations. See Walter Stahr, *Seward: Lincoln's Indispensable Man* (New York: Simon and Schuster, 2012), 76–80; Jenkins, *Britain* 1:39–40; Mahin, *One War at a Time*, 4–12; Goodwin, *Team of Rivals*, 342; Foreman, *World on Fire*, 30–31, 40.

8. Foreman, *World on Fire*, 40.

9. Greeley played a major role in destroying Seward's chances and thus in securing Lincoln's nomination, largely because he was one of the few truly national figures at the convention whose influence transcended the divisions between state parties. See Goodwin, *Team of Rivals*, 241–42.

10. Quoted in Jones, *Union in Peril*, 11.

11. Foreman, *World on Fire*, 30.

12. In fact, Seward had spent four hours the prior evening discussing the planned document with Henry Raymond of the *New-York Times*, as he had previously with his old ally Thurlow Weed; both men published prominent editorials echoing the chief arguments in the memo in subsequent days. Stahr, *Seward*, 270–72.

13. Quoted in Lincoln, *Collected Works* 4: 318. Fast on the heels of Lincoln's rejection of the memorandum, Seward would meet with William Howard Russell of the *Times* of London to read an Anglophobic dispatch he planned to send to the United States' London delegation; Russell found it "hostile" but judged it would be popular among northern audiences when it leaked. When rumors started arriving that Britain might recognize the Confederacy, Seward determined to "give 'em hell" and sent a letter to Charles Adams threatening Britain first with the cutting of diplomatic ties and insisting that the United States was prepared for a transatlantic war. These arguments were quickly published in the *New York Herald*, and Seward would continue to leverage his influence with the New York papers to wage a "propaganda campaign" that soon "succeeded in convincing the entire country that Britain had wronged the North." Foreman, *World on Fire*, 77; Seward quoted in Goodwin, *Team of Rivals*, 363. See also Stahr, *Seward*, 289–92; Foreman, *World on Fire*, 103.

14. Jenkins, *Britain*; Jones, *Union in Peril*; Jones, *Blue and Gray Diplomacy*; Foreman, *World on Fire*.

15. Frances Clarke makes this point in her article and subsequent book chapter on northern volunteerism. See Clarke, "'Let All Nations See,'" esp. 66–70; Clarke, *War Stories*, 16–17.

16. See Hutchison, *Apples and Ashes*, 133–35.

17. Russell wrote the letter from Charleston relating George III to southern secession

on April 30, before he could have been aware that King George's Enlistment Act would serve as the primary legal precedent for the British government's difficult task of establishing a stable policy toward the two sides in the American war. *New-York Tribune*, 28 May 1861, 9.

18. The explicit Anglophilia pursued in wartime was the flip side of what Haynes calls "the paradox of Anglophobia" that, though deployed in the first half of the century as a "useful device in the process of nation-building . . . actually served to reveal the preexisting fissures in American society." Haynes, *Unfinished Revolution*, 294–95.

19. Thomas M. Boaz, *Guns for Cotton: England Arms the Confederacy* (Shippensburg, PA: Burd Street, 1996), 3.

20. In a meeting with President Davis and Secretary of War James Seddon, Lee argued that an invasion of Pennsylvania would rejuvenate Confederate efforts to win foreign recognition. See McPherson, *Battle Cry of Freedom*, 647.

21. The meeting took place at Russell's home, partly to avoid the appearance of an official audience, and he made no commitment, though the proclamation of neutrality followed soon after. See Doyle, *Cause of All Nations*, 42–43.

22. Henry Adams, *The Education of Henry Adams*, Modern Library ed. (New York: Random House, 1931), 114.

23. Haynes, *Unfinished Revolution*, 45.

24. See Martin Crawford, *The Anglo-American Crisis of the Mid-Nineteenth Century: The Times and America, 1850–1862* (Athens: University of Georgia Press, 1987), 47.

25. Indeed, one of these Confederate commissioners, William Yancey, had strong-armed the less vehement representatives of his state by heading off a push for a referendum and insisting that once an ordinance of secession was passed, all those who did not support it would be treated as traitors—despite the fact that they represented upwards of 40 percent of his fellow delegates. See Stephanie McCurry, *Confederate Reckoning: Power and Politics in the Civil War South* (Cambridge, MA: Harvard University Press, 2010), 61–63.

26. Adams, *Education of Henry Adams*, 114–15.

27. Jones, *Blue and Gray Diplomacy*, 36.

28. Crawford, *Anglo-American Crisis*, 50–51.

29. Jones, *Blue and Gray Diplomacy*, 38.

30. Quoted in Jones, *Union in Peril*, 23.

31. Jones notes that the Lincoln administration in particular "failed to realize that British neutrality directly benefited the Union" in part because the proclamation terms seemed to delegitimize the United States as a nation undergoing a domestic rebellion. Jones, *Blue and Gray Diplomacy*, 48.

32. Worries about both sectional unrest and Anglophobia transmitted through the press had helped inspire the *Times* of London's editor, John Delane, to tour America in 1856. See Crawford, *Anglo-American Crisis*, 21.

33. "How to Keep England Straight," *Harper's Weekly*, 22 June 1861, 386.

34. Tamarkin, *Anglophilia*, xxiv.

35. Adams, *Education of Henry Adams*, 118.

36. See, for example, *Chicago Tribune*, 22 August 1861, 1; *Chicago Tribune*, 24 August 1861, 1; *Chicago Tribune*, 26 August 1861, 1; *New York Independent*, 29 August 1861, 5; *Harper's Weekly*, 31 August 1861, 547; *New-York Times*, 20 August 1861, 1; *New-York Times*, 21 August 1861, 4; *New-York Times*, 24 August 1861, 1; *Weekly Tribune*, 24 August 1861, 7.

37. *Times* of London, 7 August 1861, reprinted in *Chicago Tribune*, 22 August 1861, 1.

38. "A Nut for Russell," *Chicago Tribune*, 14 September 1861, 1. One of the *Tribune*'s editors, Charles H. Ray, had been riding with Russell on the day of the rout and afterward publicly accused him of misrepresenting the retreat. See J. Cutler Andrews, *The North Reports the Civil War* (Pittsburgh: University of Pittsburgh Press, 1955), 100. For threats to Russell, see Knightley, *First Casualty*, 36–37.

39. *Weekly Tribune*, 24 August 1861, 7.

40. Russell did not think much of Greeley, privately calling him a representative of the "nastiest form of narrow minded sectarian philanthropy, who would gladly roast all the whites of South Carolina in order that he might satisfy what he supposes is a conscience but which is only an autocratic ambition." Quoted in Brayton Harris, *Blue and Gray in Black and White: Newspapers in the Civil War* (Washington, DC: Brassey's, 1999), 31.

41. See for example, Whitman, "Long, Too Long, O Land," "A Broadway Pageant," "Flag of Stars! Thick Sprinkled Bunting," "World Take Good Notice," and "Turn O Libertad," in *Drum-Taps* (1865), 45, 61, 65, 67, 70. See also Whitman, "Lo! Victress on the Peaks!," in *Sequel to Drum-Taps* (1865), 23.

42. Whitman, *Memoranda* (1876), 62. Whitman may have been referring in part to a July 30 *Tribune* editorial in which Greeley buoyed northerners by reminding them: "It is not characteristic of Americans to sit down despondently after a defeat.... Reverses, though stunning at first, by their recoil stimulate and quicken to unwonted exertion, and in the end our achievement is the greater for the temporary rebuff." The poet was understandably misled about the undamaged confidence of New York editors, however, for Greeley also wrote a famously despondent letter to President Lincoln on July 29 offering his help "if the union is irrevocably gone" and if "an armistice of thirty, sixty, ninety, one hundred and twenty days—better still for a year—ought to be proposed with a view to a peaceful adjustment." Quoted in James M. Perry, *A Bohemian Brigade: The Civil War Correspondents—Mostly Rough, Sometimes Ready* (New York: J. Wiley, 2000), 44.

43. The *Times* had grown increasingly suspicious of the unionist reporting of their longtime New York correspondent, Bancroft Davis, which was one reason Russell had been sent to the scene. Davis would resign, unmourned by his former employers, at the end of the year. See Crawford, *Anglo-American Crisis*, 127–30.

44. Whitman, *Memoranda* (1876), 63. Given that "it is difficult to describe or exaggerate the force of the shock which Russell's letter produced," it is impossible to suppose that Whitman was not acutely aware of Russell's reporting in the *Times*. See Andrews, *North Reports the Civil War*, 100.

45. See Whitman, "Walt Whitman," *Leaves* (1867), 26; Whitman, "Quicksand Years," *Drum-Taps* (1865), 30.

46. Whitman, *Memoranda* (1876), 62.

47. One English best seller proposed that secession was inevitable based on geographical facts and human nature, as well as historical precedents, and cited the history of ancient Greece to argue that "no Federal Union has ever been formed, on a large scale, of States which had approached a mature condition; it has always been the resource of communities young and feeble"; as the author noted, this was not a novel argument but widely held among theorists and statesmen. James Spence, *On the American Union: Its Effect on National Character and Policy, with an Inquiry into Secession as a Constitutional Right and the Causes of the Disruption*, 3rd ed. (London: Richard Bentley, 1862), 11.

48. Frances M. Clarke comprehensively summarizes the climate of transatlantic hostility toward the northern cause in order to explain the international orientation of publicity surrounding the United States Sanitary Commission and other northern volunteer organizations. As Clarke's analysis shows, efforts to vindicate the American political system emerged in response to foreign criticisms but also provided a forum to address long-standing northern anxieties concerning American national identity. See Clarke, *War Stories*, 116–43.

49. Thus Martin Crawford notes that "between 1861 and 1865, *The Times* found itself in the unenviable position of being the leading object of northern attacks on British policy." Crawford, *Anglo-American Crisis*, 135.

50. G. M. Towle, "Our Recent Foreign Relations," *Atlantic Monthly*, 1 August 1864, 243–44. The tendency of foreign observers to regard the war as a final test of the republican "experiment" was widespread, though they understood that term in different ways. See Doyle, *Cause of All Nations*, 7–8.

51. Towle, "Our Recent Foreign Relations," 243–45.

52. Towle, "Our Recent Foreign Relations," 250, 249, 251.

53. James H. Moorhead, *American Apocalypse*, 81, quoted in Clarke, "'Let All Nations See,'" 90.

54. Nevin quoted in Noll, *Civil War as a Theological Crisis*, 76–77.

55. Towle, "Our Recent Foreign Relations," 252.

56. Whitman, *Memoranda* (1876), 63.

INDEX

Aberdeen, Lord, 133, 134
abolitionists, 67–70, 77, 82, 140, 157, 235n46, 246n2. *See also* antislavery movement; slavery
Adams, Charles Francis, 204
Adams, Henry, 204, 206, 210
Adams, John, 204
African Americans, 65, 69, 88, 90, 94
Albert, Prince, 122, 125
Alexander, Michael, 33, 241n2
American Phrenological Journal, 165
Anderson, Benedict, 12–15, 225n44, 225n45, 225n47, 240n2, 241n1
Anglicanism, 58
Anglophilia, 115, 202, 208, 243n26, 258n18
Anglophobia, 115, 177, 198, 209, 211
anti-Americanism, 121, 123–24, 126, 170
anti-Catholicism, 18, 109, 226n57, 241n3
antislavery movement, 19, 65–66, 68–70, 75, 78, 81, 88, 138–39, 173, 193, 256n84. *See also* abolitionists; slavery
antitraditionalism, 40, 43, 62, 82, 234n28, 236n4. *See also* presentism
architecture, 17, 30–33, 110; Gothic Revivalist, 48, 228n5
aristocracy, 42, 44, 121, 165–66, 173; European, 94, 96–97, 178; southern, 81, 94, 96–97, 143, 172, 202
Assmann, Jan, 8
Associated Press, 33, 242n12
Atlantic, the, 215, 216, 217
Auerbach, Erich, 12, 15, 224n41
Auerbach, Jeffrey, 115, 122, 125
Augustine, 224n41

Badger, George Edmund, 89
Baltimore, 41
Barry, Charles, 32
Bede, the Venerable, 224n41
belonging, 10–11, 116, 128, 144, 181, 241n4
Benjamin, Walter, 12

Bible, 68, 85, 88–89, 142, 151; and slavery, 255n71. *See also* New Testament; Old Testament
Big Ben, 23, 227n59
"Bleeding Kansas," 20, 131, 138, 141, 143, 148–49, 154, 157, 192, 196, 201. *See also* Kansas
"Blood Money" (Whitman), 82–88, 90, 91, 94–96
"Border Ruffians," 131, 141, 146, 148, 149, 150
Boston, 58, 59, 66, 72, 171, 172, 174–79, 252n35. *See also* Whitman, Walt: "A Boston Ballad"
Brexit, xi
Bridgman, Richard, 193, 232n2
Brooklyn, 192
Brooks, Preston, 156
"Brother Jonathan," 118, 210
Bryant, William Cullen, 78
Buchanan, James, 137, 139, 141, 193
Buckingham Palace, 28, 110
Bull, John, 43, 118, 119, 174, 193
Bull Run, memory circuit of, 209–14, 217
"Bunker Hill Monument Address" (Webster), 63, 79, 80, 174, 252n29
Burns, Anthony, 171–80, 183, 252n36
Bush, Harold K., Jr., 61
Butler, Andrew, 156

Cadava, Eduardo, 63
Calhoun, John C., 81, 89, 132, 133, 148
Calvin, John, 86, 239n32
Canada, 137, 149, 158, 198, 207
capitalism, 7, 13, 50
Carlyle, Thomas, and Emerson, 72, 192, 193, 233n6, 255n76
Catholic Emancipation Act (1829), 106
Catholicism, 18, 86, 106, 109, 226n54, 226n57, 228n2, 240n3
Chartism, 35, 229n16
Chicago Tribune, 211
Christianity: antitraditionalism and, 45–49;

261

Index

Christianity (*continued*)
  and conflict, 133–34, 136, 142; Emerson and, 56–62; and national memory, 3, 11–19; and sacred history, 57, 224n41, 225n44; Whitman and, 82–86, 88–91, 95–96
church and state, separation of, 28, 151. *See also* religion, and politics
Church of England, 54, 56, 58, 107
circulation, 38, 68, 113, 119, 123, 130, 156. *See also* under *New-York Tribune*; *Times* of London
Civil War (the American), xi, xiii, xiv, xviii, 16, 21, 103, 197–98, 202, 211, 216–17; and Great Britain, 203–10
Clarendon, Lord, 134, 135
Clarke, Frances, 90, 217, 260n48
class, 35–38, 55, 71, 123–24, 137, 166
Cobbett, William, 36
Cobden, Richard, 113, 114, 116, 229n20
Colley, Linda, 36
communication, mass, 10, 51, 102
communion, 11, 58–60, 83–85, 87, 90. *See also* Eucharist
Communism, 76
Communist League, Second Congress of, 50
Communist Manifesto (Marx), 50, 53, 240n1
Compromise of 1850, 75, 76, 78, 80, 88, 92, 132, 139, 145, 172, 174, 175
Confederate States of America, 196, 200, 202–9, 226n58, 257n13
Constitution, U.S., 69, 80, 88, 89, 146, 150, 183
"Constitution and the Union, The" (Webster). *See* Speech of March 7
Corinthians, First, 255n74
Crimean War, 133, 134, 136, 138, 149, 153, 158, 169, 211
Crystal Palace, 108, 110–11, 113, 117, 121–22, 125, 128
Cuba, 115, 169, 182; annexation of, 136–39, 253n40
culture: Anglophone, 181, 197; local, 9; national, 3, 15, 21, 32, 44, 48, 121, 126, 161
Curran, John Philpot, 70

Daily Tribune. *See New-York Tribune*
Dana, Charles, 92, 95
Davis, Jefferson, 206
Davis, Kathleen, 224n41
Declaration of Independence, 183, 213
Delbanco, Andrew, 92
Democratic Party, 40, 41, 63, 77, 144, 150, 155, 193, 248n38
diplomacy, 135, 138, 198, 200–201, 203, 205; transatlantic, 21, 196, 197, 202, 216, 256n5
Douglas, Stephen A., 139, 145, 150–51
Duke of Wellington, 122

Eagle, 77
Eckel, Leslie Elizabeth, 254n66
Economist, 242n9
Edwards, Jonathan, 83
Eliade, Mircea, 13
Eliot, George, 162, 163, 168, 189, 254n68
elitism, 40, 124
Emerson, Ralph Waldo, 4, 19, 22, 55, 63–64, 74–77, 85–88, 101, 161–65, 172, 174, 178, 185–91, 194, 233n13, 233n14, 234n35; "American Scholar," 64; and Carlyle, 72, 192, 193, 233n6; "Divinity School Address," 64; and Christianity, 56–62; *English Traits*, 53, 54, 72, 161, 164, 193, 232n2, 233n6; "Lord's Supper," 58, 60, 72, 82, 85; *Nature*, 63, 64, 65, 67, 69, 71, 79, 86; "The Poet," 74; on slavery, 65–73; *Second Series*, 74; and Whitman, 74–77, 87, 163–64, 172, 174, 185–94, 254n64, 255n71, 255n76
Engels, Frederick, 50
England, 34, 38, 72, 114, 158, 165, 166, 169, 182, 191, 204, 207. *See also* Great Britain
Enlistment Act, 257n17
Erkkilä, Betsy, 76
ethnicity, 51, 63, 91, 109, 125
Eucharist, 83, 84
evangelicalism, 48, 231n52

federalism, 140, 147, 181
federalists, 63
filibusterism, 138
Foreman, Amanda, 200, 228n5
Fort Sumter, 4
Fourierism, 42, 121
France, 35, 112, 117, 133, 136, 138, 157, 200
Frederickson, Andrea, 29
freedom, 65–67, 151–53
Free Soil movement, 40, 75, 77–78, 80–81, 93, 139–41, 153
Fugitive Slave Law, 78, 80, 89, 93, 95, 171, 172, 174, 176
Fuller, Margaret, 92, 93, 95

Garrison, William Lloyd, 66–71
Gat, Azar, 15, 222n17
George III, King, 175–78, 257n17
Georgia, 72, 146, 175
Gettysburg Address, xii, xiii, 219n1, 219n3
Gillis, John, 5
Gilmore, Paul, 114
God, 66, 142, 163, 217
Gothic Revival, 2, 9, 14, 19, 27, 30–32, 48, 54, 71, 163
Grant, Susan-Mary, 102, 153
Grant, Ulysses S., 18
Great Awakening, Second, 46, 48, 66

Index

Great Britain, 33, 36, 43, 49, 70, 126, 138, 141, 158, 161, 191, 200, 216; and the American Civil War, 203–10; and catholicity, 105–8; Emerson on, 53–57; and foreign affairs, 134–36; and hypernationalism, 121–24; and Whitman, 165–68. *See also* England

Great Exhibition of the Works and Industry of All Nations, 19, 103, 121, 128, 136, 210, 242n9; hypernationalism and, 124–25; news coverage of, 108–11; telegraph and, 112–18

Greeley, Horace, 1, 3, 29–30, 37–38, 43, 49, 51, 72, 75, 117, 150, 152, 155, 198, 220n3, 220n4, 229n20, 247n23, 259n42; and the Great Exhibition, 119–21; and hypernationalism, 123–25; and mass communication, 34–35; and national memory, 39–41; and presentism, 18–19

Greenfeld, Liah, 29, 111, 132

Halbachs, Maurice, 223n20
Hanlon, Christopher, 4, 131, 232n2, 242n17, 246n3
Harper's Weekly, 207
Harrison, William Henry, 40
Harvard Divinity School, 57
Hatch, Nathan O., 46
Haynes, Sam W., 4, 205, 236n53, 258n18
history, sacred, 3, 19–20, 28–30, 31, 52, 57–58, 69, 71–72, 74–75, 78, 82–83, 105, 107, 129, 143–44, 154, 162, 164, 193, 196, 208, 213, 215; antitraditionalism and, 45–48; Christianity and, 11–15, 57; Emerson and, 60–66; Whitman and, 85–88
Hobsbawm, Eric, 223n25, 224n34, 228n5
Holzer, Howard, 144
Hope, A. J. B. Beresford, 163, 226n58
Howe, Julia Ward, 196
Husch, Gail E., 62
Hvithamar, Annika, 13, 223n25, 224n39, 227n4
hypernationalism, 17–18, 20, 102, 108–9, 116, 125, 129, 146, 149–50, 157, 160, 181, 195, 200, 218, 241n7; and the Great Exhibition, 124–25; and Greeley, 121, 125

Illustrated London News, 34, 117, 118, 119, 130, 138

Jakelic, Slavica, 225n43
James, Henry, 230n45
Jefferson, Thomas, 40
Jenkins, Brian, 200
Jesus Christ, 58–61, 82–90, 94, 95, 151
Jones, Howard, 200, 258n31
journalism, 34, 43, 66, 75, 92, 118
Judas, 81, 83–88, 94, 96

Kansas, 20, 131, 133, 140, 142–47, 149, 151–60
Kansas-Nebraska Act, 139, 141, 148, 150, 172, 179, 180
Klammer, Martin, 77, 78, 237n8, 237n9

language: English, 16, 44, 114, 126, 167; print and vernacular, 14; shared, 44, 105, 106, 114, 127, 166, 167
Last Supper, the, 60, 82, 83
Leader, 163
Leaves of Grass (Whitman), 4, 20, 75–76, 78–79, 87, 97, 103, 160, 163, 165, 167–73, 176, 178, 181–94, 218
Lee, Robert E., 203
Leonard, Thomas, 145
Liberator, 66, 68, 69, 70, 235n47
Life Illustrated, 182
Lincoln, Abraham, xii, xiii, 140, 194, 196, 198–99, 204, 206, 256n1, 257n13
literature: American, 75, 162, 165, 166, 172, 180, 190–91, 218; British, 161–62, 164–67; national, 53, 64, 164, 167, 169, 181, 190, 217
Log Cabin, 40, 41, 42, 105
London, 23, 28, 32, 108, 114, 119
London Chronicle, 158
London Weekly Dispatch, 189
"Lord's Supper" (Emerson), 58, 60, 72, 82, 85
Loughran, Trish, 140, 148, 241n1, 247n24, 248n48
Loving, Jerome, 173, 236n3, 237n8, 238n25, 254n66, 255n76

Marki, Ivan, 188
Marx, Karl, 50, 51, 53, 102, 125, 136, 232n63, 240n1
Matthew, Gospel of, 86, 94
McCormick, Cyrus, 120
McElrath, Thomas, 34
McKanan, Dan, 82, 235n40, 240n52
media, 111
memorialists, 3, 10, 21
memory: collective, xiii, 5, 6, 49, 127, 166, 184, 220n7, 222n15, 232n62; national, xiii, xiv, 2, 5–9, 11, 14, 16, 17, 51, 57, 102, 106, 127–28, 147, 149, 157, 160, 166, 168–69, 178, 181, 196–98, 200–201, 208, 220n7; —, and Greeley, 39; presentist mode of, 2–3, 8, 10–11, 19–21, 43, 49, 63, 79, 86, 102–3, 128, 131, 147, 164, 168, 170, 178, 186, 220n7, 235n46; traditionalist mode of, 2–3, 8–11, 14–15, 17, 19, 21, 43, 49, 51–52, 54, 56–57, 63, 65, 78, 82, 127, 147, 166, 183. *See also* presentism; traditionalism
memory circuits, 108, 184; and Bull Run, 209, 212, 214, 217; transatlantic, 15, 16, 21, 102, 128, 178, 196
Mexican War, 77, 131

Missouri, 143; and "Border Ruffians," 131, 141, 146, 148, 149, 150
Missouri Compromise (Compact), 139, 147, 154
modernism, 223n25, 225n47
modernity, 2, 6, 7, 10, 12–14, 50, 56, 110, 224nn34–35
Morris, William, 122
Morse, Samuel, 41, 112, 242n16
Mott, Frank Luther, 43
Muslims, 136

Napoleon III, 134, 136
Napoleonic Wars, 135
Nature (Emerson), 63, 64, 65, 67, 69, 71, 79, 86
neutrality, diplomatic, 200–209, 258n21
Nevin, John Williamson, 47, 217
Nevins, Alan, 197
New England, 67, 70, 83
Newman, John Henry, 107, 240n3
New Orleans, 77, 95, 123
New Orleans Crescent, 77, 95
New Testament, 13, 56, 62, 65, 72, 83, 86
New York (city), 1, 34, 37, 38, 177
New York Evening Post, 78, 81
New York Herald, 41, 257n13
New-York Sun, 37
New-York Times, 136
New-York Tribune, 1, 34, 37, 39, 41–42, 51, 72, 105, 119, 130, 133, 145–48, 151–53, 155–59; circulation of, 35, 120, 149–50, 154, 220n4, 228n12, 230n35; and Whitman, 19, 22, 75, 76, 78–79, 81–82, 90–97, 163, 171, 179–80, 184
Nietzsche, Friedrich, 223n23
Noll, Mark, 68, 81, 142
Nora, Pierre, 5, 245n57
Nord, David Paul, 66, 235n40
Norton, Charles Eliot, 254n66
Nudelman, Franny, 256n2

Oakes, James, 256n84
Old Testament, 14, 56, 57
Ostend Manifesto, 137, 247n31
Ottoman Empire, 134, 136, 140
Oxford Movement, 33, 107. See also *Tracts for the Times*

Packer, Barbara, 61, 72
Paine, Thomas, 70
Palmerston, Lord (Prime Minister), 134, 135, 207, 246n13
paranoia, xii, 35, 109,
Paris, peace talks, 135, 158. See also Treaty of Paris
Parker, Theodore, 140, 177

Parliament, 1, 3, 27–29, 31, 32, 35, 49
Passover, 58, 60, 83, 85
Paul, the Apostle, 59, 224n41, 238n31; letters of, 13, 86; Whitman on, 83–86, 191
Pelikan, Jaroslav, 234n29
Peyser, Thomas, 115, 116
Philips, Kevin, 158–59
poetry, xiv, 163, 165–73, 183–93
Political Register, 36
Powers, Hiram, 120
Presbyterianism, 231n55
presentism, 2–3, 17–19, 49, 52, 77–78, 106–7, 169–70; and collective memory, 14, 43, 48, 49, 132, 220n7; and national memory, 2–3, 8, 10–11, 14–15, 17, 19, 20–22, 43, 45, 49, 56–60, 71, 79, 102–3, 106–7, 128, 131, 142, 144, 147, 160, 164, 168–70, 178, 184, 196, 198, 201, 202, 213. See also memory, presentist mode of
privilege, 36, 49, 55, 94, 121, 123, 166
proslavery movement, 19, 68–69, 80, 89, 139–40, 142, 143, 146, 148, 155–56; and Christian churches, 66. See also slavery
Protestantism, 14, 18, 62; American, 45, 47, 68, 81–82, 86, 121, 142; British, 109, 134; liberal, 48, 90; presentist, 226n48
Providence, divine, 11, 12, 62
Pugin, Augustus Welby Northmore, 19, 30, 32–33, 39, 46, 49–51, 54, 56, 63, 65, 107, 110, 122, 228n4; *An Apology for the Revival of Christian Architecture in England*, 226n54, 228n5; *Contrasts*, 71, 228n2
Puritanism, 45, 83, 121, 226n54, 231n50

Quakers, 234n25, 238n29
Queen Victoria, 122, 125

race, 68, 122, 137, 166, 173, 193, 232n2, 237n9. See also "Blood Money"; slavery; Speech of March 7
Raglan, Lord, 135
recognition, diplomatic, 21, 200, 203, 206, 209, 258n20
recruitment affair, 137, 169
Reformation, the, 32, 60, 62, 225n44, 225n45
religion, 8, 13–15, 47, 54, 61, 225n43; journalism and, 48, 55, 161, 162, 164; and politics, 28, 29, 48, 54
Republicanism, 18, 124, 138, 154, 193, 194, 207, 214, 216, 217; "Black Republicanism," 145
Republican Party, 143–44, 153, 158, 198, 256n84
revivalism, 46, 47, 48, 107, 163, 235n40
Revolutions of 1848, 56, 76, 94, 173, 183
Richardson, R. H., 151
Richmond Enquirer, 157

Russell, Lord, 204, 206, 207
Russell, William Howard, 134, 202, 210, 211, 212, 213, 214, 246n11, 257n13, 257n17, 259n40
Russia, 134, 136, 138
Rust, Albert C., 155, 156

Saturday Review, 163, 164
Schaff, Philip, 47, 217
secession, 80, 96, 181, 199, 200, 204, 205, 260n47
Second Church (Boston), 58, 59
sectionalism, 103, 131–32, 145, 169–70, 172–73, 178–82, 191, 195, 198, 207
secularism, 13, 221n9
Select Committee on Newspaper Stamps, 36
Seneca Falls Convention, 93
Seward, William H., 39, 40, 198–200, 210, 216, 256n1, 257n7, 257n13
Sherman, Roger, 81, 89
Simms, William Gilmore, 180–81, 253n47, 253n48
Sims, Thomas, 72, 172, 175
Six Acts of 1819, 36
slavery, 75, 131–33, 139–44, 148, 178, 182, 193, 216; and the Bible, 255n71; Emerson on, 65–73; and Kansas, 152–56; Whitman on, 19, 20, 75, 77–83, 86, 88–94, 169–75. *See also* abolitionists; antislavery movement; proslavery movement
Smith, Anthony D., 9, 14
Smith, Ryan K., 226n57
Sontag, Susan, 232n62
Southern Quarterly Review, 180
Spain, 137, 138
Speech of March 7 ("The Constitution and the Union," Webster), 80, 81, 82, 91, 96, 97, 174, 237n11, 237n12
spiritualism, 240n52
steam, 3, 10, 34, 37, 41, 108, 111–13
steamers, 118, 147, 212
Sumner, Charles, 156, 157

Tamarkan, Elisa, 4, 115, 224n32, 243n26
taxation, newspaper, 3, 16, 30, 108, 229n20
Taylor, Charles, 15, 140, 142, 221n9, 234n35
technology, 9, 108, 111, 116
telegraph, 10, 34, 41–42, 108, 111–13, 123, 147, 177, 242n16
Tennyson, Alfred, Lord, 167, 168, 190, 211; *Maud*, 165, 166
Terdiman, Richard, 7, 220n7, 223n20, 243n25
Times of London, 16, 34, 36, 37, 55, 58, 108, 112, 119, 120, 130, 210, 211, 244n36; circulation of, 124, 233n6, 245n42
Toryism, 174, 202, 226n55, 257n13
Towle, G. M., 215, 216, 217, 218

Tracts for the Times, 33. *See also* Oxford Movement
traditionalism, 2–3, 8–10, 19–20, 48–49, 51–52, 56–57, 61–62, 64, 76, 78–79, 87, 90–91, 96–97, 101–3, 182, 217. *See also* memory, traditionalist mode of
transatlantic cable, 113, 123, 200, 214, 242n16, 242n17
transatlantic time lag, 16, 17, 18, 20, 21, 102, 108, 119, 126, 160, 199, 213, 214
transcendentalism, 49, 53, 57, 61, 233n13, 234n25
Traubel, Horace, 182, 238n29
Treaty of Paris, 207, 216. *See also* Paris, peace talks
Turkey, 134, 136, 157
Two-Penny Trash, 36

Unitarian Church, 57
Unitarianism, 64, 177

violence, intersectional, 20, 143, 156
Virginia, 171, 179, 211

Washington, DC, 41, 89, 93, 133, 140, 144, 147, 150, 155, 192, 193, 204, 208
Webster, Daniel, 64–66, 76, 81–83, 84, 86, 88–91, 93–94, 96–97; "Bunker Hill Monument Address," 63, 79, 80, 174, 252n29; "The Constitution and the Union" (Speech of March 7), 80–82, 91, 96–97, 174, 237nn11–12
Weed, Thurlow, 39, 40, 41, 42, 63, 77, 80, 92, 93, 105, 144, 145, 156, 198
Weekly Tribune, 51, 142, 146, 148, 179. See also *New-York Tribune*
Weisbuch, Robert, 44, 222n13, 226n52, 231nn49–n50, 253n46
Westminster, Palace of, 1–3, 5, 23, 27, 28–29, 31–33, 36, 39, 50–51, 54, 62, 65, 101, 108–10, 228n4
Westminster Abbey, 27, 28, 36, 54, 110, 175
Whig Party, 18, 39, 40–42, 63, 92–93, 105, 144–45, 156, 198, 226n55
Whitman, Walt, 18–22, 179–81, 184, 196–200, 213, 216–18; "Blood Money," 82–88, 90, 91, 94–96; "A Boston Ballad," 171, 173–78, 182; and Christianity, 81–86, 88–91, 95–96; and Emerson, 74–77, 87, 163–64, 172, 174, 185–94, 254n64, 255n71, 255n76; "An English and an American Poet," 165, 168, 170, 183, 185, 189; and Great Britain, 165–69; "House of Friends," 91; "Leaves-Droppings," 187–89; *Memoranda during the War*, 211, 212, 259n42; and Paul the Apostle, 83–86, 191; "Poem of Apparitions

Whitman, Walt (*continued*)
in Boston, the 78th Year of These States" 183; "Poem of the Dead Young Men of Europe, the 72d and 73d Years of These States," 183; "Poem of Many In One," 186–87; "Resurgemus," 76, 77, 91–97, 171–72, 174–75, 178, 182; on slavery, 77–82; "The Slave Trade," 182; "Song of Myself," 184, 186. See also *Leaves of Grass*

Yancey, William, 258n25
Young England movement, 17, 33, 226n55

Zechariah, book of, 91

www.ingramcontent.com/pod-product-compliance
Lightning Source LLC
Chambersburg PA
CBHW021349300426
44114CB00012B/1140